# WORKING CONSTRUCTION

# WORKING CONSTRUCTION

WHY WHITE WORKING-CLASS MEN
PUT THEMSELVES—AND THE LABOR
MOVEMENT—IN HARM'S WAY

## KRIS PAAP

ILR PRESS, an imprint of
CORNELL UNIVERSITY PRESS
ITHACA AND LONDON

First published 2006 by Cornell University Press
First printing, Cornell Paperbacks, 2006

Printed in the United States of America

Library of Congress Cataloging-in-Publication Data

Paap, Kris, 1968–
    Working construction : why white working-class men put themselves and the labor movement in harm's way / Kris Paap.
        p. cm.
    Includes bibliographical references and index.
    ISBN-13: 978-0-8014-4467-8 (cloth : alk. paper)
    ISBN-10: 0-8014-4467-5 (cloth : alk. paper)
    ISBN-13: 978-0-8014-7286-2 (pbk. : alk. paper)
    ISBN-10: 0-8014-7286-5 (pbk. : alk. paper)
    1. Construction workers—United States—Attitudes.   2. Working class men—United States—Attitudes.   3. Men, White—United States—Attitudes.
    4. Masculinity—United States.   5. Construction industry—United States—Safety measures.   I. Title.
    HD8039.B892U66 2005
    331.7'6240973—dc22

                                                                    2005037543

Cornell University Press strives to use environmentally responsible suppliers and materials to the fullest extent possible in the publishing of its books. Such materials include vegetable-based, low-VOC inks and acid-free papers that are recycled, totally chlorine-free, or partly composed of nonwood fibers. For further information, visit our website at www.cornellpress.cornell.edu.

Cloth printing           10 9 8 7 6 5 4 3 2 1
Paperback printing       10 9 8 7 6 5 4 3 2 1

PRINTED IN U.S.A.

*To Ian and Avery*

# CONTENTS

# ACKNOWLEDGMENTS

In the process of bringing this work to a publishable state, I have benefited tremendously from the contributions of many persons—first and foremost, in-depth readings by Jerry Marwell, Jane Piliavin, Jane Collins, Mitch Duneier, and Maria Lepowski. Helpful readers of earlier drafts include Herbert Hill at the University of Wisconsin, Michael Burawoy from the University of California, Heather Hartley (now of Portland State University), Amy Cantoni and Lisa Schreibersdorf at the UW Writing Center, Ronni Tichenor at the SUNY Institute of Technology, Linda Goldenhar (formerly of National Institute of Occupational Safety and Health [NIOSH] and currently at the University of Cincinnati), and Judy Wolf, a writing colleague and friend. Jon Harrington served formally and informally as my personal editor for several versions of the manuscript: without his willingness to work weekends and middle-of-the-nights on my behalf, this project would be less coherent and less done. And it was H. Andrew Michener at the University of Wisconsin who made the essential connection between men's language of productivity and the everyday constructions of their sexuality, invaluable to my larger understandings of the relations between profit, class inequality, and masculinity.

Later versions profited from the efforts and attention of Mary Gatta at the Center for Women and Work at Rutgers University, Herman Benson at the Association for Union Democracy, Fran Benson at Cornell University Press, and two anonymous reviewers. Portions of the book also received valuable feedback from members of the Construction Economics Research Network (a project of the Center to Protect Workers' Rights and the National Institutes of Occupational Safety and Health), among whom Dale

Belman of Michigan State University deserves a particular thank you for his support and assistance.

An earlier version of chapter 6 was previously published as "'Voluntarily Put Themselves in Harm's Way': The Bait-and-Switch of Safety Training in the Construction Industry," in *Sociology of Job Training*, Research in the Sociology of Work, Vol. 12 (Oxford, UK: Elsevier, 2003). The editor of that volume, David Bills, provided valuable feedback to drafts of that manuscript, as did two anonymous reviewers.

As a construction worker, a scholar, and a person, I have often been blessed with professional and personal support. Emily Kane, now of Bates College, provided the intellectual foundation for most of the questions I ask in this and other projects. I am grateful to Linda Goldenhar for her mentoring in safety research and the use of her focus group data. Eduardo Bonilla-Silva and Michael Kimmel have been profound role models and gracious advisers. Mary Gatta and Eileen Appelbaum at the Center for Women and Work at Rutgers University have my boundless gratitude for creating an institution in which outspoken women are celebrated and promoted. I particularly thank Jerry Marwell, an advisor without whom this project would not have been possible. He has been very tolerant of my need to find my own path intellectually and personally and provided some of the best pieces of advice and instruction that I continue to share with my students.

At the SUNY Institute of Technology, where I have been able to find some time and space to complete the manuscript, particular thanks go to Linda Weber, Maureen Helmer Cool, Bob Jones and Renee Jones in the print shop, Ron Foster (the librarian who can locate anything), and Ronni (a/k/a "Ronald") Tichenor (invaluable colleague and friend, a delightful motivator and competitor, and a source of sanity when it was otherwise hard to find).

Almost last but certainly not least, I have benefited tremendously from a family that has been willing to release me from family obligations in order to work on this project. Thank you, David, Ian, and Avery; and thank you, Bill and Penny. From a distance, my sister, Kim, and my dad, Tony, provided support and legal information. Jo, my stepmom, provided endless encouragement and buoyancy, and my mom, Sandy, has given me many things—among them the assumption that women *can* do anything and have the right to do so. Without that, I would be a different person and there would be no book. Additionally, Ken LeBlond created much needed momentum early on and his faith in me is the foundation of this.

Finally, it would be egregious for me to end these acknowledgments without addressing the men and women in the building trades who have made this book possible: the apprentices and instructors who pushed me along and treated me with respect (and often with humor); the foremen and co-workers who shared their tools and their tricks; everybody at Family Builders; the white women and people of color who created the path on which I was able to enter the industry; and a special thanks to the tradeswomen's support group and Nancy N., its guide, with whom I started my construction career. Thank you all.

KEP

# WORKING CONSTRUCTION

# Introduction

## WORKING CONSTRUCTION

It was dark and cold, roughly 6:30 a.m. on a midwestern January morning as I pulled into the parking lot of the construction site run by Remodel Co. My rusty old Toyota Tercel crunched across the compacted snow until my headlights came to rest on the temporary trailer that held the office of the job superintendent. I had been told to report to this trailer for my first day of work for Remodel Co.—and my first day in the construction industry.

Needless to say, I was nervous, as most people would be when starting a new job in a new industry. I was also about to enter a new world: as a young white woman raised largely by a single mom and an older sister in a middle-class neighborhood, I was aware that my decision to leave graduate school for a career in construction—the apparent epitome of masculine culture and working-class life—was dramatic. My success in such an enterprise was far from guaranteed. I was unsure of my abilities and the conditions I was about to face. Could I succeed technically? Would I know or be able to figure out the tasks in front of me? Would I be strong enough or be able to build the strength required?

I was equally concerned about the social tests that were likely to confront me. Would I be fairly or unfairly tested by my new co-workers? Could I survive emotionally in a world widely seen as hostile to women? What sorts of hazing and harassment—sexual or otherwise—might I endure? I knew both anecdotally and from books that a woman entering a male-dominated job often ended up with her equipment stolen or sabotaged and often had to put up with such "unpleasantries" as dead rats in her lunch box. I wasn't a big fan of rats, dead or alive, and I wasn't sure how I'd handle trials like this (should they occur).

Trying to guess the answers to these questions was made even more difficult by the fact that I had little real information to go on. What I knew about the company for which I would be working, Remodel Co., came from comments made at the meetings for women hoping to enter the trades. I hadn't heard much outside of its reputation as being busy and therefore a good company to work for. I also knew relatively little about the industry beyond what it produced, the stereotypes about its culture, and what I would be doing as a commercial carpenter's apprentice. This notable gap in my knowledge was caused primarily by the fact that the nature of the industry has been largely—at least lately—undocumented by academics. Three ethnographic works published in the late 1970s and early 1980s by men who had previously worked in the industry all comment on the initial influx of women, but none could provide insight into the longer-term participation of women or the current culture of the trades.[1]

Trying to anticipate the culture of the construction workplace was also complicated by the fact that much of the current research focuses on "quantifiable acts" such as worker output, injuries, and other parts of life easily measured by persons outside the workforce. This emphasis is caused at least in part by issues of liability (who wants to pay for a researcher accidentally killed by a falling I-beam?) and disinclination on the part of companies and unions to be the focus of outside research. As a result, my best information came from a small collection of books about women in the trades and a handful of novels and autobiographical accounts.[2] Additionally, of course, I was armed with the stereotypes about the work and workers that I had learned growing up in a middle-class suburb.

As a result of this reliance on stereotypes, 1970s literature, and autobiographical accounts, I anticipated co-workers who were big, hypermasculine, politically and socially conservative, and hostile to anyone who didn't look like the historically traditional worker—to women in particular. Not all these expectations were nonsense, of course: history offers numerous descriptions of desperate union workers becoming physically violent to protect their turf, whether against corrupt employers in the early twentieth century, scabs crossing the line, or foreign-made automobiles at the end of the twentieth century.[3] Although white-collar workers and executives have also been a dangerous lot (including an apparent tendency for employers to incite violence with or among the workers), since I didn't see myself as heading for a white-collar arena, I wasn't terribly concerned about the alleged wrongdoings of those workers and managers.[4] My very real fears—though I wouldn't have admitted them then—were of being beaten up by the stereotypically big and burly guys in the worksite parking lot.

## The Social Realities of Working Construction

### Taking a Social Beating

I soon found, fortunately or unfortunately, that the beatings I would take and the turf battles I would have to fight would be social, psychological, and political rather than physical. It is not clear to me that I paid a much lower price as a result. From that January morning, I would spend the next two and a half years struggling to prove myself as an apprentice in an environment where outsiders (designated "affirmative action" workers in response to the much-maligned policies) were determined before the fact, during the fact, and after the fact to be incapable of doing the work. It wasn't just that I would need to prove myself; it was that actually proving myself competent would turn out to be almost by definition impossible.

I would also spend the next two years attempting to negotiate a constantly changing set of social conditions in which I, as a female on site, would be the object against which the men's masculinities would be measured and against which their masculinities would be proved. This meant that men who felt they needed to assert their heterosexuality would "come on" to me publicly. Men who felt they needed to assert their masculinity as being "above women" would be publicly hostile or insulting. All of this became as much a part of my job as swinging a hammer or running a saw.

What was most surprising to me about these experiences was *not* that these battles were painfully personal; after all, one would expect them to be personal since they generally involved unwanted discussion of or contact with my physical body or private life. Instead, I was surprised to realize that these battles, often highly public, seemed to have little to do with *me-as-me* but rather involved *me-as-symbol*. Because I was a female working in a highly competitive world that was unequivocally male dominated, I found that I represented what "successful" (that is, heterosexual) social men were supposed to "achieve" or possess. Because I was a female working in a culture in which women were often characterized as sexual achievements, I found that I represented what the men were supposed to "do." I wasn't allowed to represent workers in general but rather what the workingmen worked for, what they allegedly kept at home, or that which they "fucked" or "screwed" as an expression of their sexuality. In the obvious ways, of course, I was simultaneously a symbol of what men were *not* supposed to be, best represented by the insults they used against each other—"girl," "woman," or, in the more crude vernacular, "pussy." Thus my symbolic role on the worksite, my job within a job, was to be the focal point around which the battles of masculinity were staged. It was as if I existed socially on site solely to assist the men in their own social negotiations of their public masculine identities.[5]

This symbolic "job within a job," representing the Anti-Masculinity, was tiring. It took a toll on me beyond the days of work themselves, a notable toll that I was no more able to prevent than I was to ignore. In fact, my attempts to respond to these challenges were themselves publicly contested, since my responses either supported or challenged the larger status quo. Moreover, my attempts to "let it roll off" (following the advice of some male workers and most supervisors) were criticized by men who warned that my own status was diminished by not attempting to hold my own. The informal rules of the jobsite required that I ignore the instances of harassment and discrimination, yet the rules of public masculinities (to which I was also, however ironically, bound) required that I stand up to my challengers. The complex and often contradictory realities of the industry meant that neither of these responses, nor any hybrid response I was able to conceive, was likely to be successful. It was a situation in which there were no right answers and little that I could do to actually change the day-to-day social conditions of work.

## Masculinities at Work: Entrenched, Dominant, but Far from Monolithic

It was, no doubt, my sense of vulnerability as a woman that made me more immediately aware of the tensions between men and women in the workplace and less immediately aware of the tensions among the men themselves. Although the stereotype of the industry as preferencing and protecting male workers turned out to be undeniably true, my preconceptions of the men as unified in these matters were false. Rather than being monolithic in their interests, the men of construction were starkly divided along the social lines of class position and race, of age and skill, of speed and trade—and often by any and all other dividing lines made meaningful in a given context.

The most surprising aspect of the men's relations was that one of the most significant elements of social structure—that of the class inequality between the men in construction—appeared to be virtually unrecognized. In spite of the tremendous class consciousness attributed to union men in stereotypes, I found that the differences between the men who did the work (the men "in the field") and the men who supervised the work (the men "in the trailer") were largely undiscussed. There were no rants about the "boss man," no Marxist slogans, and few—surprisingly few—critiques of management. Although the workers did complain about individual members of management, they did not complain about management as a whole or about the larger structural relations between the workers and the men who supervised them.

This omission is striking because the interests of these two groups are often directly in opposition. At lunch breaks, for example, it is in the workers' interests to take an extra five minutes, whereas it is in the employers' interests to have workers back on the job punctually, if not earlier. Similarly, in the pacing of work, workers benefit from a more leisurely pace, but employers' interests maximize the level and rates of output. Although I did observe workers acknowledging the differing interests in their own individual situations, they seemed unwilling to acknowledge the larger tensions around (for example) speed, profit, and safety. The men did not openly discuss how their daily risk-taking put money in other men's pockets. Instead, the hallmark of the relationship between the white working-class men on the job and the middle-class white men in the trailer was the emphasis on gender and race-based unity, with a tendency to downplay or even deny the contradictory class interests.[6]

This tendency of the white working-class men to identify "up" the chain of command rather than focus on their own economic circumstances is probably the product of a number of forces but appeared in my observations to be tied to the declining nature of the political and economic circumstances themselves.[7] That is, rather than focus on the declining wages of union construction work or the concomitant loss of union power, or even the general loss of social regard given to working-class persons over the last few decades, the workers of construction appeared to focus on being unified with those who supervise them and profit from their work. It was as if they hoped to derive the power and prestige of management by association.

A second set of reasons for identifying up the chain of command is seen in the historical tendency of the white working class to identify itself as white first and workers second, in a partially successful strategy to emphasize the racial "deservingness" of the labor movement.[8] A similar, gendered benefit has been gained in declaring the construction industry the province of men who require a family-supporting wage, relying on the increasingly outdated beliefs that women are home with their children and that men's wages should be able to support an entire family. Since these arguments supported outcomes of both family wages and gender segregation, it is clear that maintaining a masculine identity has had political and financial advantages for these workers.[9]

Identifying upward cannot be explained simply by the men's desire to become management, although that may be part of it at least for some. It is not the case, however, that a good number of the men in the field will actually make it into the trailer. Instead, a profitable company requires that there be substantially more men working in the field than there are supervising. And, as always, it is the men with supervisory backgrounds and even college degrees who are most likely to begin and end up in the trailer. The men who are most skilled and successful in the field may, of course, eventually win themselves a space in the supervisors' trailer, but it appears to be far more likely that the best workers in the field will simply earn themselves a measure of job security doing exactly what they are doing: working with their hands and tools in the company of other men.

## Organizational Structures, Hierarchical and Insecure

The pressure to strive for job security—even if it keeps the worker in the field and not in the trailer—cannot be lightly dismissed. The men's gendered and racialized work performances were socially and economically meaningful in part because they represented the workers' attempts to negotiate a social proximity to the supervisors' trailer, as well as—on the other side of the equation—the workers' apparent distance from the layoff line. Striving for positive relations with management is the product of organizational (company and union) structures that are both hierarchical and wholly insecure. Because of the seasonal and fluctuating nature of the work (jobs are often halted for bad weather; different sorts of workers are needed at different stages of a job), union employers have the ability to send workers back to the union hall (that is, to lay them off) without providing any warning or justification beyond the statement that "work is slow." And that no one is able to verify whether or not the work actually *is* slow creates a tremendous vulnerability—essentially a total lack of protection from arbitrary firing—for the workers, who are thus dependent to greater and lesser degrees upon the goodwill of their supervisors. The pressure is on to prove oneself as a good, worthy, and cost-efficient worker.

Proving oneself as a worker is not easy, however, and it is most certainly dependent on the goodwill and skill of one's co-workers. In contrast to the image of construction work as tangible and easily measurable, its products of work are generally team products and largely dependent on successful coordination with other workers. This coordination requires assistance from both the members of one's own crew and the members of other trades. Success in any specific task is also likely to be reliant upon the quality and performance of the materials. Thus, the "simple" measurement of what one has done must incorporate—and attempt to control—all these factors.

Because one's work performance is dependent on others, the workplace is highly political. Because the employment itself is insecure, the culture of work is competitive and even cutthroat. Workers must attempt to prove themselves with support—or despite opposition—from others. But proving themselves is further complicated by the fact that the social relations among the men are shaped by a collection of competitive and often contradictory hierarchies: a man is likely to decrease his status in one category as a result of increasing his status in another. For example, the workers were ranked according to trade, a hierarchy in which electricians have more prestige than carpenters, who have more prestige than laborers, and so forth. Within the social hierarchies of the field the men were also ranked by speed and task competence and by their temporary locations on the company totem pole. Since employment in construction is always temporary, however, positions on a totem pole are part theory, part speculation, and always subject to change. And since the values of the varying masculinities themselves are largely contextual, moving "up" is neither easy nor clear.

Still, a few rules of thumb are generally useful in determining an individual's status. Journeymen outrank apprentices; supervisors outrank workers; and among the supervisors, divisions exist between those who wear their tools and those who are able simply to watch the men work. Through all of these rankings run the negotiated meanings of gender and race, categories that are sometimes fluid enough to permit the entrance and "naturalization" of outsiders but, more often than not in my experience, tend to use the presence of outsiders to reinforce the industry's self-concept as white and male dominated. Even the outsiders themselves—white women and men and women of color—are often involved in hierarchical disputes in determining (also contextually and temporarily) which group of outsiders is to be seen as most "inside." All these variations affect how each individual worker is perceived and treated.

### A Labor Process Infused with Economic, Social, and Organizational Forces

The insecure and competitive nature of the workplace does more than simply influence the social or emotional experiences of doing the work; it has real effects upon the way that work is done. It shapes and sometimes mandates how workers relate to their bodies, to their tools, and to the materials. For example, it sometimes means that looking busy is as important as being busy and that any sort of movement, even a movement that might actually be counterproductive or causing mistakes, is seen as better than no movement at all. This means that one might wisely make work when there isn't any—sweeping where sweeping is unnecessary, or moving piles of 2×4s whether or not they need moving—just in case the job's superintendent happens to walk by.

This pressure to prove oneself as a worker—combined with the virtual lack of protection from arbitrary firing—also affects the ways that workers are and are not able to utilize the safety protections on the books. In my own experience, it was clear that workers often worked harder than they should have—according to Occupational Safety and Health Administration (OSHA) regulations as well as conventional wisdom, engaging in risky or hazardous practices to demonstrate that they were willing or able to do such tasks. For example, a worker might opt to carry a 4×10 or 4×12 sheet of drywall by himself, rather than interrupt another worker. Workers often carried heavy items up ladders—creating the very real possibility of losing one's balance and falling—rather than take the time to find or set up a safer means of moving the materials. More mundane but no less meaningful examples include failing to wear earplugs in noisy environments or face masks on dusty worksites—situations where the potential for damage is both clear and cumulative. Damage to hearing and respiratory capacities can be both immediate and built up over time from exposure to even routine and seemingly innocuous hazards. Getting earplugs or a face mask from the trailer, however, takes time from work.

In the short term, the practices involved in demonstrating one's value mean that an individual worker sacrifices physical safety in an attempt to seek economic security within organizational structures that do not provide it. In the longer term, this means that the contract is renegotiated by individual workers and groups of workers in ways that undercut both the contract and the union. The contract is renegotiated because workers individually and collectively remove the protections that have been won for them by refusing to utilize them consistently or across time. When a contract that is agreed upon by the whole is dismantled little by little by individuals—however much constraint or freedom they feel in making their decision—the ability of the union to create or enforce a contractual agreement is weakened.

In looking at the bigger picture, it becomes clear that these practices damage the union movement and the working class as a whole. That such mundane worker actions take place is on its surface an economic phenomenon shaped by social structures and economic pressures. That the workers fail to acknowledge these pressures and their concomitant sacrifices is a cultural and psychological issue, tightly intertwined with gender, racial, and social class identity.

Recognizing the intertwining nature of work practices with racial, gender, and class identities is important because doing so highlights the unified nature of work elements that many scholars and practitioners tend to treat as separate: the labor process and the social performances of workers' various identities. Because these practices are a part of the workers' proving themselves as workers, as whites, and as men, the processes of work and sacrifice in the construction industry reveal a larger truth of workplace life. Most simply, these processes reveal how *the way that work is done* (what Michael Burawoy has termed the capitalist labor process) cannot be understood separately from the ongoing and situational negotiations of gender, class, race, and power.[10] Work *and* gender, sexuality, race, and social class are things that are "done" and "accomplished" during the 7:00 a.m. to 3:30 p.m. day.[11] Work is not a simply physical or economic process: Rather, work is inextricable from the social and historical relations in which it occurs.

Additionally, workers' willingness to forgo basic protections highlights the distinction between what might appear to be actors' "rational interests" (for example, their economic interests in class-based organizing or building a strong labor movement) and their apparent preferences for the social and psychological wages of dominance in the forms of white and male privilege. As I will demonstrate, workers not only continually reproduce the market arrangements in their contract (what Burawoy has called creating consent for the contractual relationship under capitalism) but also *undercut* these arrangements, renegotiating them to their own detriment, by working harder and in less safe ways than the contract requires.[12] This undercutting matters, not least because it challenges the conventional wisdom that workers work against managerial interests and in favor of their own.

## The Methods and the Role of the Researcher

### Deciding to Enter the Trades

My decision to become a construction worker was equally the product of personal and professional interests. I was interested in the way things worked, I wanted a good job, and I wanted to be *competent* in shaping the world and space around me. Having seen my single mom struggle with contractors she was sure were fleecing her and knowing she felt unable to challenge them, I knew I wanted to learn how to fix my own leaky faucets, the holes in my own walls, my own roof. I wanted to be a carpenter.

I also wanted to understand why women *didn't* make this choice more frequently, when it seemed to be well known that earning a wage at a "woman's" job made it hard to pay the bills, whereas earning the wages of a man's job made paying bills possible. This latter question had actually been the basis of my master's thesis, a small survey and a set of interviews I conducted with roughly forty women leaving high school with no plans for college. What I found in those interviews was rather surprising: not only did these women entering the workforce have little information about the wages of jobs or the difference in wages for male or female dominated jobs, but they were also able to say directly that "people would think they were crazy" if they were to become an electrician or an auto mechanic. Thus they were aware of and responding to social pressures. Even when they knew about the wage gap, it appeared that the young women with whom I spoke were more willing to walk away from money than they were to look "crazy."[13]

As I started to think and write about the data from these interviews, I had what I must admit were probably some fairly condescending thoughts. For example, I wondered, "How could these women so obviously let other people shape their decisions? How could they simply be willing to be what other people thought they should be?" The obvious implied contrast in all these questions was me: I assumed that I had been acting in a much more informed and proactive manner. Then I started to think about my own decisions. I realized I knew nothing about the School of Engineering on my campus—or really anything about engineers—because I "knew" in some unspoken way that it was "irrelevant" for me and that I didn't "belong" there. In fact, people might have thought *I* was "crazy" if I had announced that I wanted to learn about engineers and then become one. Hmmm. People might think I was crazy. And here I was getting a graduate degree (not surprising in my family or neighborhood) in sociology (hardly surprising for my gender). I actually knew nothing about what engineers or sociologists or college faculty would earn.

The more I thought about my own decisions, then, the more I realized that I had made essentially the same sort of decision as the young women I had interviewed, I was simply protected somewhat by the class structure. By this I mean that although I, too, had chosen a path fairly segregated by gender—one that my peers and family would find acceptable—unlike the women I studied, I had reason to believe that such a path would allow me to support myself simply because of the "middle class" identification of the job. The gendered wage gap at my educational level was more likely to mean a lower standard of living than an actual inability to support myself.

Because the questions of occupational segregation mattered to me in an applied sense, I knew that I wanted to work on research projects that would enable women to transcend the gendered barriers of jobs (and of poverty) and become economically self-sufficient. Trying to figure out why women weren't entering male-dominated jobs was an important part of this. However, an ideological wrinkle soon appeared in my plans: The more I thought about young working-class women's occupational decision-making and the ways they limited themselves according to gender and class constraints, the more my own constrained choices disturbed me. My choices reflected the preferences of the people around me, yet I was expecting women with fewer resources to do *more,* to go beyond the social and emotional security *that I myself had chosen.* The question that followed me around was this: How could I tell these women that they should leave their female-typed jobs and step outside of the roles that society had offered them, *if I would not?*

Because these questions came at a time when I was already questioning my role within the world around me, they carried more weight than they might have at another, more entrenched time in my life. Thus these were not purely intellectual or theoretical questions for me. Instead, they became personal questions bound up in my conceptions of broader intellectual honesty, in a sense of the person and of the woman that I wanted to be. Combined with a strong interest in remodeling physical spaces and a growing desire to be competent in a broader range of life's tasks, these questions made becoming a construction worker a reasonable choice.

## Becoming a Carpenter

Within a few months of these soul-searching processes, I enrolled at the local technical college in a noncredit class designed to introduce (and recruit) women to the trades. An eight-week program that met for three hours on Monday and Wednesday evenings and for eight hours on Saturdays, the class had sections on each of the different trades. It provided skill training in areas such as framing a wall, running wire, or working with sheetmetal, in addition to the use of power tools, physical fitness and heavy lifting, professional communication, blueprint reading, and writing a résumé to emphasize how past work experiences will transfer into the construction field. Panels of tradeswomen came and spoke to the class, and tradeswomen who were available taught the classes relating to their own trade.

The course thus provided not only role models and contacts but also confidence and the skills needed to start as an apprentice in the construction industry. Additionally, the time and attendance requirements were used to demonstrate to employers the women's commitment to being a part of the industry and to provide both the women and the employers a greater sense of confidence in the women's ability to succeed in an apprenticeship. This course also provided the local tradeswomen's advocates a vehicle for directly addressing the unions and the employers about women's employment, a strategy described by Vivian Price as essential to publicly affirming (and thus eliciting) unions' and employers' commitment to hiring women.[14] As a result, these connections helped the women and advocates circumvent the traditional blocks to hiring that have been well documented in the trades.[15]

During this time I also attended a once-monthly Friday night support group for women interested in nontraditional work. This was a place where women shared hints on the different tests required, information about who was hiring, and which companies were reportedly "better" or "worse" to work for. Women already working told stories about their experiences on the job and offered support (and sometimes condolences) to others. This meeting was facilitated by the woman who coordinated the eight-week course and who often met with employers to help them recruit and retain women workers (or to convince them to hire women in the first place). This support group thus provided similar structural benefits to the class described above.

Bolstered by my experiences and the women I met, I signed up for and took the math test required for the union carpentry apprenticeship. The test consisted of high school geometry in addition to such basic math skills as multiplication, division, subtraction, and addition. I passed and received the slip of paper called a "hunting license," necessary to seek employment as a union apprentice. Although each trade (and often each local) has its own hiring procedure, the hunting license used by the carpenters' local is among the less restrictive approaches, because one needs only to pass the math test and find the first job in order to enter the apprenticeship. Although locating the initial job is not necessarily easy or immune from basic discrimination, this route offers fewer barriers than those into other trades. For example, the electricians' union in my area required more complicated tests and panel interviews, from which a ranked waiting list was created. Many of the "ranked" trades open only a specific number of apprenticeship slots on a semiannual or annual basis, regardless of the length of the list. Although all trades depend on the strength of the market to determine the number of apprenticeship positions, the ranked trades rely on a form of union and employer consensus to establish the numbers for the union local. The carpentry hiring, in contrast, is restricted only by the individual employers' sense of the market.

In spite of all of my anxieties about being able to land a job at all, my career in construction began much sooner than I had anticipated. In January I went to the regularly scheduled meeting of the tradewomen's group at which the president of a local "female-friendly" construction company was the guest speaker. In a half-joking manner (not untouched by false bravado), I asked him whether he was hiring. To my surprise, he invited me to come to his office the following week. Because his was considered a good company to work for, and I didn't see this opportunity coming so quickly again, I went.

## Working Construction as a New, Female Apprentice

Over the next two and a half years I worked as a carpenter's apprentice at various union construction sites in the upper Midwest. I was employed by three different companies with varying workforce sizes and market specialties, and I did a wide range of tasks. I swept, did wood and steel framing, set and stripped concrete forms, hung drywall, set countertops, hung doors, laid shingles, did demolition, and "humped" plywood, 2×4s, and whatever else needed to be humped up and down the site.

It is essential when interpreting this text to recognize that it is written by someone who was a worker, not a researcher, during this time. That is, I was not on site as an observer or an intellectual, but rather was employed full time as an apprentice, enjoying all the privileges and responsibilities of that position. I did not enter the industry with the intent of writing an exposé of masculinity or whiteness or safety, although I was interested in why women did and did not want to work in these jobs. I had rather haphazard plans of completing my apprenticeship and using my academic background (then a master's degree) to find a nonacademic career: maybe running work in the construction industry, maybe doing consulting, maybe taking a government job connected to women and nontraditional work.

My thoughts about what I might do later were far less important, though, than what I was required to be doing at the time. As a worker and not a researcher, I was required to *work*. This meant that I worked eight-hour days, and more when more was required. I worked when the others on my crew worked, in very hot and very cold weather. I worked when I was exhausted, when I was bored, sometimes when I was nervous, and sometimes when I was in pain. Thus, my descriptions of the processes and experiences of work are different than they would be if I had simply been able to observe. I now, for example, have a different understanding of the word "hard" when it is used in the phrase "hard physical labor."

I soon realized that I was in a fortunate (if often uncomfortable) position. As a worker, I understood things about work that my friends who were studying work didn't have a very good sense of. In particular, I found that the realities of working-class work were significantly harder, more damaging, and less protected than my middle-class peers believed. As I read through more of the literature on the industry, I also realized that my perspective as an "outsider" helped me to call into question some aspects of the culture that were foreign to me but taken for granted by previous writers on the industry. Thus I began to realize that my experiences might be able to illuminate more than the processes of women's occupational decision-making.

One of the first things I learned on the job, for example, was how some aspects of work contradict not only the official version of work—the version one might receive from the job foreman or superintendent—but also the accounts one receives from the *workers*. Both employers and workers provide accounts that represent their own individual and collective interests. One example is the actual versus theoretical "curing" time for concrete—the amount of time poured concrete is allowed to harden before the plywood and steel forms, the shell into which the concrete is poured, are removed. Not surprisingly, the textbook- and manufacturer-recommended length of time is significantly longer than the times that appear to be used in practice. These practices—similar to the worker practices that Michael Burawoy describes as "making out"[16]—often contradict the employer's and/or union policies. As a result, this is something I might not have noticed or been told had I been simply interviewing or observing.

There is also a whole range of things that I wouldn't have been *allowed* to experience if I had been on the jobsites only as a researcher. One can assume, for example, that I would have been exposed to less—or at least less serious forms of—harassment. I would not have been asked to engage in work practices that were in violation of both OSHA procedure and OSHA principles. I probably wouldn't have become aware of the insecure nature of employment or how it can complicate otherwise commonsense decision-making. I learned, uncomfortably, how one can come to rationalize actions that involve clear and real risks of injury or even death—because of a perceived lack of choice in the matter. All of these experiences, however uncomfortable at the time, have been invaluable in shaping my understanding of the world of working construction.

## Limits of the Female Apprentice Perspective

That I was on site as a worker is also important for the methodological foundations—and thus the ultimate conclusions—of this book. First, because I was working for roughly eight hours each day, with an additional hour (or three) for travel, I did not have the freedom to engage in the hour and a half of notetaking for each hour in the field that is recommended by many research methodologists.[17] Had I attempted to do so, I would have left myself roughly three hours for sleep *and* all of life's other tasks. Nor was I able to sneak off during the workday to write down my thoughts and observations, as my time was tightly accounted for, and I was often directly supervised. And since my work responsibilities never included writing, I could not hide note taking among other tasks, as researchers such as Herbert Applebaum had been able to do in the 1970s.[18] Instead, what I draw data from are the journals that I kept during this time, much like the journals I have kept for most of my life (I discuss all this in greater depth in the appendix on methods).

Clearly then, these data reflect my own encounters with the construction industry. They are the observations of one white woman working as a union carpenters' apprentice for three companies in a few midwestern cities. Although I have attempted to triangulate the data through conver-

sations with other apprentices (male and female), other journeylevel workers (carpenters and otherwise), supervisors, and superintendents as appropriate, my observations begin and end with my own experiences.

## Caveats on Interpreting and Generalizing These Data

Like all ethnographic data, my observations and explanations are bounded
by the context from which they are drawn. The companies, worksites, and
even the work crews I describe here are clearly the product of their time,
the location, the racial composition of the area, the race and gender politics, and the economic pressures and structures of the region, including the
relative strength of the union locals at the time. My observations are specifically shaped by the fact that I was a *union* carpenter's apprentice, that
I worked in the Midwest, and that I worked in an area not traditionally
dominated by labor or working-class politics. My experiences and the resulting data might have been different in another time and place, under
different influences.

### Influences of the Trade

My data are certainly influenced by the fact that I worked as a carpenter,
rather than an ironworker, an electrician, or a plumber. Carpenters' work
is generally broader and more variable than that of other tradespersons
(with the exception of laborers, who are often able to do a little of everything on site so that they can assist all trades as needed). Although carpenters often specialize in one aspect of building (see chapter 1), it is
carpenters who put together the concrete forms for the foundation wall of
the building and take them apart when the concrete has cured. Commercial carpenters frame the walls, lay the floors, hang the sheetrock on the
walls, install the doors and windows, side the outside, and lay the shingles
on the roof.

   This variability affects my data in two ways. First, because I was able to
work as a concrete carpenter, as a hanger of sheetrock, and as a finish carpenter, my experiences are likely to represent a good deal of the variation
across the trade. Second, as a carpenter I had the opportunity to observe
and interact with a large variety of other trades. For example, carpenters
frame the walls through which electricians and plumbers run their wire
and pipe; carpenters hang the sheetrock that is finished by tapers and

painted by painters. Thus I am confident that I had a reasonably good view of the commercial construction industry within my region.

From the perspective of a carpenter, I am probably more aware of the trends in subcontracting and de-skilling than workers in other trades might be. For example, increased reliance on technology in workplaces has required some workers in other trades to gain highly technical electrical skills or to create and monitor the HVAC (heating, ventilation, and air conditioning) systems necessary for sensitive electronic environments.[19] These jobs are likely to have retained—or created anew—the sense of highly skilled work central to the stereotype of union construction work. On this same job, however, there are likely to be carpenters who do only concrete work or only sheetrock or only roofing—certainly more of the skill sets associated with manual laborers than with craftsmen.

These increasing levels of specialization (or decreasing levels of skill) among carpenters have had notable effects on the size and strength of the union. Union carpenters have been at a greater risk of losing work to nonunion firms, especially residential work, at least in part because of the skill level required at entry. As one worker explained, "any guy who doesn't know what else to do can buy a Skilsaw [the brand name of a circular saw], hang out a shingle, and call himself a carpenter." Labor scholar Herbert Hill argues similarly that some of the mechanical trades (with more expensive tools and training) have been able to retain greater control over their hiring procedures and regulations. As a result, it appears that the mechanical trades have been somewhat more successful than other unions in retaining a largely white base of workers.[20] Thus it appears that this vulnerability of the carpenters' union has led not only to the loss of union control of specific companies and jurisdictions but also to the union's receptiveness to—or perhaps their inability to resist—the increasing diversity of their workforce.

## Importance of the Brotherhood: Union Effects

It is meaningful that this book is written from the perspective of a union apprentice, most obviously because the existence of the formal union apprenticeship system let me be on the job. Union apprenticeships, although they are often given to men with family ties to the industry and thus previous work experience, are open to persons with no formal training or skills. In fact, outside of journeymen who have the skills to simply "buy" their union cards, all apprentices are required to go through the multiyear training program established by the union in coordination with the state and the employers' council. In my area, this was a four-year program for carpenters and a five-year commitment for other trades such as electricians. This makes union apprenticeships both a legitimate and a valuable path for persons who, though without any previous training or experience, are interested in entering the construction industry. Apprenticeships are not exclusively union, but they are predominantly so: While only about 20 percent of construction workers are union members, roughly 75 percent of apprentices come through union programs.[21]

I also opted to enter construction through the union (United Brotherhood of Carpenters and Joiners of America, or UBC) because I felt that it gave me a more scrutinized path of entry. Because of the trade unions' histories of race and gender discrimination, they are often scrutinized by government agencies or other third parties attempting to ensure fairness in hiring. Since unions generally control hiring streams, monitoring union hires is easier than enforcing antidiscrimination policies across individual employers. In my own case, I hoped that this meant my application would not (or could not) quickly or easily be cast aside simply because I was female. Events at roughly the time I was hired suggest that I wasn't entirely wrong on either count—within about a year of my entering the union, another trade in the area was investigated by the federal Equal Employment Opportunity Commission (EEOC) after only white men were taken from the waiting list into apprenticeships.

Of course, I also hoped that this protection might extend to later hirings as well as the initial one, given the formally bureaucratized hiring and out-of-work procedures used by (or at least in place at) most union halls. In theory, when workers are laid off from a job or by a company, they call the union hall to be placed on the out-of-work list. Workers are then removed from the list in chronological order or as requested by employers (by specialty or to address affirmative action needs) to the next available job. This supposedly objective process was important to me as an individual from a "less desirable" category of workers, because it theoretically lessened the difficulty I might have getting hired by companies uninterested in hiring females. Upon later reflection, however, I realized that my own three placements occurred because of personal contacts and networking rather than by going through the union. The extent to which these hiring halls are actually used, as well as whether they actually combat or *extend* discriminatory practices, has been the subject of much writing and discussion.[22]

My decision to go union was also designed to provide me with more protection in terms of safety and working conditions. The union contract includes regulations regarding pay, discrimination, hiring, firing, and so forth, and it is intended to govern all local or regional employers who have signed on with that union. It is my perception (and I would argue that the perception exists throughout the industry) that smaller, nonunion companies are less likely to be monitored by government agencies. Similar to the monitoring of hiring practices, the presence of the union as a semiautonomous third party can simplify oversight for outside agencies, whereas the smaller, nonunion companies may be more likely to interpret rules and regulations differently, and perhaps more loosely. This is of course a difficult perception to validate, as documentation is limited and complex: the fact that union companies appear to have higher worker-compensation claims appears to be an artifact of reporting patterns as much as anything else.[23]

Finally, I chose to work union because I had previously been a union activist within my local of the teachers' union and am a firm believer in unions as a means to democratize and make more egalitarian the world of work. In fact, my desire to go union may have preceded the choice of construction work: I was drawn by the promise of a democratic, activist, and empowered workforce. Although my idealism has been somewhat dimmed by the ways in which many unions have been and continue to be heavily involved in the reproduction of inequality—the product of both individuals' actions and antidemocratic structures—I still believe firmly that working for greater equality (and, in the case of the United Brotherhood of Carpenters and Joiners, for a democratic and representative union) is both unions' potential and their mandate.

## Regional Effects

There are also likely to be area-specific effects that influence what I describe. For example, in contrast to larger urban areas, the medium-sized city in which I did much of my work has never had a solid working-class, industrial population base—as did, for example, Chicago or New York City. There are not the generations of union workers and families nor the concomitant union history and sentiment to bolster the otherwise flagging unions. Instead, the area was dominated by largely educated and white-collar communities, and the unions active there were themselves largely white collar and tied to county, state, and federal government employment.

Although it is difficult to know exactly how my experiences might have been different in a major metropolis or a city with a more traditional blue-collar history, it is possible that the union locals in which I *was* working were weaker and less able to intervene for workers than they would have been in those other settings. Alternatively, it is possible that a community with a longer history of working-class unions would have had more of the problems tied to exclusivity and discrimination which I describe.

The data I report were likely influenced as well by what one might describe as the political culture of the area. The jurisdiction in which I worked is widely perceived as being politically liberal (if not "politically correct"), and this regional characteristic can be expected to influence the union culture. Specifically, conditions described within this study are likely to be more egalitarian, less gendered, and potentially less racist than in some other cities and locales. On the other hand, since the population is largely white in both the county and the state, it is possible that what I have observed is dramatically *less* racially egalitarian than are larger cities with larger and more politically powerful nonwhite populations. Still, some data suggest that my observations vary more in form or degree than in content from similar observations in other places. For example, in larger, racially diverse urban areas the construction industry appears to be integrated by worksite but not by trade. This means that white men and men of color work on the same jobsite but that they do different work and belong to different trades, with the trades of lower skill and less prestige becoming the province of the nonwhite or immigrant men.[24] In any case, my data are by definition circumscribed and call for further elaboration by future workers and scholars.

### Introduction to the Companies

My observations and conclusions are also shaped by the three companies for which I worked, all of different sizes, with different market specialties and different work cultures. The work that I did for each company was linked to its size and specialty: at the one I call *Remodel Co.*, I spent the majority of my time doing steel studs and drywall, with a healthy dose of roofing thrown in for variation. At the company I call *Concrete, Inc.*, virtually all my time was spent pinning together and stripping apart the plywood-and-steel forms into which semifluid concrete is poured. At the third company, the one I call *Family Builders*, I did the largest variety of tasks, including trim work, which is widely considered to be the most skilled (insofar as one must make detailed and accurate adjustments to the materials) and the "easiest" (insofar as one is generally working indoors in reasonably safe, clean, and even potentially comfortable circumstances).

Although it was the case in my experience that the size of a company correlates with both its work and its culture, drawing this sort of conclusion is complicated by the fact that even smaller companies can serve as general contractors on jobs, meaning that a small company may be brought in to coordinate the work of the other, often larger contractors. It is generally carpenters and carpentry contractors that serve in the role of general contractor, interacting with and supervising the companies doing the plumbing, painting, and electrical work (for example). Because distinctions between task domain, workforce size or "manpower," and organizational culture are complex, I don't attempt to theorize about the causal relationships between these variables but rather rely upon the variation within my experience to discuss the different forms and possibilities of work and work culture within the construction industry.

*Company Sizes and Specialties.*   The first company I worked for, Remodel Co. had approximately two hundred workers and did mostly commercial remodeling, with some from-the-ground-up work. Although we did on occasion handle a small residential job for a special client (generally an individual with whom the company management worked on larger commercial projects), almost all the work done by this company involved medium-sized commercial or business projects. Its specialty was the renovation of retail units in shopping malls (including free-standing buildings), theaters, restaurants, and churches.

Concrete, Inc., was the largest of the three companies I worked for, employing roughly five hundred "men"—the generic term for workers in construction. It specialized in larger structures, such as corporate business offices and headquarters, medical clinics, parking ramps, and state or federal government buildings. With a focus on poured concrete and large steel-beam structures, the work done by Concrete, Inc., is referred to as *heavy construction* by those in the industry. It involves generally bigger, dirtier, and somewhat less precise work than the "lighter" aspects of carpentry such as cabinetmaking or trim work. Although smaller crews came on site to do the finish work or remained after the earlier rough work was completed, the bulk of the company's "manpower" was utilized on the concrete work.

The third company I worked for was a family-run concern of roughly thirty workers and office staff. This company, Family Builders, did more residential work than the other two, although its specialty was also in the commercial sector. Family Builders' residential work was somewhat of an anomaly among union companies due to the higher risks and tighter profit margins in the residential sector. In its commercial work, Family Builders tended to focus on smaller-to-medium retail units such as bars, restaurants, and stores. The company had its own shop where it made its own floor base and other wood molding, in addition to building and laminating counters and other large forms. Although all three companies performed the same range of tasks, the carpenters working for Family Builders were likely to have a larger range of assignments (and thus talents) than they would have had at either of the two bigger firms; thus, they came closest to the image of craft workers perpetuated by the academic and general literatures on construction. Closer examination, however, reveals that they, too, were subject to the pressures of specializing and de-skilling—albeit to a lesser degree than their counterparts at Remodel Co. and Concrete, Inc.

*Organizational Cultures of the Three Firms.*   The three companies varied not only in size and likely tasks but also in their cultures. Remodel Co., the midsized firm, was known for working in public and semipublic settings and thus had what might be considered a paraprofessional culture. Although the company owners repeatedly referred to the workers as a "rougher" sort of men or "pigs" (terminology I discuss in greater depth in chapter 6), they also had high standards for the public behavior of their workers with clients. As I assert repeatedly in later chapters, it was not the case that the lines of propriety were not understood by the men who worked for this company (or the other companies); it was simply a case of when, where, and by whom the rules were—or were not—enforced. Both in the field and in the office of Remodel Co. (where I had numerous opportunities for discussion with the female clerical support staff), it seemed clear that women were "welcome" to work in the field of construction as long as they understood the differences between men and women—that is, the sorts of behaviors that the cruder sort of men were likely to engage in. This clearly meant, too, that women working in the field were not supposed to expect the higher standard of behavior to be applied in *their* presence, just that of the clients.

Because Remodel Co. tolerated harassment and discrimination, these behaviors were common. But the management at Remodel Co. was also clear about the liabilities of harassment, and they did not intend to be held liable. For example, they, like the other companies, maintained formal regulations against harassment and used them as needed when problems arose. But it was my distinct impression that the sanctions for such behavior were also applied strategically. If a man was able to use harassing behavior in a manner such that no formal complaints were made, no sanctions would be used to displace him. In the one situation where a formal complaint was filed (it was actually in my own situation, when I learned that a foreman was claiming responsibility for my pregnancy after I lost work time because of a miscarriage), the company stonewalled me and sent the foreman in question "on the road," a clearly less desirable position than being able to work near his home. Thus the company protected itself, and both parties in the field were sanctioned.

At Concrete, Inc., the nature and location of the work permitted a different sort of organizational culture. Because the company boasted roughly five hundred workers, the sites were large and physically remote from the office. Workers therefore almost always reported to the worksite directly and virtually never to the company's office or shop, as they might for Remodel Co. and Family Builders. In fact, it was possible that a person could work a number of years for Concrete, Inc., and never see the inside—or even the outside—of the corporate office walls.

This distance between worksite and office appeared to be significant for the ways in which harassment and discriminatory behaviors were understood and tolerated. The physical distance from the office created a buffer of safety for those wishing to engage in such behaviors. In my experience with Concrete, Inc., working under a superintendent who tolerated and even exacerbated the tensions between the various categories of workers, this meant that workplace problems were problems only if they made it back to the office. From what I could gather by observation, in conversation, and by a virtual lack of consequences for much of what occurred on site, they never did. As a result, harassment and discrimination seemed to be a workplace sport, rather like "girl baiting," which was defined as little more than fun. Although the formal policies of the company remained in place, they had the same effect as those at Remodel Co.: protecting the company and minimizing the changes made to workers' behaviors.

It was at Family Builders, founded by a man who had since turned the company over to his children, where harassment and discrimination (at least along gender lines) simply did not occur. This was not because Family Builders drew its workers from an entirely different labor pool; they did not. Although the firm tended to retain a good number of its workers when the economy permitted—and certainly offered working conditions that engendered worker loyalty—Family Builders hired its workers from the same union locals as the other firms. The difference in its company culture appears to be tied to the owners' policy of no tolerance for harassment or discrimination. This policy was generally attributed to the older brother running the firm and was taken seriously by the workers. Management left no room for doubt that these policies and their enforcement should be treated as real. Although the workers and managers tended to use some of the same phrases as the other companies to talk about harassment and discrimination policies (such as stating that someone would be fired immediately if such problems occurred), Family Builders was the only company where I saw any indication that such action might in fact be taken. As a result of their approach, virtually none of the prohibited behaviors took place during the time that I was working there.

As I argue in greater depth in chapter 5, this is perhaps the single most important point to be made in the interpretation of worker "nature"—that workers (like other people) appear to be easily socialized into and out of dominant-group behaviors. That is, union construction workers appear to be "pigs" when they are called upon to be pigs, and they simply aren't when being a pig is truly prohibited. These performances are therefore not reflective of the workers' "essence" but rather are tied to the larger social structures in which the workers exist. More important, perhaps, these performances reveal the connections to the larger structures of inequality that both privilege and constrain the men.

Upcoming chapters demonstrate that the men of construction gain substantial public and psychological wages by performing the stereotype of the union construction worker.[25] This stereotype not only empowers these men over white women and people of color but also adds a dimension of social, historical, and even moral meaning to the work, as D. W. Livingstone and Meg Luxton describe in their work on the gender consciousness of steelworkers: "The unpleasantness and the brutality of the working situation is sometimes reinterpreted into a heroic exercise of manly confrontation with the task. . . . Difficult, uncomfortable or dangerous working conditions are not seen directly as employer-imposed hazards for the workers, but as challenges to masculine prowess.[26] Construction workers are able to tie into the larger cultural imagery that establishes them as real and natural (if unrefined) men. They serve as the symbol of hard work, of individualism, and in a larger sense of the American nation, which built itself from the ground up (ignoring, of course, the more problematic accounts of history that take indigenous and slave populations into account).

These same performances that empower the workers also constrain them, however, and add to the power of those who employ them—specifically but not exclusively the men of the managerial class. White male construction workers are constrained first as individuals, because this performance of the stereotype (what I refer to later as performing "pigness") is not an option; instead, it is a mandatory part of demonstrating one's fitness as a man as well as a construction worker. In this setting as in other settings, men who do not conform to dominant models of masculinity are themselves sanctioned and devalued.[27] In a wholly insecure organizational structure, this matters.

These men are also constrained as a class. Even though their racialized and gendered performances elevate them as men over women and as white men over men of color (at least in working-class settings), these performances serve to subordinate them further as workers. As I demonstrate in chapters 5 and 6, the performance and reproduction of the construction worker stereotype causes the men to work in ways that undercut their longer-term individual and collective political and economic interests. Thus, such performances are ultimately beneficial for management. It becomes clear, as Cynthia Fuchs Epstein has argued, that "heightening gender distinctions sometimes provides a means of controlling the workers, of undermining their resistance and maximizing consent on the job."[28] Because of this simple truth, then, the nature of public masculinities in the construction industry would appear to reveal more about power and dominance, privilege and constraint, and the social constructions of identities than it does about any "true" or "essential" manhood.

## Outline of the Text

This book delineates the culture and practices of union construction workers in ways that reveal the gender, racial, and class-based tensions I've pointed out in this introduction. In chapter 1 I describe the economic and political contexts of contemporary union construction work, focusing on how such work is *perceived* by outsiders (and perhaps by the men themselves) and illuminating the ways in which the industry's realities differ from the myths. I emphasize particularly the unusual nature of hiring and firing in construction, and how these structures shape the options available to the workers.

In chapter 2 I explore the social relations of production, focusing on the way that workers and groups of workers come to be recognized as "good" or "bad" workers through collective conversations and practices. Affirmative Action politics, hazing and harassment, and informal training are among the topics included in this overview.

Chapter 3 expands on some of these ideas by exploring the ideologies about "outsiders" (largely white women and men of color) that I encountered while working as an apprentice. These circularly supported ideologies were used not only to justify discrimination and harassment but also to make it invisible. Thus these ideologies also serve to *neutralize and make acceptable* discriminatory practices that at least some of the men would appear to have opposed in their lives beyond the construction site.

Chapter 4 looks at how the bodies working construction shape and are shaped by the social structures in which the work occurs. I explore both the external changes to the body (such as weathering and strength) and the interior changes whereby the body comes to understand its own physiological reactions as supporting the gendered and heterosexualized structures. By focusing on the physical conditions and experiences of doing the work and how these experiences are inextricably tied to the notions of manhood and heterosexual sexuality, I reveal how doing construction work pays a *physiological and psychological* wage by making the worker look and *feel* like a man. This matters collectively as much as individually, because it provides an external—and more important, internalized—validation of the work culture. As a result, these feelings of masculinity serve also to validate the larger ideologies about who does and does not belong in the industry.

In chapter 5, I examine the way male workers and managers talk about the white men working in the field of construction and show how their ideologies—apparently positive on the surface—maintain and even expand class inequalities while protecting the white and male privileges that exist. The true costs of these class inequalities are illustrated in chapter 6, which focuses on the formal and informal rules about safety practices in construction. Drawing on my own experiences in the industry, as well as the media coverage of a fatal work accident in the same region, I argue that what appears to be a masculine rejection of safety procedures is really a constrained set of decisions, scripted by pressures for speed and the industry's lack of protection from arbitrary firing.

In sum, the white male workers' use of gender and race divisions in their attempts to empower themselves not only obscures their economic interests but makes virtually impossible the working-class solidarity that could strengthen them over the longer term. I discuss this in chapter 7, along with the psychological, social, and economic payoffs of race and gender privilege. Here I elaborate on the *wage of whiteness*, a concept coined by W. E. B. Du Bois, expanded by David Roediger, and amended recently and succinctly by Eduardo Bonilla-Silva.[29] I add to it a *wage of masculinity*, complete with its financial, psychological, and even physiological rewards. I conclude with a discussion of the implications for labor and class politics in the United States.

## Two Final Notes for the Reader

### On My Use of Language

In my descriptions and analysis I have chosen language that both reflects and reproduces the cultural tensions of the construction industry. First, I use the pronoun "he" throughout, except at points where I am specifically referring to a broader scope of workers or trying to call the reader's attention to the presence and experience of women. I do this not because I believe male pronouns to be neutral or "generic"—on the contrary, I believe them to be powerful and exclusive. To use mixed pronouns (i.e., "he or she") or a more neutral "they" would mislead the reader into seeing the environment as something other than heavily gendered, virile, macho, and unavoidably male. To pull readers into a world that does *not* sound and feel entirely male would be to take them into a world that is *not* the union construction industry.

This unavoidable maleness of the workplace culture is striking and pervasive. In spite of being a woman who has long argued for the recognition of appropriate pronouns, while working in construction *I found myself beginning to refer to the world in masculine ways*. At first it happened only at work or on construction-related topics, but it soon spread to other contexts. Additionally, I began to adopt the language of "doing" female things at work, (e.g., getting *her* done, calling *her* a day). This use of language (as I argue in chapter 4) is tied to the production of masculinity both socially and physiologically. These changes meaningfully shaped the way that I experienced my job and myself. It is with a healthy respect for the power of language, therefore, that I have chosen to use it to reinforce my descriptions.

Second, I use the word "worker" in general to refer to white workers, and overwhelmingly this reference will be to white male workers. This usage reflects a history of gendering and racializing language; in fact, it may simply sound generic to many Americans. Rather than simply reinforcing such an assumption, though, my intent is to highlight the historically and socially constructed nature of these categories, as well as, again, to re-create the flavor of the construction industry as it is experienced.

A third way in which I intentionally use language to reproduce the environment is by adopting the language of the culture itself—including the use of the word "macho" as it is ingrained in the cultural picture of the cowboy-style construction worker. I use it consciously in the North American sense rather than according to the Latino definition, although I am aware of and sensitive to the distinction.[30] Much of the speech can also be graphic, sexual, and violent. Swearing is pervasive on worksites, and some of that appears here. To the extent that this language shapes both the culture and its participants, its inclusion seems unavoidable. I apologize in advance for any discomfort this may cause the reader.

## On Generalizing (or Failing to Generalize) beyond the Industry

In my last aside to the reader, I should like to make it very clear that I am not suggesting that construction's issues with gender, class, and race are wholly different from those in other industries. As any review of the literature makes clear, the conditions of discrimination and harassment on the basis of gender and race are hardly exclusive to a single industry; they may occur more overtly within but are certainly not limited to the building trades. Research has consistently revealed that these issues are present in many if not most industries and occupations. See, for example, Rosabeth Moss Kanter's study of executives and secretaries; Jennifer Pierce's exploration of litigators and paralegals; Robin Leidner's investigation of insurance sales and fast-food work; Judith Hicks Stiehm's work on women in the military; and Cynthia Cockburn's analysis of gender and change in the printing industry, among many, many others.[31]

In construction, of course, the discrimination is often more obvious than it is in other industries: discrimination and harassment are often right out there where you can see it and hear it—or, to put it bluntly, where it can grab you quite literally in the behind. In other fields (academics, for example) very different language is used to draw boundaries between the dominant and subordinate groups. The procedures through which workers are evaluated are, in some settings, equally subjective and arbitrary; thus the production of the "good worker" and "good scholarship" in academics can sometimes resemble construction work more than one might think. This is not to argue, of course, that construction is not generally or overtly sexist (or racist or homophobic), since this identity is part of the construction worker stereotype that I describe in chapter 5. Instead, I would like to emphasize that the construction industry should not be used as a contrast for other industries or occupations in which power is exercised and negotiated in more complex and subtle ways. As much as construction workers are tied to a vision of a universal masculinity, they are also treated as authentic bearers of racism, sexism, and homophobia. This attitude, as my text reveals, is not only incorrect in its reference to other groups and industries but is also at the heart of the contradictions that plague construction worker identities and performances, and, ultimately, their political agency.

# 1

# THE POLITICAL AND
# ECONOMIC RELATIONS OF THE
# CONSTRUCTION INDUSTRY

In the 1970s, union construction workers were in their heyday. They were earning well and doing respected work. They were even labeled the "aristocracy" of the working class by a midwestern academic, E. E. LeMasters, who spent time hanging out and shooting pool in a working-class tavern to write a book that purported to be about "blue-collar life styles."[1] During this same time, a union electrician—also in the Midwest—was drawing upon his own experiences at work to write what would later become *Hard Hats,* an ethnographic account of union construction work.[2]

In both accounts the authors appeared to draw on as well as contribute to the standing stereotypes of the day. Jeffrey Riemer, the electrician-turned-sociologist, provided a workplace equivalent to LeMasters's tavern observations, describing the men of construction as hearty, rough-and-tumble characters who take the world head on. About this same time, Herbert Applebaum, an anthropologist with supervisory experience in the industry, wrote a monograph that concurred with Riemer's view, adding that the men were always ready to laugh, liked a good party, and enjoyed food.[3] Thus construction workers, when described by men who had previously worked in the field, were heralded as the hypermasculine average Joe, with an eye for women, a taste for liquor, and a talent for workplace pranks.

More important perhaps, all three of these accounts described union construction workers as having the world by the tail when it came to making a living. They portrayed union construction as providing significant freedom, good working conditions, great pay, and a convivial environment where working-class masculinities set the rules. In fact, the workers were seen not just as having *a lot* of freedom and control on the job but instead as having almost *too much* control. In one example, Riemer described how union construction workers not only determined many of their working conditions but also when—and if—they would work. He relates the following about how "rain days" (when work was called off because of the weather) were determined on one of his work sites: "A member of the carpenter crew . . . drew a circle in the dust on a particularly cloudy day and stated, 'When three rain drops fall in the circle, I'm going to the tavern.' And he did, and others joined him."[4] Workers were seen as having so much control over their work that they could not only call a rain day, they could declare it to be raining *when it wasn't*. It is hardly an exaggeration to say that they could be like gods on the site, able to bend the elements—or at least the naming of the elements—to their will.

My experience, roughly twenty years later and also in the Midwest, revealed a very different world of construction work. I wrote in my journal:

It is Monday morning a little before 7 a.m., and we are all sitting in the mantrailer (the portable building where we store our personal gear and take coffee breaks), waiting for the word on whether or not we will work in the rain. Martin, the foreman, finally comes into the trailer, and after a few morning comments, says, *"Well, let's hit it, it's not raining that hard."* This is followed by several rounds of jokes from the workers about Martin's signature line in these situations: *"It's not raining until I tell you it's raining."*

So we head out to work for a few hours until it is raining so hard that even Martin has to acknowledge that it is raining. The downpour is torrential as we sit in the trailer, waiting for the weather to break enough for a run to the temporary parking lot, now a giant mud puddle filled with trucks and cars.

Two of the workers have not returned to the mantrailer, however, and are known to be working up in a cherry picker (also known as a "manlift") some distance away.

*"Where the hell are Foxy and Al?"* barks Martin, the foreman, clearly agitated.

*"They're up on [————] Street* [a distant part of the job]," the lead laborer responds.

*"What the hell are they doing out there in this rain?"* yells Martin in even greater irritation.

*"How are they supposed to know it's raining without you there to tell them it's raining?"* the lead laborer barked back, hiding a bit of a smile.

Even though the workers (and particularly the lead laborer) are clearly joking with the foreman, there was more than a kernel of truth in the joke.

In fact, on this job it really was the case that we were not even supposed to *say* that it was raining. After all, to point out that it was raining would be to suggest the need for calling the day, and therefore each such statement made by workers was met with the foreman's standard line: *"It isn't raining until I tell you it is raining!"* Thus in my experience, in contrast to Riemer's, workers were neither allowed to call the day nor, in general, able to avoid working in the rain.

This comparison of rain days is significant because it illuminates some of the changes that have taken place in union construction since the 1970s. In contrast to Riemer's, Applebaum's, and LeMasters's descriptions, by the time I walked on site the workers were no longer treated like or seen as gods. Instead, on this job and virtually all others, the job's timeline appeared to be the god, and it was the foreman (or, more likely, the job superintendent via the foreman) who set the rules. By the time I worked union construction, the rules were not in favor of the worker.

## Contemporary Conditions of Union Construction Work

In this chapter I draw on my own experiences to illuminate the contemporary political and economic realities of union construction work. In contrast to Riemer's portrayal of the overly empowered workers of the 1970s, I describe workers whose work has been sped up, de-skilled, and subcontracted; whose real wages have dropped; and whose unions' membership—and union protections—are dramatically lower than expected. I describe workers who are in control of neither the worksite nor their own working conditions. In fact, I argue that a close look at the actual conditions of the workplace—especially when compared with the officially stated policies of the unions and employers—reveals that construction workers, even union construction workers, are actually less, not more, protected than many other classes of workers. I begin by describing the feature of work that I believe is at the center of most other relevant working conditions: the structural insecurity of construction employment.

### Structural Insecurity

It is very likely that the most significant—and least recognized—feature of union construction work is the workers' lack of protection from arbitrary firing. This is neither a passing trend nor dependent on the individual employer or union representative. Instead, it is a feature of the work that is built into the contract. On every job and at any time, union employers in construction have the ability to lay off any worker without warning, grounds, or severance pay. I refer to this as *structural insecurity* because it is built into the legal and contractual relationship between employers, unions, and workers.

It is important to note, however, that the contracts do not actually read that anyone may be laid off at any time for any reason. Instead, the contracts offer two distinct paths for the removal of a worker. One is the doctrine of "just cause" or progressive discipline. According to this doctrine, a problematic or nonperforming worker is to be warned, first verbally and then in writing, and, after being allowed the opportunity to improve his performance, can then be terminated in a manner considered to be fair. In order to be legal, of course, the cause for the firing can only be something related to work performance. It cannot be tied to the worker's gender, race, or protected forms of action such as union organizing or filing complaints about discrimination, harassment, or safety violations. This path, in my experience, is never used.

The second path through which a worker may be removed is that of the "layoff," which requires no formal justification in regard to worker performance or action. The layoff path is designed to respond to the constantly changing workforce needs of the industry. Since construction is by definition a dynamic workplace, each job will almost by definition require a different number of workers each month, each day, and potentially each hour. And, as the work moves from demolition to grounds preparation, to foundation, to framing, and to finish work, different types of workers are required as well. Since construction is also affected by weather, work tends to stop for rainstorms and other dramatic or dangerous conditions, as well as slowing down for winter in many northern states. As a result of these changing conditions and labor needs, then, employers have the ability to take on and lay off workers without having to resort to the procedures of progressive discipline. Employers may draw workers from—and return workers to—the union halls as needed in order to best staff their worksites under these constantly changing conditions. Employers need only say that "work is slow" or the like, and workers are no longer employed.

Although the processes of "laying off" and "firing" continue to be distinct in theory and in the contract, in practice they are the same. Workers are not generally warned or terminated for cause but instead are told to return to the union hiring hall because "work is slow." No other justification needs to be offered. This conflation of layoffs with firing translates roughly into a freedom of management to *let go of anyone at anytime for any reason—*

and for the workers a complete lack of protection from arbitrary firing. This path, in contrast to progressive discipline, offers no protection for persons who might be vulnerable to discrimination, such as those deemed less desirable by reason of their racial or gender identity or their union activism or political activities.

Workers are aware of the company's discretionary power and that the discretion can be used for a variety of reasons unrelated to labor needs. The widespread recognition of these policies is revealed by the fact that one need only make reference to the firing procedures to hear a seasoned construction worker recite—sometimes with a smile—"I've never been fired, but I've been laid off when they were hiring!" This means, of course, that he was laid off with the justification of "no work" even as newly hired workers were streaming through the gate.

This structural insecurity has immeasurable effects upon worker behavior. Since the workers are not protected from arbitrary firing, they are reliant on the goodwill of their employer for their ongoing financial security. And because of the transitional nature of worksites, the need for this goodwill is significant. As Herman Benson has shown, "Construction workers no sooner start working on one job than they worry where the next will come from."[5] Thus the goodwill of one's employer and the ability to "get on steady" with an employer (be retained across building projects) are no small matters.

The dependence of workers on the goodwill of their employer is certainly increased by the declining strength of construction unions and of organized labor as a whole. If unions were stronger, they could potentially enforce the formal processes through which workers are to be hired and let go. Workers are further weakened in their relationships with employers by the processes of de-skilling and subcontracting, both of which have generally reduced the skills used by the average worker. And fewer skills reduce the worker's ability to locate a new employer, should he displease—or choose to walk away from—his current boss.

## Declining Union Strength

Although Jeffrey Riemer's description of the circle in the dust is no longer an apt summary of union workers' power in the workplace, it is meaningful today because it reveals the dramatic changes that have taken place over time. As I mentioned, my observations of construction took place approximately 20 years after Riemer's. Although in roughly the same area, our union experiences were quite different, in part because mine occurred in an era significantly less friendly to union activity. I was a union construction worker long after President Ronald Reagan used replacement workers to break the air traffic controllers' strike in 1981, an action that is widely seen as having devastated the effectiveness of threatened strikes or walkouts. This was also after globalization began the international *Volksmarch* of manufacturing jobs, first to the southern United States and then to factories beyond U.S. borders. By the time I entered the workforce, the co-occurring antiunion sentiment and cultural emphasis on consumption seemed to have caused the working-class consciousness to shift away from fighting for the American Dream to being willing to dream about making it big through the lottery.

These changes have had real numeric results in addition to the obvious ideological shifts. For example, in the years between 1970 and 1999, union membership in construction declined from 39 percent to 19 percent.[6] This means that over the course of three decades, unionization in the construction workforce has been cut in half: now only two out of ten construction workers are part of a union. The decline in unionization matters because labor unions provide protective benefits for their members and even, it appears, for nonunion competitors. Union membership is known to be correlated with better pay for union workers.[7] Union membership is also believed to be correlated with safer work environments, although this is considered somewhat difficult to verify because of widespread underreporting by both union and nonunion employers.[8] More important, perhaps, the improvements tend to spread to competing companies in the nonunion sector; as a result, the benefits of unionization include higher pay and benefits within the regional construction market. When unionization declines, then, nonunion workers are likely to suffer along with the union members.

More specific effects of unions' decline can be seen in the areas of their jurisdiction: wages, hours, and working conditions, the three primary topics over which unions are allowed to bargain; all other issues are discussed at the discretion of management. It is important to recognize, of course, that these categories may be more analytically than actually separate. For example, a decline in wages makes overtime more imperative for some workers, and an increase in overtime tends to increase the risk of injury, a primary component of working conditions.

*The Decline of Union Wages.* At the end of the twentieth century, union construction workers' wages, like most working-class wages, took a big hit. In fact, statistics reveal that the purchasing power of union wages declined roughly 25 percent between the 1970s and the early 2000s.[9] That these jobs continue to be seen as highly desirable is tied in many ways to their strength *relative* to other working-class jobs. That is, these jobs remain a highly attractive option for persons entering the workforce after high school in part, if not largely, because other job opportunities have declined in value or disappeared altogether.[10]

The stereotype of the construction worker as earning exorbitant sums of money does not, however, reflect current realities. Although people often remarked about the vast amounts of money I "had to be making" as a union carpenter, the reality was that I started the job earning roughly six bucks an hour—40 percent of the journeyman's scale at that time. In spite of the great fanfare for union construction wages, I was coming in not far above minimum. And this was a job for which I had to purchase several hundred dollars' worth of hand tools *and* often drive up to ninety miles to the worksite. My health benefits didn't kick in for a few months; I had to pay into the retirement fund for which I would not be eligible until I had worked ten full years; and I had union dues and other fees to boot. In other words, I wasn't rolling in money as people seemed to think.

I *did*, however, have the health benefits after a few months, and I was in a job that would eventually provide retirement if I stayed. I received on-the-job training, and my pay was contractually scheduled to increase every six months until it reached the journey-level scale—then roughly $17.80 an hour plus benefits. And this deal even improved slightly while I was in the union: during my second year, the apprentice scale was adjusted to begin at 60 percent (about $10.50 an hour) in response to a perceived difficulty in recruiting new apprentices. Thus those who began after me started under even better conditions.[11]

This hourly wage, however, cannot easily be converted into one's annual wage. Many jobs permit a mathematical calculation of hourly wages multiplied by hours per week (usually forty) and weeks per year (usually fifty). Construction work, in contrast, is vulnerable to both logistical and weather-related shutdowns, and construction worker earnings are estimated on a thirty-nine-week year. As a result, the average journey-level wage in my area would have been estimated at $27,768 in gross pay, rather than the $35,600 that could be earned in fifty weeks. This amount is clearly above the average earnings of many Americans and even significantly above those of many nonunion construction workers. So, even though my then-current and future pay was not what I or others might have imagined, the job was and continues to be a good option for working-class workers. This desirable status is best considered a measure of relative rather than absolute conditions, though, as the remainder of my text makes clear.

*Increasing Overtime.* The second aspect over which unions have the right to bargain is that of hours—a right that is in reality somewhat limited, since construction workers largely work according to the needs of the job. Unions' weakness in this area is reflected in the industry-wide increases in overtime. Although this could appear to be desirable, given the extra (time-and-a-half) pay, overtime is problematic because of higher risks, increased pressure on workers and their families, and, perhaps most important, the fact that overtime is not in practice as voluntary as it is in theory.

Although the carpenters' union contracts in my region stated clearly that no worker was required to accept overtime, the option to work overtime is clearly only as voluntary as the employers consider it to be, given the total lack of firing protection that exists for workers. Because workers know that they work at the whim and pleasure of the employer, employers don't need to put overt pressure on them to accept the overtime (OT). Workers are well aware of the pressures to get the job done according to schedule, and they are also aware of the penalties and bonuses for supervisors who complete a job behind or ahead of schedule, respectively. Thus, OT was in my experience technically voluntary but in reality as mandatory as other days and work times. Workers worked OT when asked and, strikingly, seemed never to use their vacation or sick days. They took seriously the time pressures of work and reported in when the boss asked them to.

The questionably optional aspect of OT is significant for workers' overall well-being. Although OT can certainly enhance income, the increasing use of it is likely to diminish workers' longer-term economic positions through the addition of injury and illness risks.[12] Injuries not only cost a worker through lost and largely uncompensated sick time but also through the potential for decreased future earnings if he should be partially or fully disabled. Thus the risks are clearly economic as well as physical. An aspect of union construction work largely unrecognized outside of the industry is that days lost to sick time are uncompensated, and thus the cost is often borne by the individual worker. Workers are not paid by their employing company for time missed due to illness or work-related injury. They are compensated from a union fund *if* they miss *more than one full week* of work, but less than one full week of absence is simply out of the pocket of the worker—likely explaining at least some workers' tendency not to take sick days when the sun was shining.

Although it is generally assumed that workers' compensation provides financial protection in case of injury, the apparent trend in the industry—documented in research as well as my own experience—is that employers prefer to keep injuries off the books and offer to pay workers' direct medical costs instead of filing an official work-injury claim. This practice not only transfers work-related medical costs to the workers' health insurance plans rather than the company's insurance (an issue significant at the national level) but also prevents workers from accessing the additional funds allocated to support workers injured on the job. Thus, workers who are injured on the job—a risk increased by overtime—pay out of their own pockets for the majority of short- and long-term costs. These costs could be significant, I observed, because the union monies that served to replace lost wages *did not come close* to replacing all the wages; instead, they were a fraction of what would have been earned on the job—roughly only $140 a week while I was an apprentice.

In spite of all of the very real economic reasons that workers might oppose increasing levels of OT, overtime continues to be a common response of employers. It is widely recognized that the pace of the industry itself has sped up over recent decades and that there are notable pressures to build buildings in ever shortened lengths of time. As a result, in a study completed at the end of the 1990s, the AFL-CIO estimated that more than 25 percent of union construction workers were putting in overtime in the average week.[13]

Overtime also increases the pressures on workers with families. Given that the questionably voluntary OT is taking place in an industry already considered hostile to those with family responsibilities (e.g., the lack of sick days or flex time, and the often extensive travel required to job sites), it is likely that insistence on overtime is undesirable, even for many of the people for whom the additional money would be most welcome. It was certainly my sense while working in the industry that the vast majority of my male co-workers did *not* have stay-at-home wives (as the stereotypes might predict) but rather spouses who were working in some capacity. As a result, especially for workers with children, the burdens of housekeeping and child care were likely to be disproportionately shunted to their spouses—and therefore to workers in other industries.

*Working Conditions.*   The third aspect of work over which unions are permitted to bargain is that of working conditions. Again, the comparison between Riemer's example and my experience suggests one way in which unions' and workers' strength has declined. A significant component of working conditions is occupational safety, and one might assume that matters of safety would have little to do with union strength, because the industry is allegedly heavily regulated by federal safety guidelines. That was not, however, my experience. Thanks to its constantly changing worksites, the construction industry poses a unique challenge to potential governmental and other outside regulation. Even if inspectors focus on one contractor, for example, that contractor is likely to have multiple jobs in progress in different locations, and each job is an evolving set of tasks for workers and inspectors alike. When these factors are combined with a dramatically underfunded regulatory agency (OSHA), both workers and supervisors accurately perceive the risk of a surprise inspection as low. As a result, occupational safety is largely "regulated" by those working at the site—the workers, foremen, and superintendents.

Because the regulation of safety appears to be largely left to companies, unions, and workers, the ways that occupational safety precautions are trained for, informally negotiated, and ultimately performed are meaningful indicators of the social and employment relations within the construction industry. At best, these relations are variable and problematic. To the extent that they are negotiated on site, the union tends to be physically absent, so informal negotiations fall to the workers and their immediate supervisors. To the extent, then, that occupational safety procedures become recoded as performances of masculinity and loyalty (see chapter 6), the union becomes a lesser party in determining the conditions of work.

*The Spiral of Union Decline.*   The loss of union strength in construction is significant beyond the industry in part because it appears to be a self-perpetuating phenomenon. That is, the weaker the union, the less able the union is to mandate enforcement of worker protections. And if they are not able to enforce the mechanisms already on the books, weaker unions are unable to push for increased worker protections. Consequently, the less that the union is able to do for the workers, the less likely workers are to commit their time and energy to the union cause. In fact, by the time I entered the union, being a "union man" seemed to have lost most of the cachet it had been rumored to have. It seemed instead to be associated with a sense of low energy and low initiative—hardly the image you want connected with your name in an industry with little protection from arbitrary firing. As a result, worker involvement in my local appeared to be fairly unenergetic and equally unenthusiastic. Lack of worker involvement, of course, even in a relatively undemocratic union such as the United Brotherhood of Carpenters, does not bode well for the union movement as a whole.

This cycle of weakness was evident in the area where I worked because the companies were able to respond to worker or union pressure with threats of decertification—an election process through which employees vote for or against the presence of the union, often with significant lobbying from both sides. The process of a decertification vote is always risky for unions, since it reopens the question of the union's right to represent the workers in negotiation with management. Decertification elections are even riskier in weak union environments where workers—even pro-union workers—are vulnerable to pressure from employers either to vote against the union or simply not to vote at all. Because of workers' complete lack of protection from arbitrary firing by the employer, the risk of decertification is intense, and the threat of decertification elections is effective against workers or unions pushing for their rights.

In one such example, a union company in my region was known to have a nonunion sister company in a nearby city. There were constant rumors that if the company were to be further agitated by the workers or union, it would go nonunion—a supposedly simple process for this company, since it could just shift its work to the nonunion side. Regardless of how likely (or even desirable) this option might have been for the larger company, its ability to float the threat—or even the rumor of a threat—appeared to have a significant effect on the workers' collective vision of the union's strength.

Rather than being the bastion of powerful working-class masculinity that it appears to have been in the past, then, in my experience the union and those associated with the it (worker activists and union representatives or "reps") were often seen as "sissies"—men who couldn't make it on their own in the real dog-eat-dog world of construction capitalism. And dog-eat-dog was the authentic playing code, the legitimate set of rules by which the men were to compete. Attempts to bring in external controls, whether union rules, employment law, or OSHA regulations, were seen as signs of weakness and incompetence, of men's inability to negotiate the workplace relations on their own. Thus unions, once a symbol of strength, had become a symbol of weakness.

## De-skilling, Subcontracting, and the Disappearing Craft Worker

It is important to note that although unions have some control over formal apprenticeship training and the skills and information taught in apprenticeship classes, unions have no control over the skills required of or used by their workers. Unions cannot mandate that workers actually use the skills that they are taught or even that they work in more than one subfield.

As a result, union construction work, in spite of the stereotypes of highly trained craftsmen, has succumbed to many of the same pressures that face other industries. A combination of de-skilling (simplifying the tasks assigned each worker) and subcontracting (using different employers and crews to perform different parts of a job) has transformed the construction industry much as it has many other fields of work.

At the end of *Hard Hats,* Riemer warns that the drive for productivity, speed, and lower costs in the construction industry are destroying both the union craftsmen's work skills and their concern for quality.[14] It may be the case that the increasingly litigious nature of American business has since then at least partially corrected the declines in quality described by Riemer and others, since this was not an aspect of work about which I heard many—if any—complaints. The tendency of construction jobs to be de-skilled and streamlined is marked, however, and was clear in my observations of the workforce. These trends have also been noted by other scholars of construction. For example, research by Marc Silver in the 1980s revealed that the circumstances associated with craftwork (such as being in control of one's own work and environment) *did not appear to be common* among construction workers; they were more highly correlated with supervisory or foreman positions. In short, the qualities that have been widely associated as defining construction, those of a "craft environment" with worker control, seem to reside in construction where they do in other industries— *with management.*[15]

*De-skilling across the Three Companies.*    In contrast to the image of the old carpenter who can do all the different jobs on a site, larger-scale carpentry work is now generally performed by task groups where each worker performs *one and only one* task. This appears to be true of both union and nonunion sectors and of both residential and commercial work, and it was certainly true of the three different companies where I was employed. At Concrete, Inc., the largest, specialization and de-skilling were at their most extreme. Because the bulk of this company's carpenters did the heavy physical labor of pinning together and stripping apart the plywood and steel concrete forms, working for Concrete, Inc., generally meant working with concrete. In fact, some men who had worked more than twenty years for the company had never done anything else. This matters because it means that the men likely had no skills that they could market to a different sort of commercial carpentry employer, should they seek work elsewhere. One of the men, a foreman, had allegedly never learned how to hang a kitchen cabinet—a simple task that requires no more than the use of a level, a nail to find the studs, and some long screws. Working for Concrete, Inc., was no longer carpentry in a general sense, then, but was specifically "concrete carpentry"—fairly low-skill work that could limit a worker's options beyond that company.

At Remodel Co., the 200-"man" company, there was enough variation in the work that many carpenters had skills in at least a handful of different areas. They were likely to spend a good amount of time doing steel studs and drywall (framing walls and hanging sheetrock in commercial establishments) but were also likely to spend time roofing, doing some smaller concrete jobs, and even hanging doors and installing windows, if they had the skills. In this way, Remodel Co.'s work range appears to have been more normative for the commercial carpentry industry. Its workers saw the tendency to specialize as more or less beneficial depending on the work to which they were assigned. For example, "Silver," an apprentice with whom I worked, expressed concern that his speed at laying shingles (roofing) would cause him to be put on a roofing crew more regularly—a job he didn't want. For those on the drywall crews, however, though the work was often dull (hence the nickname "dumbboard"), the conditions were reasonable, as they were almost by definition indoors and thus likely to be heated or cooled or at least protected from the elements. This meant both that the work would be somewhat more comfortable and that it would be steadier, without days or partial days lost to the weather. In comparison, because of the additional fall hazards caused by rain, sleet, or snow, roofing work is likely to be called sooner and more frequently in bad weather. Because sheetrock is now used almost universally, sheetrock work was likely to be steady and easily transferable. But even though sheetrock work was seen as more desirable than roofing or concrete work, the issues around de-skilling and subcontracting were the same, meaning that the workers still had fewer marketable skills than previous generations had developed.

At Family Builders, the small, sibling-run company, the trend was less evident, and the workers were more likely to resemble the older-style craftsmen. This appeared to be in part due to size: because the company was small, workers were more useful if they were able to handle a variety of tasks as the need arose, and a good number of the workers there had and actually utilized a range of skills. There were certainly carpenters with better trim skills than others had, or a better sense of framing and structural issues, and some whose skills were largely limited to rough carpentry (e.g., framing and concrete). Not surprisingly, perhaps, the level of worker specialization appeared to vary with the degree to which the workers were "on steady" with Family Builders. A small core of workers employed almost permanently by the company, subject to layoffs only during the most severe work slowdowns, were likely to have a broader range of skills than the carpenters who were pulled from and sent back to the union halls.

It is also significant, however, that the work skills at Family Builders were different because the company was different. In contrast to the other two companies, where profit seemed to be the driving force in decisions and interactions, Family Builders seemed to focus on acquiring enough work to keep the workers busy and to keep people employed. The name "Family Builders" is fitting not only because the company was run by three siblings but also because they actually worked to maintain a family atmosphere. The boss knew some if not most of the workers' children, people knew other people's dogs, and when the alternator went out on my old car, the laborers directed me to a used one that one of the young laborers "dropped in" my car, using shop tools—after hours, of course. In all these ways, Family Builders differed from the other contractors I worked for and, from what I could tell in conversations at the union hall, from other contractors in general.

*Effects of De-skilling on Individual Workers.*  De-skilling and the subcontracting of work in the union construction industry can certainly be seen as beneficial for companies and clients in terms of the speed and profit of work, and even potentially in the quality of work, since each worker has more experience in a narrower range of skills. At least in theory, though each worker can do less, he should be able to do it better because of the concentration of his skills and experiences. These practices also reduce training costs, since specialized workers require less on-the-job training. Even if the workers continue to receive union apprenticeship training, then, de-skilling should result in significant savings on the job.

De-skilling and subcontracting also have notable—and notably less positive—effects on individuals' daily experiences as well as their larger marketability and security. De-skilling certainly means that a construction worker's job is less interesting: concrete carpenters will tend to only do concrete work, roofers will roof, and those who do steel studs and drywall may see little else. Thus, de-skilled construction work is less desirable work in an experiential sense. It is also less desirable for workers because their limited sets of skills will affect their ability to "job shop," to look for work with different employers. For example, more specialized workers may be limited to a handful of employers within a given metropolitan area. This limitation is caused both by the reduction in the worker's skills (the fact that he has only concrete or framing labor to sell) and by the fact that the market will likely support only a small number of specialized contractors. A medium-sized metropolitan area, for example, might be able to support only a handful of companies doing only concrete work and would thus provide concrete carpenters only a handful of potential employers.

*Effects of De-skilling on the Unions.*   Because construction unions have maintained their strength in part through their ability to monopolize and mobilize a trained labor force, the trends of de-skilling and subcontracting pose a significant threat to their stability. These trends are difficult ones for workers and unions to combat. Although my union local developed a collection of classes (on hanging a door or doing trim work, for example) in order to help the carpenters gain broader skills, this is a supply-side solution to what is largely a demand-side issue. And, ironically, this practice might actually undercut the union itself, since many members appear to use the broader skills to find work "on the side." This practice is strictly against union rules, prohibited because workers working "on the side" are seen as competing with the union employers for jobs and undercutting the union wages by using their training—often financed by the union and union employers—to do nonunion work. Thus, the development of these classes, like many if not most of the changes I discuss, seems to be working against union interests.

## Proving Oneself in an Insecure Environment

It is particularly meaningful (and unfortunate for the workers) that these changes in union strength and labor processes are occurring together, as they tend to feed into each other and further exploit existing weaknesses. The layoff loopholes in the traditional employment rules, which I term "structural insecurity," exacerbate and are exacerbated by the weakness of unions. If not for these structural insecurities, even weak construction unions could use the rules in the contract to limit or prevent the arbitrary firings of workers. Similarly, if unions were not weakened, they could strive to make the layoffs caused by work fluctuations more regulated and less arbitrary.[16] If the work were not being de-skilled, workers and unions could retain greater control of the work and the market. But if anyone can be trained to hang drywall within a matter of hours, the unions' ability to offer apprenticeships and training—and their ability to pull workers out in a strike—are made meaningless by a quick and easy supply of replacement workers.

Because the uncertainty of construction work appears to be best mini-mized by "getting on steady" with an employer (meaning that one is no longer sent back to the union hall between jobs but instead is kept on with the company and merely moved to different projects and worksites), the boss's opinion of the individual worker makes a difference. The fact that getting on steady often had as much to do with currying the boss's favor as it did with skill or productivity was well recognized: in fact, the phrase "getting on steady," was used to describe not only the state of ongoing em-ployment but also the practices and social relations that led up to it. Work-ers would sometimes accuse each other (jokingly and not) of "trying to get on steady," a clear reference to what is called apple-polishing or brown-nosing (or even less polite terms) in other circles.

As a result of this very real need to maintain the pleasure of the em-ployer, workers tended to engage in work practices that would demon-strate their commitment to the job. This occurred most obviously, perhaps, with issues of safety and comfort (as discussed briefly in the introduction and further in chapter 6). In many situations, of course, these are simply variants on the same spectrum. Issues of comfort in the short term are sometimes, though not always, matters of longer-term health and safety. Workers simultaneously demonstrated their loyalty to employers and their value as workers by demonstrating their willingness to work through dis-comfort and sometimes great risk.

## Loyalty and Comfort: Good Workers Don't Pee

One of the ways in which construction workers appear to demonstrate their loyalty to an employer is by limiting the number of times they go to the bathroom each day—most easily controlled, of course, by a restriction of fluid intake on the job. This becomes especially noticeable on very hot days, when drinking is actually encouraged—not just as a health measure but as an alternative to calling the day because of the heat. Thus water is used to protect both workers' and employers' interests—not necessarily in that order. The tensions around this matter are evident in the following ex-cerpt from my notes:

> By the time the morning is over, I am wholly drenched in sweat. Not only is the high for the afternoon in the mid 90s, but it is also humid, meaning that the heat index [a measure of the experience of heat] is above 100. Down in the holes working on the foundation, we feel no wind. Up on the deck where the carpenters are laying the plywood for the next pour, the sun beats

down and radiates up off the plywood. A couple of the men over 60 will go home before noon, but the work largely continues as usual, though a little more slowly and with a few more breaks.

One of the journeylevel women on the site is one of the earlier people to leave. She tells me later in the week that she leaves before the men in part to avoid the macho pressure that exists to stay and in part in the hopes that it will allow the older men to leave, if someone has left already. Her sensitivity is increased, I am guessing, by the fact that she is romantically involved with a man who works for the company and is apparently in his 50s or older.

The concerns with heat are of course both comfort and safety. On another site on the same day described above, a construction worker in our area died of "natural causes," which presumably means he did not fall or get buried by concrete. Because bodily organs and processes are strained by working under extreme conditions, it is reasonable to assume that social and economic practices might be tied to these natural causes. Heat and cold matter for the bodies of those who work.

Although I—like workers a few decades earlier—*technically* had the right and freedom to determine whether or not I stayed on site during severe weather, the *informal rules* at work made clear that working through bad weather was an important display of loyalty and commitment to the employer. This is something that I was told a number of times by different foremen and men in the field: the more advanced workers knew it meant that they could slow down if they needed to but that physically staying on the job was seen as a demonstration of loyalty and fitness. On one occasion I was told directly by Harry, the foreman, that I should simply slow down and take water breaks, and in fact, it was only on days like these that water stations became visible on site, with large plastic containers and paper cones available for our use.

The appearance of water on such days was initially surprising—because contractors did not supply or promote (in *practice*, though they did in theory) drinking water during the day. The fact that it was only on severe days that we were encouraged to take water breaks highlights the pressure that ordinarily existed *against* water—and then, of course, also bathroom—breaks. Because all construction workers are paid by the hour (and thus also by cumulative minutes), trips to the bathroom tend to be regarded with suspicion as potentially unnecessary incursions into the employer's paid time. Workers taking "too many" breaks or breaks that were "too long," according to their foreman or co-workers, often received comments to that effect. Such comments perhaps appearing reasonable in a pay-by-the-minutes arrangement, certainly contributed to the fact that the men with whom I worked seemed to require neither water nor trips to the bathroom. Both practices are of course, important aspects of prevention for short-term heat-related illnesses and for longer-term and potentially fatal kidney ailments.[17]

### Loyalty and Risk: Blow-drying My Hair in the Bathtub

A second way in which workers often seemed to demonstrate their loyalty to an employer was by bypassing traditional or more mundane health and safety practices, such as the use of mandated fall protection, earplugs and masks, safety guards on power tools, and the proper handling of electrical equipment. As I illustrate in greater depth in chapter 6, there is often a great deal of pressure to bypass protections seen as unduly cumbersome (a nebulous and subjective set of criteria at best) in order to "get the job done." Although employers formally prioritized their workers' safety, in reality the informal communications among workers and between workers and foremen was that "safety" was to be balanced with an assessment of the actual risk. That is, workers were to guesstimate what would happen if the formal safety procedures were not followed as well as have a sense of the time and money saved by the shortcut. Thus, safety procedures were generally to be used only when the risk of serious injury (or the risk of OSHA inspections and fines) made it the more fiscally conservative option.

Violating safety rules in all but the most egregious conditions became a commonplace way of displaying loyalty to the employer through one's recognition that speed and efficiency were to be valued more highly than the petty details of formal safety policies. And, although I understand that company and union officials who read this are likely to claim that such practices are *never* encouraged on their sites, I would argue that although they were never *formally* encouraged in my experience, neither did I ever observe or work on a site where such calculations were not universally in use.

An example of such decision-making that stands out in my mind comes from a day when I was working one-on-one with Harry, a foreman at Concrete, Inc. The work we were doing on the foundation of a larger building had me wearing hip waders (the kind worn for fishing) and standing waist deep in water, operating an electric hammer drill. Since I have a reasonable amount of knowledge about electricity (enough at least, to keep me from drying my hair while in the bathtub), this situation seemed, well, awkward at best. I had a vision of myself as the subject of a grainy black-and-white,

1950s-style safety movie in which I was the example used to warn future workers of the paths to immediate death. Of course, I also knew enough about electrical hazards to know that immediate death was potentially the better option, as I had learned in my apprenticeship class that an electrocuted body cooks from the inside out, causing excruciating pain and grotesquely disfiguring the body and skin. As I worked in the water, I knew that I should be hoping for immediate heart failure if something went wrong.

So I went back and forth in my head for a while, debating between "This seems *really* dumb, Kris" and "*Certainly* he wouldn't ask me to do something that would put me at such great risk." I finally decided to voice my concern in a fairly passive and indirect way. I don't remember exactly what I said, but it was something like, "Are you sure this is safe? It just seems a little uncomfortable, using a power tool while standing in water." I don't remember exactly what Harry said in response, but it involved cursing me out half under his breath and telling me just to get out of the hole; he would do it himself. So I got out of the hole and gave him the hip waders and the hammer drill, but I had the distinct feeling that I had lost this exchange, regardless of whether the work was safe. If it was safe, then I had just proved myself to be a wimp and a sissy, exactly what I was supposed to prove I *wasn't* in demonstrating my value as a team member. If using a power tool in water *wasn't* safe, though, I had probably lost even more, since I'd just proved myself potentially unwilling to take the fall for my foreman and had put him in harm's way instead.

Stories like this one, stories in which I or another person engaged in an activity that was both against safety procedures and often grotesquely violating common sense, were all too familiar during my time working construction. Such stories are important, I believe, not only for highlighting the fact that the OSHA standards are not about "paper cuts" or similar injuries, as OSHA's detractors would argue, but also for highlighting the changing conditions faced by a once-powerful set of union workers. Union construction workers, formerly working-class aristocrats, are now resigned, it appears, to working in the rain and blowing their hair dry in the employer's bathtub.

# 2

# THE SOCIAL RELATIONS
# OF PRODUCTION

**B**efore I entered the construction industry, I believed the common wisdom that women gossip more than men. I suppose I was simply buying into the standard workingman stereotype, since I largely expected my male co-workers to be straightforward and straight-shooting, with little time or energy for conniving workplace politics. I assumed that they'd talk matter-of-factly to one another, perhaps about work, work logistics, and maybe sometimes about sports, cars, politics, and women. I did not, however, expect them to spend so much of their energy, in public and private, discussing themselves and each other as workers, as people, and as *men*. On this matter, like many of the assumptions I had made before entering the industry, I was very wrong.

Not long after formally joining the union, I revised my assumptions to reflect that men gossip at least as much as women. They simply call it bullshitting, shooting the shit, or even "having a conversation." But their conversations, contrary to popular belief, are no more benign than the catty, backstabbing talk often attributed to women. To the contrary, the men on my worksites spent significant amounts of time discussing who was honest, who was mean, who cheated on his wife (and with whom), as well as who had drinking troubles, legal troubles, or some combination of the above. Even more important, the men spent a lot of time and energy figuring out and challenging social hierarchies of power and status—determining who was better or faster or knew more about what than whom. The questions of *who* was a good worker and *why* he was a good worker were always up for and under negotiation.

This ongoing determination of good-worker status is particularly meaningful because it reveals how the qualities of a good worker are largely socially rather than objectively determined. In this way, it makes sense to think of the production of construction work as simultaneously a *material construction* (producing a physical object) and a *social construction*—producing social relations and the ideologies that support them. The men not only use their workplace energies for economic and social production; they also labor to reproduce their social status, social and economic circumstances, and even the social structures that surround them.

This recognition of the social production of work is significant because it challenges one of the fundamental assumptions of workplace culture: that workers' status should be *and is* based on some objectively measured form of "merit." From this perspective, merit is revealed as something *negotiated and achieved* rather than simply measured. The collective workplace discussions of "merit" and being a "good worker" do not, of course, recognize these labels as socially constructed or tied to social processes but treat them instead as a valid and objectively measurable reality. The social identity of having merit and being a "good worker" (as well as having a lack of merit, or being a "bad worker") continues to be seen and treated as "true." This matters because such processes are able to effectively reproduce and obscure the racialized and gendered hierarchies of the industry. An exploration of the social relations of work demonstrates how the status of the good worker is not only continually renegotiated but also inseparable from the negotiations of race, gender, and class identities.

## Making the Good Worker: The Social Construction of Merit

The production of construction work may seem straightforward and easy to evaluate, but in reality the processes of work are complex, multilevel, and dependent upon many elements and persons for a successful outcome. For example, tasks and projects in construction are rarely done by one person working alone but rather by many people working simultaneously or in close sequential fashion. On any one job there might be architects and engineers, project managers and foremen, superintendents and supervisors—all weighing in on how things are to get done and in what order. There might also be laborers, electricians, ironworkers, plumbers, concrete carpenters, sheetmetal workers, painters, and trim carpenters—among others—contributing their labor and skills to the production or renovation of the project. And the success of the collective effort is clearly dependent on the success of each of these individuals. For everything to turn out, it is generally the case that many people must complete their tasks with good timing, good fortune, and no error. Thus even when the products of work are clear and visible—such as a poured foundation, a new roof, or a building built from the ground up—exactly who should take the credit (or blame) for the work is never as simple or as cut-and-dried a conclusion as it might first appear.

Because the credit and blame for work are not easily assessed, the social negotiations of good-worker status are vulnerable not only to the more obvious forms of social control (such as workplace authority) but also to the structures of gender, race, and class. In short, there is a different version of the Golden Rule in operation here: the cliché that "he who has the gold makes the rules" appears to be quite true in worksite status negotiations. It is often those who have workplace-based social status (in a variety of possible forms) who are most influential in determining what and who is valued. Put another way, he who has the status determines the status.

As a result, the determination of who is a good worker is often tied more to *who one is* than to how well or how fast one works. The processes that determine who does the best work are not entirely separate from how closely the worker meets the preconceived ideal of the construction worker or how much he fits the cultural and historical (often contextual) definition of the "insider." In my experience, one's value as a worker was often directly tied to how white you were, how male you were, and how appropriately and publicly you demonstrated your appreciation for the values and cultures of the setting—values that included, as I will illustrate, individualism, competitiveness, and an insensitivity toward individual risk, injury, and pain.

I observed a variety of ways in which these categorical forms of merit were determined. Sometimes the bestowing of merit happened in a prima facie fashion: workers seen as "insiders" (those who "fit in," given their gender and race) appeared likely to be seen as "good workers" by virtue of their appearance and group membership. The opposite was true, of course, for outsiders. Outsiders were often determined to be bad workers (until proven otherwise, perhaps), because of their gender and/or the color of their skin.

At other times, merit was applied through the use of differing attributions for success and failure, particularly in regard to the interpretations of mistakes. For example, it was clear in my observations that insiders were more likely to be given the benefit of the doubt when they failed or made a mistake at work. A phrase I heard used among insiders was that you weren't working if you weren't making mistakes. In other words, mistakes are part of the job. Outsiders (those who did not belong to the dominant gender or race groups) seemed by comparison much more likely to be held personally accountable for their errors. Attributions of outsider failures were likely to be tied to the individuals' personal skills, intelligence, and their sense of commitment to the work.

These patterns were most visible on the jobs with Concrete, Inc. Though one might assume that it was the roughness of the work that produced the roughness of the culture (an assertion I heard numerous times from men within the industry), the distinction across companies does not appear to be the product solely of the nature of the work. The more aggressive culture did not appear to be solely the product of the size of the company, either, although the *social distance* of the workplaces from corporate headquarters (a potential correlate of company size) probably made it easier for the workers and supervisors to ignore formal harassment, discrimination, and safety policies, if they were so inclined. Although these factors do shape the environment, it was my clear sense that the processes of social reproduction were more visible in part because differences between the categories of workers were salient: Concrete, Inc., utilized federal and state monies for some of the larger jobs and thus was under a greater burden to demonstrate equal opportunity. Stated more simply, then, the greater hostility expressed against white women and people of color appeared to be tied to the fact that there were a number of white women and people of color present—one of the few jobs I was on where this was true, in contrast to the always single-digit and often single-person "diverse" populations on other sites.

These numbers had a significant effect on the climate of the worksite. It was quite disturbing, however, to realize that the change did not have the positive effect generally predicted but a rather more incendiary outcome. The greater numbers of outsiders on the job not only served to make the issues of affirmative action, harassment, and discrimination more salient to all the workers but also appeared to raise the sense of cultural and economic threat experienced by the white working-class men. As a result, latent fears were made real and visible, and passive hostilities were released, both in individual and in structural ways.

### Whiteness and the Good Worker: Determining Merit at Concrete, Inc.

One of the clearest examples that I have of the social negotiation of merit comes from a hot summer afternoon on the large public job run by Concrete, Inc. I was working in a shallow trench with Harry, the foreman on our small crew. We were setting and "pinning together" the steel and plywood forms that serve as a mold into which the concrete is poured and set. This meant that we were moving and placing two-foot by four-foot pieces of plywood rimmed with steel, getting them in place, and connecting them with small triangular steel pins. We were working on what would eventually be the building's foundation, a series of large concrete cubes connected by stretches of four-foot-high walls that would run under the first floor of the building. As concrete carpenters, we did little other than set up the forms and then tear them apart after the concrete had been poured and at least partially hardened. Workers from other unions, such as the laborers and the concrete finishers, did the vast majority of the tasks in between.

Roughly twenty yards away, a crew of laborers was pouring a larger stretch of foundation wall, a piece for which the four of us on my crew (Harry, Brent, Morris, and I) had put together the forms over the preceding day. All of a sudden yelling erupted from the pour; the laborers and their foreman began swearing up a storm, calling out for the carpenters on our crew. Harry scrambled out of the trench and headed over to them; I climbed out and followed him. By the time we got to the site, it was clear that at least two pieces of the plywood-and-steel forming had separated under the pressure of the concrete's mass. Wet concrete was rolling out from a gap in the forms.

Known as a blowout, the failure of the forms to hold together can be deadly in large pours because of the tremendous volume and weight of wet concrete. Especially in a deeper trench, concrete can even quickly crush or cover a worker. I had been previously told by a veteran worker that if I were in a deep trench when a wall was being poured and I heard a popping sound, I should run like hell—or be buried. In this instance, however, the pour and the hole were small enough that the cost of the blowout was not death, and no one was at great physical risk. Still, the blowout represented the loss of time and effort put into the forming, as well as the time and effort of the men currently working on the pour. Additionally, completion of the pour would be delayed, a load of concrete lost, and damage done to the job's overall timeline, as work and "manpower" would have to be temporarily shifted to other tasks. So someone was certainly getting hurt, though not physically.

A number of the laborers grabbed shovels and jumped into the trench, working quickly to reclaim what concrete was salvageable. Harry jumped in beside them and worked on pinning the forms back together. He called for me to hand him 2×4s and other material to shore up the wall of the form. I did so diligently and with my greatest speed; like everyone else, I wanted to be seen as part of the solution and not part of the problem. And

I was trying to do two things at once here: I wanted to be visibly busy and helpful, in order to avoid immediate and public attack, but—knowing the rules of the highly political "blame game"—I was also trying to be as unobtrusive as possible in order to be less likely to attract wrath as the determination of blame played out among the men.

*"I Think I Know Who Did It": Public Constructions of Blame.* Clearly, no one wanted to be blamed for losing time and money on the job, and workers began throwing out different versions of what happened, with variations on culpability across the accounts. When the site superintendent walked over, the workers were arguing loudly among themselves about what had happened and who was to blame. "I think *I* know," said Harry angrily, "*that* guy over *there.*" He turned and pointed toward Morris. Morris was one of the union local's few black carpenters and one of the four workers on our small crew. It was striking, of course, that Harry said "that guy" and not "those guys," since Morris had been working all morning with Brent—a white carpenter—to complete the section of form that blew out. Harry didn't provide any information about how he "knew" that it was Morris and not Brent who was responsible. This was an especially interesting question, since Harry had been working with me all morning.

If one were tempted to give Harry the benefit of the doubt and not interpret his comment as being about race, one might draw upon the workplace "recognition" that Morris was not at all a good carpenter. He was seen by the other men—that is, by the white men—as surly, lazy, not terribly skilled, and almost entirely without motivation. And if one observed Morris, these accusations would appear to be at least partially true. He didn't go to any great lengths to look driven, and he didn't give off the frenetic sense of running that a lot of the workers did. He seemed apathetic and at times hostile to the enterprise. I found him neither terribly friendly nor in a personal sense very likable.

It was also clearly the case, however, that one could not observe Morris without recognizing the disdain and hostility that were heaped upon him, both overtly and covertly. Comments were made publicly that were biting and accusatory, and equally biting and accusatory claims were made privately, too, more patently revealing the underlying codes of race.

The more I watched Morris over time, then, the more uncomfortable I became. On one level, his presence offered me a tiny edge of status: though I was as a woman largely unwelcome on the site (a point made clear to me by co-workers and company officials alike), my status as a *white* woman meant in some settings—though not all—that I was likely to be highlighted as "more welcome than"—meaning more welcome than the black men who were the "Affirmative Action workers" only slightly less numerous than the white women in the local unions. This placement of different groups of "Affirmative Action workers" in competition, however uncomfortable it made me, was something that I soon recognized across settings in the industry. I came to understand it as an ongoing set of contextualized interactions that meant my relationships with the men of color on site (again, most generally black men, in this region) were often strained or charged with an air of potentially hostile competition.

My relationship with Morris was additionally strained by what it made visible to me about *me* and about the public functions of whiteness. Though I wished to distance myself from this surly and apparently unmotivated worker, I could not do so publicly without publicly contributing to a reaffirmation of whiteness and the value of whites-as-workers. I knew without question that I did not want to do this. Yet, I felt uncomfortable around Morris also because I came to see him as representing what I might become if I were not vigilant in my drive to perform, to improve, and to produce. I desperately wanted to succeed in this industry and had made many sacrifices to be a member of this union. The more I worked in a setting that denied me an identity of competence or a sense of basic worth, however, the more I saw how easy it would be just to give the collective of white guys what they seemed so focused on—a white woman who neither cared about the job nor put in great efforts to do it well (the quintessential "Affirmative Action" worker, in the collective view). Since they were so damn convinced that a woman couldn't be fired or laid off for fear of a lawsuit, it was tempting some days just to milk it, to flip them off metaphorically, and to do as little as I could get away with—exactly what I saw Morris doing. In this way too, then, Morris represented a very real potential part of me that I didn't want to become.

Morris was clearly central to many of my co-workers' views of themselves, too, though in a different way. For many of the white guys, especially the more average of the workers, Morris was a useful contrast against which they could attempt to demonstrate their own value, hard work, and skill—regardless of how hard they actually worked. This was particularly true for Harry, the foreman on our crew.[1]

Harry was himself a fairly mediocre worker, neither fast nor particularly skilled, though he could do his job well enough to get by—a dividing line that may have been determined as much by his race and gender as by his production. He gave a distinct impression of being out of shape; he lumbered instead of walking and often had to ratchet his pants back up between work movements. He, like Morris, failed to exude the frenetic sense of running that many of the other workers did; he gave off a sense of neither passion nor drive about his work. In contrast to Morris, though, Harry was able to build and maintain social ties with the supervisors, including a particularly close relationship with the job's superintendent, the top guy on this "500-man" site. And Morris himself was clearly relevant to Harry's larger social standing in that Harry publicly amplified the alleged distinctions between them. Morris was used in other situations as he was in this blowout, to represent a general lack of skill, drive, and the commitment needed to get the job done.

This seemed to be exactly what was occurring during the determination of the blame for the blowout of the foundation wall. "MORRIS!" Harry yelled, "Get over here!" With an air of resignation, Morris climbed out of the trench in which he was working and lumbered over to the blowout. At this point, people were already engaged in most of the reasonably imaginable tasks on the repair, so Morris just stood for a minute and watched. He said nothing in response to Harry's yelling and after a bit just turned around and walked away. Harry continued to yell and curse as he repaired the form, making it clear that he was really angry about it, as if being angry could prove that he was not himself to blame.

It was still unclear, of course, how Harry could know that it was Morris and not Brent—Morris's white, thirty-something partner—who was responsible for the blowout. It is possible that in addition to drawing on the workplace "truths" about Morris, Harry was also drawing upon Brent's public performances of hotdogging—working harder and faster than others in order to increase his own status. "Hotdog" is a term that is used both as a verb and as a moniker to denote those who do it. Brent was the epitome of a hotdog in my experience—not wholly a compliment, because "hotdogging" connotes not only of showing off in order to show up one's co-workers but also pushing limits unwisely, such as exerting speed and strength in a manner likely to invite injury. Hotdogs acted like "young bucks," men in the physical prime of their twenties and thirties, because, most generally, they were. Hotdogs were often aggressive and seemed eager to prove themselves capable of both dominating and supervising others they deemed weaker. And they were doing so, of course, as they approached the age at which their strength and speed would begin to decline—or at least when the status of their young(ish) masculinity would wear off. As a result, hotdogs almost always seemed to have an edge about them, an air of competing hostilely both with their co-workers and with their own aging and future vulnerability.

Because they were on the cusp of aging out of the hypermasculinity that supported hotdogging, their hotdogging also connoted a contradictory sense of machismo and desperation. The status of "hotdog" seemed to represent a terminal point in the workplace hierarchy as much as a strategic claim for power. I describe it as a terminal point in the hierarchy because, in spite of their public efforts to prove social and occupational dominance, the hotdogs did not appear to actually move up into supervision very often. Instead, the men who *were* selected as supervisors had often proved themselves much earlier by demonstrating a combination of skill and thoughtfulness about their work. The qualities that define a hotdog are not the same as those valued in a supervisor. Although the physical work of construction requires physical strength and speed, supervision in construction requires an attention to detail and sensitivity to contextual rules. For example, certain forms of traditional masculinity are appropriate among workers, but a good supervisor must also be able to function professionally among architects, local and federal inspectors, and female clients as well as clients of color. Hotdogs, by contrast, maintained their contextual dominance through speed and strength, a tendency to embrace traditionally conservative gender and race politics (at least publicly), and a heavy dose of insensitivity toward risk and pain. Thus, exactly the behaviors that successfully labeled them as hotdogs made them appear less suitable for supervisory work.

More important, perhaps, for understanding the nature of hotdogging is the sense of dissatisfaction with one's status that it implied. Unlike some of the men who seemed content or complacent with their jobs in construction, Brent seemed to have a nagging awareness that he was supposed to have been something "more," whatever that might have been. He seemed very aware of the drawbacks to aging in the field of construction work: I remember working with him once as we were tearing down the plywood supports for a second-story floor. The job was awkward, because we were up on scaffolding and had to use large prybars to peel the plywood sheets off the underside of the curing concrete slab. We were thus not only working above our heads but also had to pull the plywood sheets off the ceiling without bringing them down on top of us or knocking ourselves off the scaffolding. Not far from us a much older man was attempting the same task. Though it is hard to guess a man's age after he has worked construction for the bulk of his adult life, I would have put him in his early sixties, looking clearly worn and tired and having difficulty with the task. Brent worked a little slower as he watched the older man, then stopped and said, half to me and half to himself, *"No one should have to do this work when they are older."*

In spite of his sharing these feelings with me, though, Brent and I were in no way friends. In fact, he—like many other hotdogs—used a public disdain for and sexualization of me (as well as other women) to set himself apart from and clearly above women working on the site. Although I found that I could get along with most hotdogs when we were working one-on-one, Brent not only subjected me to the more common public sexualization but also seemed to take pleasure in engaging in these behaviors when we were not in the presence of others. He treated me like a child—a little girl, in particular—and also made consistent attempts to violate my personal space. One way he did so was reaching into and taking things out of my pouches while I was working, and even when I was bent over. Since my pouches hung off of a belt roughly around my waist, this was loosely equivalent to putting his hands in my pants pockets. Although a male co-worker once asserted that this behavior was not uncommon among the men, I never actually saw a man reach into another man's pouches, and *never* had another worker put a hand into mine without asking first. The few times when co-workers did reach into my pouches, it was out of necessity—such as once when I was holding sheetrock suspended over my head, my co-worker ran out of sheetrock screws in his pouches and needed to get screws from mine to complete the task. On each such occasion, the other worker made clear ahead of time what he was doing and why.

Brent was the only carpenter in my memory who coupled the creation of an overtly sexual and hostile environment with the frequent transgressions into my physical space. At least as disturbing was the fact that these actions for him seemed to go beyond a public proving of his identity and to provide a sense of personal satisfaction as well. As a result, I avoided contact with him when possible. Avoiding him wasn't always possible or easy, though; since we were two people on a four-person crew, there weren't many ways to arrange the group that would allow me to avoid Brent entirely. Though I was generally working with Harry, in the aftermath of the blowout, Brent and I were assigned together on another section of the foundation.

As we worked next to each other, our conversation turned to the blowout itself. "Did I do that?" he said kind of slyly and quietly enough so that only we could hear. "*We* did that together, didn't we?" he said to me with a grin and a soft chuckle, suggesting that it was also—or would soon be—my fault and not just his. "I don't know," I said, "I was working with you on it for a while and then I got called away." I tried to make it clear that I was not involved without making it sound like avoiding responsibility for something I might have done. But though I didn't want to look as if I were skirting the blame, I certainly didn't want to take the fall for something I didn't do. I had worked with Brent enough to know that he could be counted on to make me and others look bad when possible. I also knew that as a woman and an apprentice, I was an easy target.

So I was wary of this conversation and surprised when he tacitly admitted to me that the blowout had been his and not Morris's fault—that he had failed to return to and complete the job after lunch. He had instead gone on to something else, forgetting to complete the final steps or to double-check the work. Though an error like this is hardly uncommon and certainly understandable in a dynamic and fast-paced work environment, the cost of the mistake—and the public condemnation of the error—made it unlikely that someone would voluntarily take it on as their own.

*"I Don't Know Who Did It . . .".*   Not surprisingly, it soon became clear to me that Brent wasn't going to share his admission with anyone but me, and the blame would remain publicly with Morris. Though I was hardly in a great position to do anything about it, as a woman and still technically a first-year apprentice, my own outsider status meant that I could too easily imagine myself in Morris's situation. I felt personally unable simply to say or do nothing, so I attempted to raise the matter with Harry. I was initially hopeful (however naïvely) that telling him would make a difference in this situation. Harry wasn't only our foreman; he also answered directly to the job superintendent and appeared to have some sort of privileged access to his ear. I knew that the blowout would be discussed at length in the supervisors' trailer and that the issue of blame would likely be at the heart of these discussions. I was hopeful, then, that providing Harry with correct information would prevent the blame from sticking solely to Morris. But when I attempted to explain the events to Harry, he turned away with a shrug, and said quickly and dismissively, *"I don't know who did it."*

I was initially confused by this response, since he had earlier pointed publicly at Morris and been willing to make dramatically accusatory attributions on the basis of clearly ambiguous data. Now, with contrary but fairly straightforward information, Harry set the question aside as if it were neither comprehensible nor measurable. I felt sick as I realized how this worked. The phrase *"I don't know who did it"* was one that I had actually heard before in a similar situation. A month or so earlier, working on this same job, I had made a stupid mistake—not unlike Brent's here—and had caused a pour on a small concrete pad to be delayed while the form was buttoned back up. Although the delay had been less than a half-hour, a handful of workers had been forced to stand around and wait for the pour to resume.

Even beyond the fact that one half-hour multiplied by wages and benefits for a handful of workers *does* equal a costly financial mistake, such errors can also be socially expensive, because other workers often take great
delight in bitching and moaning loudly about the incompetence of those
at fault. An error thus becomes powerful fodder for the attribution of merit
and good-worker or bad-worker status. For whatever reason on that day,
though, Harry didn't want me to take the heat for it. When the laborer foreman got right in his face with a rant about wasted time, lost money, and incompetence, Harry deflected the blame, then as now simply stating calmly
and repeatedly that he did not know who did it.

On that day, as on the later pour, I didn't immediately catch what was
going on. I pulled Harry aside when we were out of earshot of the others
and admitted that the screw-up was my fault. I acknowledged that I must
have missed placing the pins on a small corner of the form. Harry didn't
respond directly, but simply turned away from me, shook his head, and
said with a shrug, "*I don't know who did it.*" As a result, no matter what the
other workers thought about my performance on that day or how much
they suspected that I was responsible, the official story out in the field was
that it was not possible to know who was at fault. Thus, in the same way
that Morris was inaccurately held responsible, I was inaccurately freed
from blame.

### Blackness and the Bad Worker

The gulf between black and white workers was not only created and re-
created through events like the blowout but also maintained by the patterned and often intentionally disparate treatment of the workers by race
and by gender. On this same job with Concrete, Inc., for example, the black
workers were slammed not only as workers but also as men. In addition to
the accusations of laziness and lack of skill, they were accused of theft, of
drug use, and of immoral conduct. This distinction was even more striking in the comparisons of Morris with Brent, since Morris was accused of
fathering children out of wedlock and living with his girlfriend—a
"charge" that I believe to be true but did not and do not know for sure.
Brent, by contrast, had received no such public criticism of which I was
aware, although he did in fact live openly with his girlfriend and their
child. Brent, again in contrast to Morris, seemed to be regarded simply as
a man trying to provide for himself and his family under difficult, though
hardly novel, circumstances.

It was also Morris about whom I heard whispered allegations of drug use, though I was never offered any actual evidence. Brent, again in a meaningful contrast, was known to have damaged his truck while driving drunk. This accident was only one of several indicators of an actual substance abuse problem, a problem acknowledged somewhat publicly by himself and others. But the factual descriptions of Brent's substance abuse never seemed to carry the condemnatory weight that the allegations of drug use by Morris (or the other black workers) seemed to carry. In fact, Brent was one of two fairly popular white men on the site who had publicly known legal problems stemming from their drinking. In neither case, however, was the drinking problem seen as relevant to or negatively affecting the man's work. To the contrary, both men were highly regarded by their peers.

In addition to workplace hostilities and what clearly seemed to be racist slander, I also observed clear differences in the informal interactions between the black and white male workers. Informal interactions are significant, of course, because they are the vehicle through which "tricks of the trade" and insider information about getting on steady with the company are communicated. I never witnessed black male workers being given the kind of mentoring or personal on-the-job training that could make the difference between a decent worker and a good or great worker. It is possible that the various black males received such mentoring in private or semi-private settings beyond my observation; however, they rarely seemed to have the sort of collegially supportive relationships with co-workers that might have allowed it. Instead, their structurally closest co-workers were often—but not always—those who made the greatest efforts to distance themselves socially and define themselves publicly as "not black." And in public settings, at least, their co-workers did not appear willing or likely to serve as mentors. Thus the black men not only experienced different (often hostile) working conditions but also appeared to receive different on-the-job training. This alone should have disproved the argument that black workers were by "nature" or temperament unsuited for the work. It did not.

## Bad Workers by Definition: Ideologies of Affirmative Action

In addition to the ways that workers and their actions were publicly constructed as "good" or "bad" through the interpretation of worksite successes and failures, and the ways that different groups were offered different on-the-job training and working conditions, workers were also deemed to be "good" or "bad" on the basis of their legal status in regard to affirmative action. By this I mean that persons who were seen as bene-fiting from affirmative action programs (white women and people of color) were generally deemed to be "bad" workers by definition. Workers seen as not benefiting (or even "suffering") from affirmative action were seen to be "good" workers. Thus the fact that one's employment *could be* addressed by affirmative action became translated into *was caused* by affirmative ac-tion; therefore, it was one's gender or race, and not one's skill or merit, that caused the hire to take place. Equally significantly, the opposite became true for white men: because their employment was not directly addressed by affirmative action, the cultural logic of the worksite equated the lack of affirmative action involvement as evidence of merit.

This logic is important both for its ability to disregard the skills and ef-forts of white women and people of color, and for its ability to certify all white, working-class men as meritorious and hard-working by contrast.[2] It does this by flipping the interpretation of affirmative action from a pol-icy intended to prevent racial and gender discrimination to a policy that promotes or even mandates it. Ironically, of course, in so doing, this logic washes away the evidence of the obvious and ongoing preferences for whites and for men; these hires become simply "objective" and tied to good work habits, rather than protecting the industry's jobs for the men who be-lieve that they deserve them.

It is significant that this interpretation of affirmative action not only in-verted the theoretical goals of the policy but also creates a condition under which its *benefits* were made into *penalties* for the participants. Because af-firmative action was seen as bringing racial bias to a setting where there allegedly was none (given the alleged objectivity of worker merit), this interpretation seemed to justify or legitimize the hostility aimed at out-siders. Because "Affirmative Action workers" were seen as benefiting un-fairly, overt hostility that might be seen as unacceptable in other settings was put forth as a "reasonable" response to the injustices created by the program. As much as its policies opened the door to persons traditionally denied entry to the field, then, they also served to reaffirm and "white-wash" the traditional patterns of bias and discrimination.

It is important for the reader to understand that I am making these as-sertions with great caution. I recognize that by arguing that the presence of affirmative action policies enabled the negative stigmatization of workers, I may enable my data to be used in support of an argument that affirma-tive action policies are in themselves detrimental to white women and people of color. To use the data in this way, however, is to fundamentally misinterpret my argument and to take the data out of context.

And their context is dramatic. Although it is true in my experience that affirmative action policies do *appear* to aid in the creation (or, more accurately, the re-creation) of a hostile work environment for white women and people of color in the construction industry, these policies also enable them to enter a work environment that has been and continues to be very effective in prohibiting their employment across settings and generations. It is widely known, and in fact part of the most common industry stereotypes, that union construction work has traditionally been hostile and even closed to women, to immigrants, and to people of color. The trades unions have a long history of using policies and practices (in legal and illegal ways) to keep the best jobs—and sometimes all of the jobs—for white, native-born men, who are seen as the rightful heirs to the work.[3] Although excluding sectors of the workforce on the basis of gender, ethnicity, and race has been outlawed since the equal rights legislation of the mid-1960s, these practices have continued through the use of informal hiring procedures, restrictions tied to patriarchal lineage (such as allowing only the children of plumbers into the union) and broader ethnic and kin networks.[4]

The ongoing nature of these actual hiring practices becomes evident when one contrasts them with formal union hiring policies. For example, the contract in my local dictated that all hiring should go through the union and that only *new* apprentices were allowed to find their own work. Yet as I have mentioned previously, all three of my jobs were obtained through informal contacts, with the full knowledge if not the support of the union reps. That was also certainly in line with the normative practices of my peers, as I learned in conversations with other workers on the job, in class, and at the union hall. Thus the formalized procedures—designed to remove workers from the union hall in roughly the order they had returned to it and thus at least theoretically reduce bias and discrimination in hiring—were notably different from many of the actual day-to-day practices. This is supported, too, by recent writings on the industry, as cited in my notes.[5]

The affirmative action practices were still clearly performing a vital function, even as they fed into the publicly expressed race and gender hostilities. For me, this made affirmative action like being between a rock and a hard place; like the sexist cliché, you can't live with it, and you can't live without it. Nevertheless, despite my concerns about how my argument might be misinterpreted, not to describe both aspects of affirmative action work would be to provide an incomplete description of my experiences and observations in the construction industry.

Understanding the applied effects of affirmative action is essential to understanding the lived nature of gender and race in the United States. In the construction industry—as well as in academics and other industries that I have had the opportunity to observe—the applications of affirmative action are contradictory and complex. As it removes some obstacles and reinforces others, Affirmative Action can be categorized neither as wholly positive nor as wholly negative; rather, it is an attempted solution that reflects the complex and contradictory state of race and gender relations in the contemporary United States.

In sum, it seems hardly possible to overstate the significance of the fact that affirmative action is *necessary* but not *sufficient* to provide white women and people of color with equal work opportunities or equal chances at success; instead, it serves simply to create conditions under which they— we—*had to be let in the door.* These policies, even if they then offered easy fodder for persons wishing to make the work environment more hostile, at least allowed us to be there. Additional work is needed to fully equalize the playing field.

### Increasing Numbers and Increasing Hostility: Affirmative Action at Work

The contradictory nature of affirmative action was particularly evident on the *Affirmative Action* job for Concrete, Inc.: because the building was funded in part with public (federal and state) monies, the project had been designated an affirmative action showpiece, meaning that greater effort than usual was made to have a diverse workforce. It seemed that all of the nonwhites and nonmales in the area's union locals were pulled onto the site for at least a short stint. There were white women working as carpenters, plumbers, and even as operating engineers—all statistically unusual in themselves and extraordinarily unusual given that we were working together. In some of these trades and specialties, after all, there weren't more than a handful of women working nationally (a fact that requires me to be particularly vague when describing the women and their jobs, in order to make more difficult their identification). Additionally, a small number of men of color were working in a variety of different trades—ironworkers, concrete finishers, carpenters. Although this is certainly a common occurrence in other parts of the country, this was a big deal in this midwestern, Euroamerican-dominated area. There was even, for a few hours on one day, a *woman* of color, though in general, it seemed the affirmative action preferences (perhaps in both a supply and a demand sense) were for white women and men of color.

According to a local employment professional (one of a small cadre of women working for expanded opportunities for women in nontraditional employment), the general contractor (Concrete, Inc.) had set the affirmative action goals for this job at 7 percent, meaning that 7 percent of the hours would be worked by nonwhite and nonmale persons. I heard several months later from the same employment professional that the hours worked by white women alone totaled roughly 10 percent of the "man hours" over the summer. Thus it is clear that the extra efforts for the diversity of the population did make a difference. And similarly, it is clear that moderate goals for diversity, when coupled with efforts and community support, are readily achievable.[6]

Striking, however, is that the goals set by the job were neither new nor radical. The goal of 7 percent is significant because it is the same percentage that President Jimmy Carter proposed in 1978 as a *short-term goal* for women's participation in the building trades nationwide. Although it was expected that this number would soon be reached, thereby establishing a baseline for expanding opportunities, the actual proportion of women in the trades has always remained around 2 percent. Thus, the fact that the 7 percent goal was reached and even surpassed was both impressive . . . and fairly unimpressive.

As I noted earlier, it is striking that the job with the best record in terms of diverse hiring was also the worst that I experienced in terms of overall harassment and discrimination. Although this could have been caused in part by the culture of the company itself, or the fact that the job was very large and physically distanced from the company headquarters, or the fact that the job superintendent (the man I call Phil) was widely reputed to dislike having women on the job,[7] none of these factors was particularly unusual in the industry. To the contrary, one might have expected all of these factors to have been somewhat neutralized by the company's public commitment to enforcing equal opportunity laws.

An examination of Concrete, Inc.'s, commitment to diversity and equal opportunity reveals, however, significant contrasts between their public and private actions, between their gender and race politics on and off the jobsite. In short, it didn't seem to be about making people happy on the job, but rather, about looking good with activists in the community. Clearly, the changes that occurred on this job were changes demanded by or negotiated with persons and groups outside of the industry, such as the local civil rights aficionados and community-level government. Although these changes were certainly made in conjunction with and support from the tradeswomen's community (and, I would assume, tradesmen of color), they were not made in response to the specific concerns raised by the persons and groups *on site*. That is, although these changes were specifically designed to address social relations on the site, they did not emerge from the social relations themselves. Instead, they seemed more closely tied to the company's larger social relations and the concerns of the larger community about diversity and discrimination in general.

This distinction is highlighted by the conditions on site in regard to sexual harassment. On one hand, I found it a real benefit that on this job there were no visible "girlie" calendars in any of the tool, lunch, or job trailers and no noticeable displays of sexual graffiti on the equipment or the trailer walls. This mattered, because in spite of the fact that the *absence* of such graffiti and graphics was clearly mandated by federal harassment rulings, they continued to be common aspects of many worksites and tool rooms. Even Family Builders had some in the company trucks, though only the deodorizers hanging from the rearview mirrors; they were significantly smaller and less obtrusive than the full-size posters that decorated many of the semipublic spaces used by Remodel Co. and Concrete, Inc., and their subcontractors. Thus the absence of such visuals on this one job was immediately apparent.

In contrast to the visual improvements, on the other hand, the culture remained one in which sexual and racial harassment and discrimination seemed to be regarded as sport: if one could do it and get away with it—the latter generally assisted by the cooperation of the supervisors—then it was only a bit of fun. This was, after all, the site on which my foreman (reporting directly to the job superintendent) referred to me with a nickname that included the word "tits," touched my backside when talking to me, failed to intervene when I was publicly asked for sexual favors, and even made public jokes about me himself (including hardly subtle references to K-Y lubrication). In short, the company didn't seem terribly concerned about sexual harassment per se, just the sort that might upset middle-class visitors and officials.

The higher numbers of outsiders also created a rather tense dynamic among the women. On one hand, I very much appreciated being able to work with and take breaks with women who had been working in the industry for years: this was one of the few times and places on site when we could remove the loneliness of being the only one to see that the Emperor of Masculinity had no clothes. On the other hand, that solidarity became somewhat forced and even awkward. Since we had spent most of our time working on our own (meaning without women) on other jobs, we had all come up with our own strategies for combatting the issues to which we frequently had to respond. We all had our own ways of dealing with the jokes, for example, and negotiating the boundaries of relationships with coworkers. When we were brought together on one site, I found I was suddenly being compared with and almost considered responsible for the other women's choices and conduct.

One woman, for example, was able to make degrading sexual jokes (e.g., the classic small-penis jokes) that stopped her co-workers flat—a strategy that certainly seemed ideal (especially to the other men) yet didn't work for the rest of us. I found that my attempts at this tactic often just made things worse, especially given my not infrequent ability to get the joke somehow backward and end up embarrassing myself more than even the other guy was trying to do. This strategy might have been fine on another job but was here measured against the fact that so-and-so *could* make great small-penis jokes. I was also measured against so-and-so who was al-legedly sleeping with one of the journey-level workers. And I was com-pared with so-and-so who could outwork most of the men and whose personable but cool exterior enabled her to distance fairly effectively the less pleasant men with whom she worked. As a result, there was this great pressure not only to like and support one another but simultaneously also to police one another and to keep sufficient distance that the failures and missteps of one of us would not unfairly be placed upon the others.

The greater number of women did not in itself create political change. Real change in women's workplace conditions would have been made here in the same way it is reached in other places: by women having more power, not just more women. Although two of the women were journey-level workers, they were only as powerful as other journey-level workers—and probably less so as women. They had greater power than some workers (mostly apprentices and some newer male workers), but it was ne-gotiated and contested contextually. Of course, they had the same power—or lack of power—that most other workers had vis-à-vis the supervisors and management, but they also stood out as women—a clear drawback in this setting—and therefore had less status and less power in a variety of circumstances. Although Jane (one of the journey-level women) could step in as needed to serve as an ally for a more junior woman, she could not al-ways be there to step in, nor could she spend the majority of her days do-ing so. As a worker she certainly could not afford to appear to emphasize women's causes more than her profit-focused relationship with the em-ployer. Likewise, she could not put her relationships with her co-workers at risk for each of the other women. This was not an environment where one willingly engendered hostility with co-workers and superiors, because one's productivity, job security, and even safety often depended on their collaboration. Also, of course, Jane had become a construction carpenter because she wanted to do the work, not fight battles.

In sum, the presence of additional women was probably nice for all of us, but it probably caused all of us some extra headaches, too.

### Internalizing Affirmative Action: Getting Used to Not Measuring Up

Perhaps the worst part of having an affirmative action connection in a hostile setting was that I found I had to struggle against *internalizing* a worker worldview that mandated my inferiority. Even though I entered into the industry at least partially aware of likely gender and race tensions, and aware that I might not be in the most supportive environment, I was surprised to find how much it ate away at me to know that I was labeled an "Affirmative Action worker." It wasn't that I minded the title; it was that it had been made clear to me that this meant I could not, by definition, do my job well.

My unintended internalization of these beliefs first became recognizable for me on the job with Concrete, Inc., on a day when I was "humping" (carrying) materials up and down the site. I had gone down to the "bone yard" (the materials area) and loaded five fourteen-foot 2×4s onto my right shoulder. To do so, I lowered myself carefully onto one knee, centered the 2×4s on my shoulder, and balanced them so that just slightly more of the weight was in the back. This allowed my right arm to hold them in place simply by being draped over the top as I stood up. I was fairly proud of this strategy, a combination of good carrying moves that I had learned from a male apprentice (the one I call Rocky) and lifting techniques that I had learned from other women. Shifting the burden of lifting to my legs not only limited the risk of back injuries but also allowed me to use my leg strength to compensate for any potential sex/gender difference in upper body strength. I liked being able to do my job well.

As I walked down the site that day, I got an unusual number of work-related cat-calls. "Hey muscles!" one of the crane operators yelled with a smile. Another crane operator farther down the site hung his head out of his cab and asked why I wasn't carrying anything on my left shoulder as well. He, too, spoke with a smile. Though the second comment should have been the clue that there was some sarcasm in play here, it didn't register. Instead, I got a familiar physical feeling in my stomach, the sense of not being able to prove myself "good enough." I silently berated myself for not working a little harder or a little faster.

The crane operators' point didn't actually sink in until Dominic, one of the laborers, pulled me aside at lunch to tell me that I shouldn't carry that much at one time if I planned on doing this work until retirement. *I shouldn't carry that much?* I wasn't being teased for carrying too *little*; I was being teased for carrying *too much*. What surprised me most was that—as sensitive as I was to my surroundings—I hadn't gotten the joke because I had been *willing to believe that I wasn't doing enough*. I worked hard to keep pace with my co-workers and to pull and lift my weight; I took pride in my ability for the most part to do so; yet I had still internalized the cultural belief that women weren't fast enough or strong enough and that therefore I was only questionably capable. Thus the biggest cost of affirmative action was not what the other workers did to me in retaliation for its policies but rather what they were able to get me to do to myself: getting me to accept the belief that I not only wasn't but couldn't be good enough.

## Bad Workers by Circumstance: Hazing and Harassment

Another way in which "good" and "bad" workers were socially constructed along the traditional lines of gender and race involved the use of hazing and harassment by other workers. Although much has been made in writings on construction (particularly writings by white male construction workers) about how union men are practical jokers who like to have a good time playing around and pulling harmless pranks on site, this characterization fails to take into account the different ways that such "joking" is applied to white women or to people of color. In my experience the nature and duration of hazing and "jokes" varied tremendously depending on the recipient. For many of the more traditional (white male) apprentices, the jokes seemed to take the form of skill-based teasing. Apprentices would be sent for tools that didn't exist—a sky hook, a board stretcher, a left-handed wrench. And these jokes seemed to be well received, as the apprentices would repeat them in the classroom. The jokes were used to delineate those who "know" the job (those who know that board stretchers don't exist) from those who are too new and too eager to please. In this way, such jokes clearly feed into the hierarchical jostling that occurs among the men on site and can be more or less friendly ways of welcoming new men into the large "inner circle" of construction work.

The jokes faced by women were in my experience quite different, often sexual, and they didn't seem to serve as a rite of passage that would end after some initial time in the industry. Instead, the jokes that constituted the hazing for women often seemed to redraw the boundaries between insiders and outsiders, with the women still on the outside. In direct contrast to the experiences of most white male apprentices in their third or fourth year, women almost by definition failed to become insiders, often continuing to be seen not only as outsiders but as constantly "new" to the industry. Each time a new worker came on site (a common occurrence, given the frequently changing jobsites and work crews), I would often find that I was treated as "new" by the newcomer, rather than the reverse. Even if I'd been on site for weeks or months, I found that I often had to go through a round of questions as if I were brand new to the site and industry ("*So, what made you decide to be a construction worker?*"). More often than not, I also received the standard complement of public comments (for example, sexual or demeaning comments at the break table) that served to negotiate the status arrangements between all the men and the new guy—and, once again, all the guys and me. As a result, the sexual jokes—fairly coded as harassment in many situations—were seen as "fair hazing" for each new man that came on site.

### "I'm Going to Call You Lightning"

This is not to say that I never endured the more traditional form of hazing, but during my two and a half years I received only three skill-based jokes, and they stick out easily in my memory. On one occasion, when I was using a drill to sink a screw into a metal "stud" (a framing unit), a few laborers walking by stopped to watch. One of them called out to me that I had the drill going the wrong way (i.e., that it was in reverse). To their amusement, I had to stop for a moment to make sure. Screws don't immediately "grab" the material when they're being sunk into metal, and so his comment had seemed possible.

On another occasion, I was pounding nails into some framing above my head—an angle of movement often awkward and particularly difficult as this was within the first few months of my apprenticeship; I hadn't yet built up the strength to maintain the full swing of the hammer at that angle. When swinging downward, of course, the weight of the hammer works with you and not against you; hammering up is quite the opposite. My supervisor, someone with whom I unexpectedly got along very well, told me that he was going to have to call me "lightning" because I never hit the same place twice. This was both fair and funny, since I *was* having a bit of trouble hitting those nails. I tried to convince him that I was simply trying to countersink the nail head, meaning that I was beating down the wood around it so that the head wouldn't stick up above the surface. Needless to say, we both knew this wasn't true.

On the third occasion, the foreman of my crew nailed my tool pouches lightly to the concrete forms while I was on break. My pouches weren't damaged, my work wasn't sabotaged, and I wasn't really slowed down enough to get in trouble. Instead, like the comment from the laborers, it was just enough to puzzle me, catch my attention, and earn a short laugh from those in the vicinity.

These three examples stuck in my mind not only because I found them to be amusing but also because they focused on how I did my job, not who I was or what was in my underwear. These jokes were different from the bulk of hazing that I received, then, because they were about my work and, ultimately, about *recognizing me as a worker,* even if giving me a hard time. The remainder of the hazing, though—virtually all the other jokes and comments I received in the two and a half years—was largely gendered and sexual in its content.[8] It was more about recognizing me as a woman and marking me as *distinct* from the other workers who were men. In many instances, of course, these jokes looked remarkably like the legal standard for sexual harassment.

### For Outsiders: The Added Assignment of Emotion Work

The distinction between hazing or jokes used on most white men and the hazing or jokes reserved for white women or people of color is significant because it creates an additional set of work responsibilities for outsiders. It adds a powerful dimension of what Arlie Hochschild has termed "emotion work" to tasks that should be (and are for many men) primarily logistical and physical.[9] Rather than simply being allowed to swing forms and pound nails, for example, I was also constantly required to interact with others in a strategic and competitive way, to fend off public sexualization, and to do so in a manner considered appropriate by a very diverse group of individuals in diverse settings. As Jennifer Pierce wrote in her observations about the legal field, "The same job is *not* the same job for male and female . . . workers."[10]

## The Benefit for White Working-Class Men

### Social Wages and Safety Nets

The ways in which workers are publicly and collectively defined as "good" and "bad" have significant and intertwined payoffs for the white working-class men of the construction industry. On a most obvious level, the processes of constructing merit serve to reinforce the value of whiteness and of masculinity. Masculinity and whiteness are not only publicly correlated with skill and goodness; they are equated. In this way working in construction provides what W. E. B. Du Bois and David Roediger have called a "public and psychological wage" for the white ethnic men who are the majority.[11] Additionally, as Eduardo Bonilla-Silva points out, this is simultaneously an economic wage, since it is the social construction of merit that helps to justify reserving these jobs for whites and for men.[12]

Working in a setting where white women and people of color are equated with incompetence also creates a social safety net for the white working-class males by offering their hierarchies of masculinity a "bottom" to which they are unable to sink.[13] By this I mean that no matter how untalented or unmotivated a white male worker may be, he is protected from total "failure" by the fact that he is by definition not female and not "colored" or nonwhite. Though this advantage is similar to the idea of whiteness and masculinity as wages, it has a different sort of effect. It isn't a benefit *over* but a protection *from*—not insignificant in an otherwise insecure world.

### Struggling for Second Place: No Solidarity for Outsiders

A third and potentially less obvious benefit of the delineation of good and bad workers by race and gender is the tendency for the workplace competition to prevent and divide otherwise meaningful alliances. The chance of solidarity between nonwhite and nonmale workers (that is, among those considered "Affirmative Action workers") is diminished by the very processes that would make such solidarity valuable.

I didn't anticipate this. I didn't even recognize it at first but came to understand it after my initial and well-intentioned (but naïve) attempts to form alliances with some men of color were rebuffed. In most, though not all, these initial interactions I was stung first by the sense of a social or emotional barrier and then often by a sexualizing comment—especially from the younger men. They would immediately make it clear that they had no interest in getting to know me and would often follow up with a comment that was either sexual or sexually demeaning. Although I certainly received both sorts of reactions in abundance from my white male co-workers, these responses from men of color were clearly different. They were *patterned:* whereas responses from the white guys were likely to be haphazardly connected (I'd maybe get one and not the other, maybe the second but not the first, maybe both, and so forth), there was a one-two sense to these responses from the men of color.

It took me a few such interactions to catch on: the responses of the men were patterned because my own actions had contextual meanings that I had not anticipated. I came to realize that my approaches highlighted their individual "outsider" status by marking us both as either nonwhite or nonmale. Additionally, my actions served to put their masculine status (their claim to insider status) at risk by associating them with me, a woman, who represented what men were not supposed to be. To be associated with women seemed to enhance a man's status only when it was a sexual connection, not when he was friends with "the girl." Thus I had potentially marked those men as double outsiders, first as being nonwhite in a setting that valued whiteness, and second as being affiliated with a woman, the symbol for weakness.

My actions also mattered in a broader and more dangerous sense because they invoked the issue of "second place," the question of which group would be seen as second in status to white men within the workplace and social hierarchies. In a sense, this question is unanswerable: all possible answers are contextual, contradictory, negotiated, and consistently unstable, as social power tends to be. In some situations, white women were valued over men of color; in other situations, masculinity was made paramount.

The assignment of second place was thus really a process, an ongoing social jostling that took place in both overt and implicit ways. In this process, the contextual values of whiteness and masculinity were negotiated—by those individuals who didn't have them as much as by those who did—by making spoken and unspoken assertions about what mattered and what should matter to persons getting by as construction workers in society.

*"Getting Pussy" and the Bonds between Men.*   The ways in which the hierarchies of gender, race, and power were negotiated were often conversational and, by construction standards, fairly mundane. In one such situation, retold to me by the black tradesman at the center of the tale, a black worker asserts his masculinity and heterosexuality (clearly within a framework of male dominance) during a conversation with an overtly racist white tradesman. Such a transparent attempt to "bond" on the level of the hegemonic (here heterosexual and depersonalized) masculinity is an effort to make workable the workplace relations between two men. It is not simply an obsequious act, but an economic necessity. Because the white man is a laborer foreman, he is in charge of the workers who often serve as support for the other trades. Not to have his—and their—cooperation would be a significant limitation for any worker on site.

In order to solicit the foreman's cooperation, then, or at least reduce the bad will, Dave, the black tradesman, talks about the importance of "getting pussy" as a central component of the workingman's life. This is important, of course, because it affirms both men *as men* and emphasizes their heterosexuality in a traditional and male-dominant way: we are men and women are "pussy,"—with all the subordination implied. Here is an excerpt of my notes to myself at the time:

> Dave (a Black tradesman) and I sit on a pile of scraped plywood forms eating lunch and talking about the work environment and the experience of not fitting in—an unusually frank conversation.
>
> He talks about trying to get along with Wally, the laborer foreman, who has been overtly hostile to him and from my observation appears to be overtly racist (as well as overtly harassing to me). Dave talks about working to get along with him, learning to just say *"look man, I didn't get any pussy last night, either . . ."*
>
> "Oh, sorry." he says, waving a hand in my general direction.
>
> I shrug and give a look of whatever, whatever it takes. I am struck by the irony of the necessity of competition between the second-category groups, a sort of ongoing debate or discourse concerning who are the "we" and who the "they." Dave communicates to Wally that "we are all men, and are all wanting the same things out of life"—that is, *"we are men and they are women."*

This event was in reality two events: the first occurred between Dave and Wally directly; the second emerged during Dave's conversation with me. In both situations, masculinity was put forth as primary to race, meaning that it is gender and sexuality, not race that should be seen as "making the man." Dave attempts to highlight the commonality among the men—that they're all just men working hard to get ahead and get "a little." In his matter-of-fact account, he is both forgetting and acknowledging that I am part of that which these men are supposed to "get." By this set of rules, I am the greater "outsider," since I am not the one who "gets" but the one who is "gotten." I am not the one who consumes others; I am the one who is consumed.

*Protecting White Pussy and the Power of Racism.*   In another situation, some weeks later, Dave (the same black tradesman) walked by while I was working. He stopped to ask casually when we were going to grab a drink, as we had agreed to do during our lunchtime conversation. This was hardly unusual for this environment.

On this day when he walked by, though, it was also an ordinary day in which I was working on a variety of tasks, more or less focused and more or less irritated by what wouldn't come apart, or go back together, or fit where it should. So when Dave walked by and casually sang out something about how he'd like to know when it is that we're going to go for that drink, I said I didn't know and kept working. A little later he walked by and sang it out again—and, a little later, again. He was clearly teasing me, maybe a little bit flirtatiously, though this hadn't been a part of our interactions before. Again, though, flirtatious interactions were hardly unusual for this environment. But after the fourth time in one day, Dave's singsong solicitations got irritating. Without really thinking, I mentioned it to Harry. I didn't expect him to react; after all, he was the foreman who gave me work instructions with his hand on my backside, ignored the overt harassment that other white workers subjected me to, and so forth—his feelings about sexualizing women at work seemed clear. So, terribly naïvely, I mentioned it as I might have said that I had a rock in my shoe: "Ugh. I'm getting really tired of him asking me when we're going to go for a drink." Harry didn't respond verbally that I can remember.

The next time Dave came by, he had to climb a ladder to the spot where Harry and I were working, in an open area on the second floor of the building. As Dave reached the top of the ladder, a particularly vulnerable spot, Harry pulled out his 21-ounce framing hammer with its long, raw steel shank and, shoving it into Dave's chest, leaned forward and said in a low and menacing tone, *"You . . . leave her . . . the FUCK . . . alone."* And then Harry paused, turned, and walked away with his hammer still in his hand.

## Contestation and Contradiction: Hierarchies of White Masculinities

In spite of the fact that the presence of nonwhites and nonmales provides working-class white men with a sort of social safety net, it is neither the case that the hierarchies of the industry are wholly bound to race and gender, nor the case that white working-class men have it "easy" or "made." As I showed in the previous chapter, all workers must constantly prove their value in an insecure market, and the working-class white men, though they are buffered by gender and race, are certainly no exception.

How to prove oneself and one's value as a white male worker is complicated by the multiple hierarchies of masculinity in the construction industry, some of which are contradictory and most of which are in effect at any one time. Out in the field, for example, it is generally a more traditional, physical masculinity that is seen as dominant. To prove oneself in this arena, the men work harder and faster, embracing varying levels of physical risk and eschewing fear or concern for injury. This is the form of masculinity in which the hotdogs are dominant.

The rankings of men in construction overall, though, involve far more complex matters than strength and skill. The men are simultaneously subject to the different hierarchies of masculinity, the traditional rankings of the trades, and the realities of unequal class relations. For example, the strongest man on site might be a laborer, more traditionally masculine than the electrician, but he would earn less and also receive less occupational prestige. As a result, the laborer is simultaneously ranked above *and* below the electrician. Additionally, both workers, regardless of their physical strength, are subject to the power and control of the superintendent. The superintendent is likely to be notably less muscular and less masculine in the more traditional, physical sense. He is also likely to receive negative prestige for being a pencil pusher, though he may have been considered a fair-to-middlin' tradesman when (or if) he was in the field. Thus the superintendent, too, is likely to be simultaneously above and below the men he supervises.[14]

All of this matters, of course, because it means that proving oneself is something that one must always attempt but can never achieve. By proving oneself to be the strongest, one is elevated on one axis of domination but called into question on another. By moving up and out of tool-wearing supervision (that is, by becoming the sort of foreman who does not need to work while he supervises), one achieves a certain level of power and status, yet loses the edge of the physical and manual skill that commands another sort of prestige. Thus, uncertainty of status appears to be the most certain aspect of the culture: no matter which hierarchy one negotiates successfully, one has simultaneously, it seems, worked oneself down somewhat in an inversely related one. There is always something to prove.

### The Contradictory Role of the Union in White Male Relations

In such an insecure world, one would expect that the collective strength of unionization would be welcomed, celebrated, and protected. But it was not. In fact, his identity as a unionized worker is potentially the most contradictory element of the construction worker's public character. Although the culture and the flavor of the unions vary by trade, it was the case among the carpenters I knew that to be union seemed to simultaneously elevate and denigrate a man in society. On one hand, to be a union man was a tremendous social wage: this is the part of the men's identities that is tied into the historical power of the industry. These are the men who built America and who could previously declare it to be raining after only three drops had fallen. These are the men who, with a high school education or less, could in past generations outearn their more highly educated peers and support their families in style.

On the other hand, attendance at and even participation in union meetings and events seemed to do little to help and could even hurt one's status—both as a worker and as a man. The negative association of unions with status was probably due in part to the declining power of the union and the fact that being a union member could not empower construction workers as it once had done. Certainly, the rumors of union-employer collusion didn't help either, since the union is supposed to be what protects workers from unfair employer requests. If the union agents are trading worker well-being for personal gain, then being pro-union might mean that one is little more than the bosses'—and the union's—patsy.

In addition to all this, of course, the union now sits rather squarely in the middle of race and gender politics. Unions, with their theoretical mandate to protect and fight for all workers, have become institutional supporters of affirmative action. What the unions might lack in genuine enthusiasm for such policies has been bolstered by government directive, the well-documented history of union-based discrimination having increased the oversight of unions by government and other outside agencies; unions are now fairly closely monitored by outside regulators. Although that regulation is certainly imperfect, it does allow the state to step in to investigate the practices of a local union. As I mentioned, it did so in the mid-1990s after a slate of roughly twenty-five new ranked-trade apprentices turned out to be all white and all male.

It is significant that the unions must simultaneously support diversity and continue to cater to their majority population—the white working-class men who feel that they're getting "shafted" by antidiscrimination goals. Unions must work to satisfy both the "Affirmative Action workers," who are likely to see the unions as bastions of racism and sexism, and the white male workers, who tend to be concerned about "unjust" or biased outside intervention in workplace politics. This tension is further heightened by the fact that the union reps themselves were in my experience still overwhelmingly white and male. And since they had all worked for years as tradesmen, they were also very much tied to the existing white and male power structures.

Because construction unions are trying to serve two fairly contradictory sets of interests, then, they are able to deliver on neither set particularly well. As a result, the beliefs of both sides feed into the suspicion that the union is just another group you have to pay into that won't ultimately work for your interests, anyway. These suspicions are only worsened by the ongoing rumors of collusion and corruption.

## Sacrificing the Labor Movement

This dilemma of the union, being pulled to serve two potentially incompatible masters, is an important part of the social relations of the construction industry. It also is tied, I believe, to the overall decline of the occupation. Because unions must work for equal opportunity and workplace protections, they must continue to fight for diversity. Because the unions are then seen as undercutting what little security the white male workers feel they have, they are seen as less valid and less valuable by those workers. Because union goals are seen as incompatible by most of the workers, the possibility of a stronger labor movement and the potential for greater occupational and economic security is set further aside.

This turning away from unionization was one of the more surprising aspects of worker culture. Despite all the problems with unions, they remain, in my opinion, industry's best hope for a more empowered and a more protected workforce. Unionization is not only a way to diminish the structural insecurities experienced by workers but a potential route to reducing or removing them altogether. As one national union official commented to me informally, the rules of structural insecurity *could* be negotiated out of the contract, but they simply have not been.

For the unions to win the battles around hiring and firing at the bargaining table, they would need a level of strength far beyond what they have now. For white male workers to recommit to unionization, it appears that they would have to forgo the social wages of whiteness and masculinity, wages that are currently far more certain (even if far less valuable) than an invigorated labor movement. Since the unions are not entirely trusted to do what they are capable of, and since they are currently unable to do much of what the workers require, it is still unclear how the unions'— and the workers'—decline might be easily turned around.

# 3

# "A BITCH, A DYKE, OR A WHORE . . ."

## How Good Men Justify White and Male Dominance

I had been working in the industry for about two weeks when a friendly-looking older carpenter sauntered up to me after lunch. He pulled me aside, looked me in the eye, and said casually yet provocatively, "*Well, you're either a bitch, a dyke, a whore, you're looking for a boyfriend, or you're looking for a lawsuit.*" I was momentarily stunned and not quite sure how to respond. Although I was certainly used to being asked why I wanted to be a construction worker, that question was usually stated simply and didn't include such a striking set of options. It wasn't entirely apparent to me *what* this carpenter was asking, or even *if* he was asking. Was I being offered a choice? Was I supposed to be answering him?

As I came to understand over time, this set of options *wasn't* actually a question, and it didn't really have anything to do with me personally. Instead, this carpenter was making an argument about the sorts of women who work construction and the roles that they should be allowed to play on site. Women are not to be taken seriously as workers, according to this argument, because they have not joined the union for the purpose of working. Even if women should prove themselves physically able to do the work (as, of course, they have done over the past few hundred years), their presence on the job should not be seen as challenging the male identity of construction, for women aren't really construction workers; they're just working construction to find a man, to prove a point, or to set up the average working man for an unfair harassment lawsuit.

Although no other worker in my experience would ever reach the level of directness and brevity of this carpenter's Bitch-Dyke-Whore taxonomy, his argument was identical to others that I saw enacted across worksites and companies over the next few years. Women were portrayed as sexual and political outsiders, their work abilities ranked a distant second in importance to their marked social status. These beliefs meaningfully influenced the cultures of the workplace. Not surprisingly, they tended both to reflect and to reproduce the male dominance of the industry.

Even more important, perhaps, since these arguments contain the evidence needed to prove themselves true (as I demonstrate below), they are able to appear to be *describing* rather than *prescribing* reality, to appear objective and nonpartisan in their approach. By providing alternative accounts of the inequalities that exist in the industry, these circular arguments serve simultaneously to justify the gender and racial discrimination that exists and to make it seem benign and otherwise blown out of proportion. These cultural explanations allow white working-class men to support and perpetuate conditions that reproduce white and male dominance without having to recognize or acknowledge that they are doing so.

This is not to say that the harassment and discrimination are entirely unintentional or that they are wholly unacknowledged by the men who maintain them; certainly there are some men who harass and discriminate intentionally and there are some who are aware of the effects of their actions. However, they need not be. These ideologies are powerful because they support unequal structures while appearing to be neutral. Thus those workers whose political and economic interests are served by inequality and whose emotional interests are served by the perception of a meritocracy are able to convince themselves that both sets of qualities are largely in place.

The Bitch-Dyke-Whore taxonomy is actually one of a number of such justificatory ideologies—ideologies that justify and generally obfuscate the ongoing inequalities in the construction workplace. The other ideologies—the Myth of the Easy Lawsuit, the Myths of Affirmative Action, the Myth of Increasing Numbers—all serve to reproduce the meritocratic self-image of the industry while ensuring that the white male workers retain the identity as the authentic construction worker. Even the language that the industry uses to explain its diversity ("Not Enough White Guys") reveals how even at its "best," the industry's workforce agenda remains dominated by white and male privilege.

## The Contextual, Contradictory, and Resilient Nature of Workplace Ideologies

Exploring the logic of the Bitch-Dyke-Whore taxonomy is meaningful because its patterns reveal important features of workplace cultural belief systems. The first such pattern is that they are contextual, meaning that they are part of larger systems of contradictory beliefs in which only some of the beliefs are accessible or salient at any one time.[1] As a result, workers can hold and espouse certain beliefs while they are at work (about affirmative action or about women who work in construction, for example) without necessarily having to take into account the beliefs that they hold to the contrary. In fact, I would argue that it is not clear that the workers I describe would necessarily espouse these views beyond the gates of the worksite.

As a result, these belief systems can more accurately be described as the in situ rules of the culture or what Erving Goffman calls the "scripts" of the worksite.[2] They are called into play when one crosses the temporary parking lot and walks through the clearly demarcated boundaries of the site; they lose their larger salience when one returns to the world beyond construction. Though it is certainly not the case that all white male workers are nonsexist or nonracist off site (any more than it is the case that all are sexist or racist on site), I was often struck by the contrasting public pressures for racist, sexist, and homophobic sentiments (or at the very least a neutral facade at their expression) and the somewhat more tolerant selves revealed in private. Many of my male co-workers had educated and professional wives and clearly appreciated women's social and economic efforts, trials, and contributions. Even recognizing that some of what was said in one-on-one interactions could qualify as "blowing smoke" in my direction, not all of it was. This is clear in part because the workers and their educated wives are part of the new two-wage economy of families and the accompanying changes in gender roles.

The contradiction between on-site ideologies and off-site lives reveals once again the structural linking of ideologies to resources and power. It reminds us that white dominance and male dominance pay not only a social or "public and psychological" wage but also a real and economic one in the form of white and male control over relatively lucrative working-class occupations.[3] Thus, these beliefs about women, affirmative action, sexual harassment, and people of color are simultaneously the folklore of the site and the functionally strategic *tool kit* of white male workers who utilize them to maintain their contextual control.[4]

The assertion that these ideologies are contextually rather than universally salient for these men does not imply, however, that such beliefs are easily subject to change. Instead, because these ideologies are able to rely on themselves for validation (a characteristic that logicians refer to as circular) they are also what I describe as slippery and resilient. By this I mean that it is difficult to pin the beliefs down in ways that make their internal contradictions apparent, and it is even more difficult to make such contradictions meaningful to those who hold the beliefs as true. After all, the white men who work construction—like most other groups and individuals—strive to create and sustain worldviews that present them with a "just world" and a coherent, unified explanation of it.[5] Where they differ from other groups on construction sites, of course, is in their *demographic dominance:* their sheer numerical and proportional control of the culture that allows them to impose these worldviews and their structural implications upon others.[6] It is in this latter way that the beliefs are able both to reflect and to reproduce the structures that create them. Several workplace ideologies have exactly these effects.

## "A Bitch, a Dyke, or a Whore . . .": Explaining Away the Women Who Work Construction

The assertion that women in construction are not really there to do the work but are there just to find a man, get laid, or cause trouble is important because it means that no woman's presence can seriously challenge the industry's male identity. The men see themselves as working to make a living but regard the women as working to disrupt or for other self-serving and sinister reasons. As a result, males see their domination of the workplace as both natural and right. Women are dismissed as whores, lesbians, or "feminists with an agenda," labels that allow the industry to downplay and discount the efforts and successes of women who have worked construction over the decades.

After observing these beliefs and practices for the better part of my two and a half years, I came to recognize that the strength of this ideology comes from three key elements. First, the Bitch-Dyke-Whore is a forced-choice question (meaning it presupposes that all women can be placed into at least one of the categories). Second, it is a closed-circuit process (meaning that women who escape one label are simply rerouted into another). And third, the label is technically unrelated to any actual realities of the woman's life but is imposed without her consent, potentially without her knowledge; it might even vary from site to site, depending on audience and intent. This does not mean that *no* woman can escape the Bitch-Dyke-Whore taxonomy, only that her ability to do so is likely to be dependent on the qualities of her co-workers (such as their ability to accept a female on site) and on the desire of her boss (e.g., the company president) to enforce the laws and policies of equal opportunity.

At Remodel Co. and at Concrete, Inc., such labels were aggressively applied and were sticky for most of the women—across sites and, in my own experience, across companies. At Family Builders, however, working under a company president who considered himself a feminist (the only male feminist I met in the industry), male workers' statements of such beliefs would truly, I believe, have put them at risk of a formal reprimand or sanction. Though I would hazard a guess that these beliefs were still relevant even there and that some such conversations simply took place behind my back, it is significant that they did not dominate the culture or my work experience as they did at the other two companies.

Outside of Family Builders, though, it was my experience that very few women actually escaped this logic, and those who did, did so by virtue of longevity, luck, determination, and a good portion of thick skin. Most important, of course, is that the few categories of women who appeared to be cautiously or reluctantly tolerated as longer-term members of the worksite were largely explained as being *extraordinary* women, a category somehow different from "women in general" and thus still unable to challenge the reality that men can do construction work and women can't.

## Signs, Smiles, Rumors, and Other Sorting Mechanisms

From my observations in the industry, it is clear that upon their entry all women are entered into this framework: each one is placed in some initial category on the basis of her behavior, appearance, or reactions to sexual "come-ons." She is then treated largely in accordance with her socially constructed (and mandated) identity. As noted above, the labels are generally applied to the women without their consent, their input, or even their knowledge.

Various processes were used, in my experience, to sort women into the different categories. In some situations, "signs" were used to mark the women, including how friendly they were or how open to talking about their lives. Private women and women who were reluctant to make "friends" were often labeled as gay; those who were open and friendly were often labeled as straight—and likely looking for sex. Sometimes the evidence was drawn from alleged behavioral cues: one time I was told that smiling was interpreted as proof that a woman was "easy"—a clear variation on "looking for a boyfriend" or "whore."

The rumor mill also played a great role in identifying each woman's "type," with rumors spread from one site and company to another, through the union or just through the social contacts of men who were friends or relatives, or who had worked with each other in the past. I often found, especially coming to a new job, that a reputation preceded me, whether or not it seemed to be my own. In one of the more amusing examples, on a large job for Remodel Co. at the beginning of my apprenticeship, I received a marriage proposal from a worker who offered to stay home and take care of my children. I laughed and thanked him but declined, of course, since I had no kids at that time. He responded with confusion since he "knew" that I was a single mom whose father brought her daughter to the worksite to see her every day at lunch! Only later did I realize that I had been observed *escorting a young girl to a bathroom* on site weeks before. The rumor mill had converted this girl to my daughter and her elderly companion to my father, a man who apparently "brought his granddaughter to visit her mother each day at lunch." With a few minutes, a few assumptions, and roughly 499 men who liked to gossip, the story of my life as a single mom was born.

Because of my very real interests—both theoretical and applied—in understanding how various relations were maintained in the industry (as well as how they were supported by men who might or might not consider themselves "good men"), I kept thinking about and observing the ways that women were categorized and dealt with by the men with whom they worked. And since this was a good sort of thing to think about while one did often monotonous tasks with one's hands, my understandings of the processes and their ramifications deepened over time. I eventually created a schematic or sort of flow chart that represented the different options as they were played out before me—and, of course, *with* me. On one hand, I consider my "Bitch-Dyke-Whore" chart somewhat tongue-in-cheek; after all, it was originally designed as much to amuse me during the more tedious hours of work as to clarify my social world. On the other hand, it does fairly accurately represent the options as I experienced them and as I believe they are laid out for women wishing to work in construction. Each option illuminates something important about the gender ideologies in place and the various forms of treatment accorded to women.

### The ManSpot Questions

The first question generally raised about a woman in construction is "Gay or Straight?" and can be posed in a number of ways. It is rarely asked directly of the woman herself but is often approached tangentially, through a variety of what I call "ManSpot" questions. ManSpot questions are used

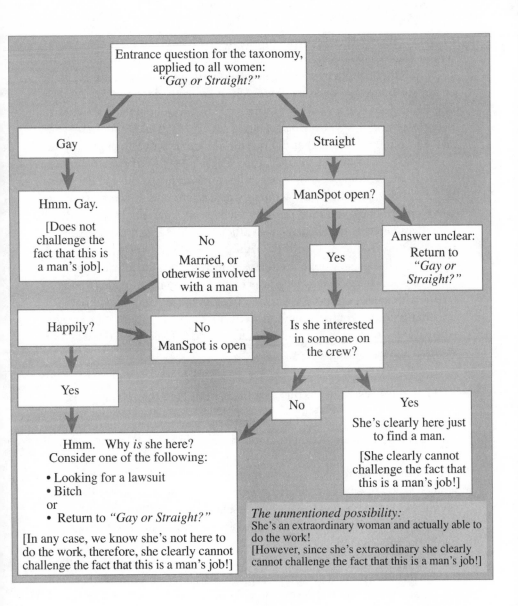

to determine whether the woman has, has had, is planning on having, or would like to have a man in her life. They are clearly predicated on the assumption that a woman is either involved with a man, looking for a man, or gay (uninterested or asexual women, it appears, need not apply). The queries appeared in a variety of forms, the most common being something like "*So, you married?*" or "*You got a boyfriend?*" My favorite of these—because I initially thought that the questioner wanted to talk about my father—was, "*So, what does your old man think about your being here?*"

All these questions, of course, are quite clearly used to determine the sexual and marital status of the woman worker. Often, they were asked directly and publicly at lunch or coffee, where one man could ask and the entire work crew was able to hear. At other times the questions were raised in one-on-one situations, with the rumor mill serving to disperse the response. On the larger public site run by Concrete, Inc., the information was solicited from the one guy who was considered to be "female friendly," meaning that he was seen as getting along with the women workers (which he actually did) and thus as having access to this information. When a new woman came on site, then, other workers turned to him to find out whether she was "gay or straight."

## "Unnatural" Women Disturb the Men—but Not the Gender Order

Women who answered "no" to the first ManSpot questions ("husband?" "boyfriend?") and showed no romantic interest in the men on site were in my experience immediately suspected to be lesbians. This label was also applied, however, to women who refused to provide much information, women who appeared to take their work too seriously, or those who were seen as being too good at it. Thus, the lesbian label, significantly, appeared to be decoupled from any actual romantic or sexual identity the woman might hold for herself.[7]

Being labeled a lesbian within this framework had the limited benefit of being a terminal point in the process: that is, it at least temporarily removed the "need" for further testing or categorizing the woman and thus relieved her of negotiating (or simply being buffeted by) the labeling process. Of course, because the categorization was neither necessarily tied to fact nor coherent across settings, the labels placed on individuals were "sticky" but not permanent or definitive. A woman was thus "freed" from labeling only as long as the gay label "stuck"—and this might change with the men on the crew, the distribution of a new rumor, or some semipublic event that could reframe her identity.

Being identified as lesbians, however, did seem to reduce the men's need to explain the women or explain them away. It was as if women identified as lesbians in construction were seen as *less threatening*—in this way at least—to ideologies of masculinity. This is to suggest not that they were necessarily more welcome in construction but rather that from this perspective gay women were seen as less immediately threatening to the gendered "rules" about men's and women's abilities: that is, to the industry's beliefs that men can do the work and women can't. Women coded as lesbians could be seen as "unnatural" women whose abilities were therefore interpreted by the culture as unrelated to what "women in general" can or should do. As a result, the success of these women in the industry was not believed to address the roles and abilities of *men in general*. Thus, these alleged lesbians might have disturbed the men as individuals, but they could not disturb the gender order.

### For Heterosexual Women, It Is All about Filling the ManSpot

Once a woman answered the initial questions (or had them answered for her) in a way that identified her as heterosexual, the subsequent questions were predicated on the assumption—or more accurately the requirement—of the ManSpot: the perception that for every woman who is not gay (that is, according to this ideology, every *real* woman) there is a "natural" spot for a man. This spot is either occupied by a man (a boyfriend or husband), or it is vacant. And the natural woman with a vacant ManSpot is—by definition—in search of and in need of a man. Thus the ManSpot question was transitional to the other man-identified paths "offered" to women: you're either married (or close to it), or seen as looking for a husband, looking for a boyfriend, or looking for sex from men in general—and thus, most simply, a whore.

In the big picture, of course, such options are all the same. Like the other options in this schematic, they're really about the ways that the men see themselves rather than about the women per se. They suggest that a heterosexual woman whose success in construction *might* disturb the gender order can be most effectively neutralized as a threat by redefining her as "pussy"—nothing more than a sexual and reproductive resource vis-à-vis the men. These options did vary slightly as to the degree of condemnation leveled against the women, but again, this judgment often seemed to be more about justifying the already-occurring treatment of the woman than it was about any real actions or conditions of the woman herself. Sometimes the labels were directly tied to the women's actions and identities; at other times they were largely if not completely tied to the men's preexisting opinions of the women.

*Looking For a Husband.*   Among the heterosexual identities, to be categorized as looking for a husband in construction is likely the most benign of the mainstream interpretations, as this implies that the woman "understands" the basic ManSpot rules and also pays homage to the manly nature of the men involved. After all, it could be seen as quite a compliment that a woman would go to the trouble of becoming a construction worker simply to find a husband. Such a woman, then, is simply taking a unique approach to the most mainstream role, investing in a tool belt and hardhat to secure her most valuable socioeconomic tool—the man.

Although women assigned to this category did not necessarily have an easier time on the worksite, a degree of respect did seem to be accorded those who were not married but were understood to be looking for a husband. This attitude might have been due to the possibility that the woman so identified would leave the occupation once she had gotten what she came for; having found her love (and her provider and the father of her children, no doubt), she would be likely, perhaps, to retreat to the domestic sphere. Since the construction industry is generally regarded as questionably safe for pregnant workers and hostile to the needs and schedules of parents (being an industry dependent on the male-without-family-obligations model), this assumption is not unrealistic. Thus the role of "looking for a husband" can be interpreted as the most reinforcing one for the masculine status quo of construction work. It both heralds men as mates and providers and marks the woman's tenure in the field as temporary.

*Looking For a Boyfriend.*   To be "looking for a boyfriend" in construction work, though similar to looking for a husband, implies a greater freedom from the traditional norms of marriage-sanctioned sexuality. The woman is seen as recognizing the potential of these men as mates (or at least as romantic partners) but, because she is not fully committed to the patriarchal marriage bargain, she might plan to stay in the industry, thereby asserting at least pragmatically her equality. Thus I argue that "looking for a boyfriend" is a potentially demeaning or punitive label for women, regarded as both challenging the status quo and threatening the homosocial nature of the environment. By looking for a boyfriend (or being labeled as doing so), a woman in construction represents the risk of competition among the males for the available female, and the risk that the bonds of loyalty between men will become subordinated to the bonds of loyalty between this woman and her man. Therefore this path, even though man-identified, can be seen as slightly more risky for the dominant cultures of masculinity.

*The Whore.* To be a whore, the third option for "filling the ManSpot," is certainly the most deviant and threatening (and condemned) of the three man-identified roles. Although the whore, like the woman looking for a boyfriend or husband, appears to recognize the manly capital of her co-workers, she does so with apparent disregard for the natural and economic hierarchies of gender, work, and family. A whore is seen as looking to please herself; not necessarily looking for just one man, she might be looking for several or many men, and it is *her pleasure* (rather than the pleasure of a man, the reproduction of the socioeconomic status quo, or her subordination) that is presumably at issue.

To interpret the whore status as an "empowering" option is to deny the status of whores. To be a whore in construction—and one might argue to be a whore in society—is to be someone who is used by others, a sexual vehicle. And in construction, similar to the rest of society, when this label is leveled against a woman, it is a master status that removes all of her other merits, and it means that she does not need to be taken seriously as a worker.

In this option as in the others, of course, it is clear that a woman does not need to actually *be* a whore or even engaged in sexual behavior to be considered and stigmatized *as* a whore.[8] In its alternative uses, then, to be a "whore" is to be seen to think that a woman can play the social game in the same way as a man (to work like a man and play around like a man). As with the other response options to the woman question, the coding of individual women into these categories has less to do with the woman's actual behavior or responses than it does with the needs and experiences of the men around her.

## Bitches and Lawsuit Seekers

The basic premise of the Bitch-Dyke-Whore ideology is that women in construction are either gay (and thus not "really" women who can threaten the gender order), or using their participation in the industry as a method of finding their sexual mates (and thus also not threatening to the gender order). Heterosexual women who do not appear to be interested in sexual or personal relations with their co-workers thus become suspect and dangerous. There are two variations on the dangerous woman theme: to be a bitch and to be looking for a lawsuit.

*The Bitch.*   The first of these, to be a bitch, is only vaguely defined and in construction—as in the rest of society—appears to be a sort of catchall term used to stigmatize otherwise unstigmatized women. Perhaps the most basic and useful description of a bitch comes from a complaint offered by an aging hotdog in his late thirties. Besides the women who were lesbians or just out to get laid, he complained, the problem with most women in construction was that they "had something to prove": that is, they were there not because they liked the work or simply to do the work but *to prove that they were capable of doing the work.* And like the rest of this ideology, of course, his assertion becomes true by definition: women who enter the industry just to do the work or to earn the living wage are forced to prove to their critics that they can in fact do the work. Thus, by definition, all women in construction can "fairly" be labeled as a "bitch." It is more than a little ironic, of course, that men are expected to use the job to prove their masculinity. Women workers are both required to prove themselves and are condemned for attempting to do so.

*Looking For a Lawsuit.*   The second and undeniably more inflammatory path for "dangerous" women in construction is that of looking for a lawsuit. As with the other labels, this identity does not need to be tied to women's actual actions or intent. One might acquire the label through the simple rejection of a come-on, a refusal to participate in sexual jokes or discussions, or a declaration that she does not find some remark or prank cute, funny, or appropriate. All of these call up the specter of the lawsuit-hungry woman.[9]

To be labeled as "looking for a lawsuit" is a tremendous liability for a woman who wants to be able to get along with men in the industry, and getting along with men is essential for most workers. To be looking for a lawsuit is seen as not only tantamount to betrayal of the occupational and union brotherhood (and it isn't called the international Brotherhood of Carpenters and Joiners for nothing) but also as being naïve to the ways of men. Frequent expressions that I heard included "Didn't she know it would be like this before she took the job?" and "Doesn't she have any idea of what men are *like?*"

It is perhaps the greatest irony of this label, though, that to be tagged as looking for a lawsuit did not seem in any way to protect a woman from harassing behavior. Although one might easily assume that a woman seen as planning to sue would have everyone walking on eggshells, men did not refrain from telling off-color jokes—or worse—to such women. To the contrary, it seemed likely to make the environment even more hostile and harassing. It was my observation that the label "protected" the women only from having their complaints heard, taken seriously, or addressed by other workers or management. After all, once a woman had been identified as looking for a lawsuit, all complaints or issues raised by her were simply rejected or rejectable on the premise that she was *looking* for trouble and no longer being "reasonable."

The fact that this ideology itself could fairly be ruled the foundation of a solid "hostile environment" charge is seen within the industry as irrelevant—contradictory logic that is central to how these circular ideologies work: they are successful because they are able to justify and maintain the very problems that they dismiss as nonexistent. Women file harassment complaints not because of *harassment,* according to this ideology, but rather out of some sort of desire to cause trouble for the well-intentioned, hardworking men. Thus the women not only represent some outside (likely "liberal") set of interests but can also be seen as "bringing the trouble on themselves," having entered the industry with this ulterior motive of looking for a lawsuit. The problem is not the harassment per se but the woman who complains. As a result, sexual harassment policies, like affirmative action policies (see chapter 2) become appropriated by the dominant culture and used to justify the very discrimination and harassment that they were intended to prevent. The Bitch-Dyke-Whore ideology not only creates a hostile environment but denies it and obscures it in a manner that becomes extremely difficult, if not impossible, to prove or disprove.

### Women Who "Make It" in Construction

To the Bitch-Dyke-Whore list originally offered to me by the older carpenter, I have added one additional category, a broad designation for the different types of women who "make it" and survive for any significant amount of time in the construction industry. What is most significant about these women, of course, is that they are deemed to be *extraordinary,* somehow more than or different from the everyday sort of woman who, by definition, cannot be a legitimate construction worker. Reasons why the women are able to make it vary slightly. Some may be related to men in the industry by birth or marriage ("somebody's wife" or "somebody's daughter"). These women are protected slightly, it seems, by the industry's insiders, perhaps because of their more traditional affiliation to the men themselves or perhaps simply because they *are* related. The irony is of course that the women who are protected by these relations are also those most likely to be familiar with the rules and culture of the setting and thus least likely to need assistance in navigating the culture of the site.

Within this category is a more surprising group—that of "college girl," an educated woman who is seen as working in construction out of choice rather than necessity. This phrase offers an interesting and gendered twist to the traditional practice of management's sons "paying their dues" or "learning the ropes" in the field before moving into the trailer or some other white-collar occupation. As such, it is also a somewhat bittersweet marker of contemporary gender and class politics for these men: not only have the rules changed enough that women must be allowed to enter the field, but they can do so in a manner that widens rather than narrows the class gulf. Not only can women take jobs in construction, but they can also do so temporarily, before moving up and out to a position more elevated and privileged than the construction work in which they were trained.

Other terms applied within this extraordinary category include "being one of the guys," suggesting that like all extraordinary women, this one *transcends* the basic category of female and approaches the status of male, even if on an honorary basis. But because she is extraordinary and not like other women, she is as unable as the women labeled gay or "looking for a man" to challenge the gender order that marks construction as the province of men. In spite of being extraordinary herself, then, she poses no threat to the assigned and "natural" roles of women and men.

### Women to be Welcomed

Although there were certainly many men who let me know I was *not* welcome in the construction industry, there were also a good many men who seemed neutral to my and other women's presence. Somewhat less frequently, but no less notably, some men actually let me know that they were glad I was on site and that they wished me well. Not surprisingly, perhaps, the language used to communicate these sentiments was—like the expression of the opposite sentiments—bound in the terminology of sex and gender. There were two times in particular when these messages were clear, one when I was encouraged to talk about my "balls," and the other when I was exhorted not to be such a . . . woman.

*Talk About Your Balls!*   On one of two occasions when I was given information about how to fit in with the men, I was working with a man I call

Vinnie, a young Italian American carpenter. We spent a number of weeks together on the large job that was my first in the industry and his first with Remodel Co. Since we were on a job that involved approximately five hundred workers, he was assigned not only to train me but also to keep me out of the range of the others (a common solution for women who experience harassment or unwelcome attention). Because we were sent out to a project physically separate from the main job, we were able to talk a lot as we worked, and Vinnie gave me advice about work, work politics, and "getting along." He knew that I wanted to run work in the future (that is, be a foreman or supervisor) and was supportive of this goal. As we grew more comfortable with each other, he would share stories of his experiences and give me lessons in the skills of running work. Eventually he came to see me as part of his larger life challenge and decided to make me into a "little Vinnie"—to confirm his own skills by guiding me, the unlikely candidate, toward success in this largely male and macho industry.

Part of his project was to prepare me for what he knew was ahead: that many men, immediately upon seeing my middle-class, white, female self, would reject me and any possibility of my competence. The battle to fit me in would be an uphill one, and the chance that people would try to take advantage of me would be great. His best attempt at protecting me (in addition to his high expectations, teachings, and help) came in the form of a sentence to disarm the men who would challenge me, to catch their attention and make them laugh, to let them know that, most of all, *I was just like them.* When male workers, superintendents, or subcontractors were claiming that their work was acceptable when it was not, that it couldn't be done on time, or that it should cost extra because of "unforeseens," I was supposed to master a look of pain and sheer disbelief and gasp, "Hey! C'mon, *you're breaking my balls!*" The lessons for use of this remark came complete with the shoulder shrug and upturned hands that said, "What do you expect me to do? Work with me here!" The goal of course, was for me to be able to say it with a straight face to the men who gave me a hard time in the future.

Out of respect for Vinnie and his sincere attempts to help, I tried practicing the sentence but, except for my closest friends, could never manage to utter it in front of others. Not only did I feel as if I were parodying an Italian-American immigrant grocer, with the exaggerated gestures and affect (I've never been a particularly good mimic), but I really didn't like the underlying *point.* I liked the ends (who wouldn't want a magic phrase to make their co-workers laugh and suddenly welcome them—*me*—into the *brotherhood*?), but I felt that I couldn't really live with the means. My graduate-student, overanalytical background took over, and I remained hyperaware of all that this expression implied. Like other references to "having balls," of course, this claim builds upon the myth that virtue, strength, and efficacy rest in a man's testicles, while offering no equivalent for women. Therefore, to use it would be to reaffirm simultaneously that I *didn't* have what it takes—i.e., "balls"—*and* that I belonged. To the extent I could "make it" and be accepted, then, I would be the extraordinary woman, the one who *almost* seems to have balls. I knew I wanted into this boys' club, but I wanted in as a *girl* (in their words) or as a *woman* (in mine). For me, membership asserted with "balls" could only be second-class.

Looking back, I sometimes think it might have been a lot easier had I just claimed "balls" and ignored the greater interpretations of where this silly expression would place me. On the other hand, I also wish I had stood my ground from the beginning. Better still, I wish that I hadn't had to make this choice at all.

*Don't Be a Pussy.*   A second big insight I received in regard to fitting in came in the form of a slightly twisted, backhanded compliment during my stint on the large job for Concrete, Inc. I was working in the hot summer sun, midafternoon, with Dane, a mellow but somewhat melancholy laborer. It was dreadfully hot, and we were stuck off to the side of the main job, pinning together forms for the building's foundation walls. The work was even more tedious than usual, since we didn't even have to make sure the forms were in the right place, just pin them together. They'd be flown into place by a crane later and given the final adjustments there.

It was just the two of us on this area of the job, and I was jokingly complaining (and complaining) about the temperature and the work. It was hot and I was bored. I was comfortable complaining like this with Dane, since he was at the bottom of the laborer totem pole and I was pretty much at the bottom of the carpenter totem pole, we had a mutual "no illusions" relationship about our levels of happiness on this job.

"Quit your bitchin'," Dane said with a big grin. "*What are you, a pussy?*" I paused and inhaled sharply, surprised and even shocked at his choice of words, but after a second I responded to his large grin with a grin and loud laugh of my own. It took me a moment, but I understood: in a backhanded way he was *complimenting* me at the same time he was telling me to stop complaining. His comment was ironic, of course, and so intended. Dane used it, shock effect and all, to recognize me as "one of the guys" by ridiculing me in the same way that the men ridiculed one another—with the threat of identification with women, with girls, with pussies. After all, one can't *seriously* threaten a woman with the risk of being seen as a woman (or, as in this situation, the semantic equivalent); rather, he paradoxically elevated me to a social masculine status by simultaneously pretending to overlook and yet slamming my actual gender identity. In this way Dane's comment transcended the usually intransigent in-group/out-group boundaries by rather boldly affirming them. Dane, obviously aware of the gender politics on site, didn't take them all too seriously. In the heat and the dirt, and in the midst of all the things that really *were* offensive to me, I appreciated that, too.

## "We Can't Say Anything Anymore!": The Myth of the Easy Lawsuit

The second circular ideology I encountered in construction, which I call the Myth of the Easy Lawsuit, is linked to the Bitch-Dyke-Whore beliefs about women through its assertions about sexual harassment and discrimination policies. Here, as in the ideas surrounding "looking for a lawsuit," the cultural contention is that these policies are skewed unfairly—in fact, radically unfairly—to the advantage of men of color and white women. The Myth of the Easy Lawsuit argues that all any woman or any man of color needs to do is say "harassment" or "discrimination," and the alleged offender is "down the road" (laid off) with no questions asked and no hesitation. This belief of course ignores the stark reality of the thousands (if not hundreds of thousands) of dollars required to file an actual suit, and the number of months (if not years) required to make any headway in the judicial system at all. Even more important, of course, the legal standard for proof of harassment requires an obvious pattern, corroborating evidence, and generally a clear injury to the worker—none of which is met by one off-color joke or curse.

The Myth of the Easy Lawsuit, however (as the name suggests) ignores the realities of litigation and focuses instead on the theoretical positions of a company's harassment policies. An examination of these policies reveals that the rules of harassment and discrimination, like the safety policies, exist in two very distinct forms—the official policies and the actual operating procedures. In spite of the fact that the company rhetoric is *always* that harassment and discrimination will not be tolerated (this is a legal position companies cannot afford *not* to take), the realities of the worksite are that the harassment is often protected, while the person raising the complaint is targeted as the troublemaker. In my observations, supervisors were often unwilling to punish someone too harshly (if at all), since the industry ideology about harassment and discrimination is that the deck is stacked against the average white guy who just tells an "inappropriate" joke or is unable to control his sexual impulses vis-à-vis his female co-workers or cannot conceal his hostility to the men of color. The assertion of this myth is that with even the slightest cry of impropriety, a decent guy's career is over.

These contradictory approaches matter because they allow companies to claim to be aggressively combatting harassment and discrimination (often with a "zero tolerance policy") while in practice they maintain a culture that actually *supports* such transgressions and refuses to punish the perpetrators. The two sides of this policy are evident in the specific, common phrases "having a guy by the balls" and "getting what you ask for."

## Myths of Enforcement: "You'd Have Him by the Balls"

The most powerful myths about sexual harassment and racial discrimination policies among men in the construction industry are that accusations are immediately addressed, require little-to-no proof, and will result in swift and dramatic punishment for the alleged offender. These beliefs are reproduced not through supporting evidence (which I would have to say in my experience—outside of the one potentially relevant instance at Family Builders—does not exist) but instead through their constant retelling in public and semipublic forums. Thus, despite fairly common occurrences of harassment *and* evidence that harassment and discrimination occur largely without penalty (and possibly even with the support of supervisors), the Myth of the Easy Lawsuit is kept alive through its constant verbal affirmation by the men who work in the field and the men who work in the trailer.

This process may be best understood by comparing it with the children's story about "crying wolf," though in this situation it is the wolf, and not the girl, that is calling out about the wolf. It happens because the men, in their day-to-day on-site banter, raise the possibility of a lawsuit almost constantly and generally as the potential outcome of the littlest sorts of offenses, such as asking if a woman is married or telling a slightly tawdry joke or, in the case of racial harassment, simply failing to give a person of color *preferential* treatment. By creating this vision of harassment and discrimination policies as unfair and extreme, the white male workers are able to reduce these issues to the level of the absurd. As a result, any subsequent and *real* attempts to raise issues of harassment and discrimination are considered to be absurd as well.

It should not be assumed, however, that the men simplistically "buy" or believe their own mythologies about discrimination, harassment, and the swiftness of the punishment. Instead, they seem to be aware both of the public status of the myths and of the contrasting underlying realities, as is apparent in the following explanation of gender and power relations given to me by a fellow apprentice. We were out to lunch with a handful of guys from our apprentice class, sitting at a table in a fast-food restaurant and talking about the men we didn't get along with at work. As I noted in my journal, "Ryan said that all I needed to do when having trouble at work was say to some guy—whoever was giving me a hard time and for whatever reason they were giving me a hard time—'*you're just doing this because I'm a chick.*' And then, Ryan said happily and loudly, while raising his hand and cupping his groin, '*you'd totally have him by the balls.*'"

What Ryan was asserting, of course, was that the threat of being accused of gender discrimination, to say nothing about sexual harassment, is so fear inspiring that I (and, one can assume, other women) could use it to my advantage in a variety of settings. It is important, of course, that he was not talking specifically about discrimination or harassment but rather referring to *any* sort of hard time, such as being assigned a "shit job" or being heavily criticized. These are the kinds of "hard time" that all workers receive but that women, according to Ryan, can avoid by making the right accusations. By his logic, all I needed to do was *raise the specter* of a harassment or discrimination complaint, and I would effectively trap and immobilize my male co-worker. I would "have him by the balls," in Ryan's words, and thus I, and not the workingman, would be in charge.

Ryan's awareness that his own assertion was false, however, was revealed by his other actions: in spite of his apparent convictions about the rigors of harassment and discrimination policies, he never hesitated to use such words as "beaver" and "cunt" in front of me; he absolutely pushed the envelope with public comments in class and *never* expressed any fear that my potential discomfort—or my perception that he was saying these things because I was a "chick"—would get *him* by the balls.

### "You Get What You Ask For"

The second version of this myth is highlighted by a discussion between a Concrete, Inc., executive and a local advocate for women who had called the executive specifically to discuss an individual's situation of harassment. I was privy to this conversation because I was the individual in question. I had left Remodel Co. after learning that a valued foreman, one who claimed to be taking me under his wing in a simply professional sense, was taking public credit for an unplanned pregnancy and miscarriage that happened to me at that time. (The man responsible for the pregnancy, who later became my spouse, wasn't a construction worker and thus was not on the radar at the company.) The foreman's assertions were offensive enough at the time—from my perspective—to warrant a complaint. Nothing of substance came of the complaint, though, outside of a rumor that the foreman had been "sent on the road" and a semi public sense that I was politically "hot" in the negative sense and looking for trouble. I decided to switch companies at the earliest opportunity.

Rather than finding refuge at the new company (Concrete, Inc.), however, I found that a reputation of "looking for a lawsuit" had followed me: after my first, fairly welcoming week on the site, I was given the cold shoulder one morning by the men I worked with. Co-workers who had talked to me previously barely noticed my presence and had to be spoken to directly before they acknowledged me. As previously noted, on a job where cooperation is essential to individuals' performance, this mattered.

One of the workers, eventually, admitted to hearing a rumor about my having filed a legal harassment claim against my former employer. The rumor was not merely that I had raised a complaint but that I had *filed a legal charge,* the beginning of a lawsuit. Equally important, there was no information about the actual behaviors in question; instead, the rumor was that I had begun the process of a lawsuit simply because my co-workers had used words like "shit" in my presence. On that basis, I was marked as dangerous even to talk to; I was a reckless, unreasonable, and unjust lawsuit just waiting to happen.

It was when things didn't improve that one of the local tradeswomen's advocates (a woman with a close working relationship with Concrete, Inc.) made an informal call to one of the company's executives with whom she was collegial. For most of the conversation, the executive expressed intolerance for harassing behaviors: "Women in the industry should not have to put up with such things!" Toward the end of the conversation, however, he added almost as an afterthought, "But then again, *you usually get what you ask for.*" Thus, according to the real beliefs behind the Myth of the Easy Lawsuit, women who raise complaints about harassment are "looking for a lawsuit" and are generally doing so entirely without cause—except that of their own making.

## Affirmative Action: Have to Hire 'Em, Can't Fire 'Em

### "Hey Joe": Good Workers Are White and Male

"Hey Joe," the laborer foreman shouted across the site, "there's a new laborer comin' out to work with you on Monday." He laughed and grinned, stopping to readjust the load that he was carrying and looking over in my direction.

"Oh yeah?" responds Joe, sounding a little uncertain.

"Yeah!" laughs the foreman. "She's black. She's a one-armed black lesbian." After pausing to watch for an effect and looking again at me, the foreman gives a half smile, adjusts his load again, and walks on. Joe snorts noncommittally, and goes about his business of picking up the site.

It turns out on Monday that the new laborer is a white guy named Louis who is a favorite of all the white guys. Talking a mile a minute and always full of jokes, he is a hard worker with a good knowledge of machinery. In contrast to the mythical black, one-armed lesbian, then, he is the cultural ideal of a co-worker.

The laborer foreman's "joke" is "funny" because it reveals the Myths of Affirmative Action in the construction culture. From this perspective, to be stuck with a black worker—particularly a woman, a gay woman, a gay black lesbian with one arm—is simply part of the miserable joke imposed on the industry by the liberal legislation of recent years. Included in this belief, of course, are the understandings that white male workers are much more likely to be successful and productive (and are thus more desirable) than less white and less male workers. Thus it is a "joke" because the foreman knows that they're really getting a "good" worker (a hard-working white guy) but is pretending that they're actually getting a "black woman," the obvious code for affirmative action or "dead weight" ("one-armed" and "lesbian," one can assume, were just thrown in to increase the hilarity).

Even more important, though, is the underlying belief that affirmative action's imposition of "diversity" is unfair because it interrupts the *otherwise meritocratic* hiring system of the unions and employers. It isn't the preferencing of white ethnic males that is unfair; it is its interruption. This is an important ideological twist, of course, not only because the argument flies in the face of a lot of legal and historical documentation about gender and racial discrimination in the building trades but also because these traditions are part of the larger stereotypes of the industry, both within its ranks and beyond. A vigorous opposition to gender and race diversity is certainly part of the stereotype of the construction worker: it makes one assume that at least on some level the workers themselves are aware of this image and history.

To be fair, though, the workers I knew did not seem to be creating and re-creating these myths entirely on their own but appeared to be well supported by the employers, who also benefit from these beliefs. After all, affirmative action (especially when publicly heralded by a company) allows an employer to proclaim to the tradeswomen's advocates, communities of color, and the larger community as well that *"we give people a fair shot."*

The efforts made (and not made) by Concrete, Inc., on their affirmative action showpiece suggest that this public image is important to large companies—no doubt because many construction clients (particularly when
public monies are involved) require companies bidding on the projects to
have harassment and discrimination policies as well as safety policies in
place.

It was my observation that companies benefit from these policies also by
being able to *lament* about affirmative action to the white working-class
male workers. By suggesting that their "hands are tied" by the larger liberal pressures from outside, the employers could suggest that they, too, understood the realities of white males as "good workers" but that they were
forced by affirmative action to give the white men's jobs to outsiders—
such as the mythical one-armed black lesbian. This sense that otherwise
fair hiring is disrupted and dictated by outsiders was common, if not universal, and expressed in both overt and covert ways.

The employers' second approach to affirmative action matters, of course,
because it increases the white male workers' collective feelings of risk and
uncertainty, feelings that are already present on site because of the arbi-
trariness of the hiring and firing structures in general. In this insecure
world it appears that both the jobs and the little protection that exists are
being given to white women and people of color—all "known" to be incompetent. Thus, as the white men of construction see it, no matter how
hard you work or how good you are, when work gets slow, *you're* potentially on the layoff list whereas the white women and people of color are
protected. These beliefs clearly serve to create greater animosity between
the white male workers and their nonwhite, nonmale co-workers. They
also serve to push the white men to work harder to prove themselves as
the "genuine article," thereby putting further pressure on a workforce already working harder and at greater risk for less pay, power, and prestige
than they would have had a generation ago.

### "Hey Buckwheat: We're the Nicest Bunch of Guys"

To the same degree, then, that the industry declares itself to be violating
meritocratic principles only when forced to do so by pro-diversity liberals,
the workers and supervisors are able to declare themselves "by definition"
not racist or sexist. And it was often the most overtly sexist and racist men
who claimed most adamantly that the "playing field is level" and that
the work environment is neutral to the gender and race of its inhabitants.
This argument became a sort of aggressive defense: it was not only rude

but downright hostile to suggest that someone had just done something potentially sexist or racist. For a white woman or a person of color to claim to have been offended was to be offensive and to be hostile and aggressive—just further proof that "outsiders" were ruining a perfectly nice environment.

One version of this claim was put forth by an ironworker foreman and his small crew, who told me that they'd "really like to have a woman join us because *we're the nicest bunch of guys.*" This suggests, of course, that the absence of women has nothing to do with the men's behavior or with the men themselves; the source of segregation must lie elsewhere. This foreman was asserting that ironworkers—at least his crew—are friendly, open, and nondiscriminating individuals who would delight in diversifying their workforce. His assertion was made more than a little ironic, of course, by the fact that he had just a few sentences earlier referred to a big, black male worker as "Big Buckwheat."

Although I am confident that the man using this expression was quite aware of its derogatory racial nature, he was probably also aware that this was a fairly safe statement because it was unlikely to be successfully labeled as "racial" or "racist." From all of my observations and experiences at Remodel Co. and Concrete, Inc., calling someone a "Big Buckwheat" was highly unlikely to receive any sanction, either informal or formal. This lack of response is due to two significant assumptions that the men of construction hold about themselves: First, everybody "knows" that it is wrong to be racist or sexist—and thus nobody is. And second (see chapter 5), since construction workers define themselves publicly as being "pigs" who are incapable of grasping the finer rules of etiquette (such as the inappropriateness of calling someone Big Buckwheat or Big Tits), such remarks can be explained not as racist or sexist but just poorly thought out and crude. No corrective action is needed; this language can just be ignored. The end result of the Myth of the Easy Lawsuit, then, is that virtually anything can be fair game, and virtually nothing is seen as a problem.

## The Myth of Increasing Numbers

A more quantitative version of the Myth of the Easy Lawsuit is found in the common assertion of the men that they "can't say *anything* anymore" because of the increasing number of white women and people of color in the industry. The claim that outsiders are entering the industry in dramatically increasing numbers and forcing changes in the workplace culture argues that the policies put in place to assist outsiders (such as antiharassment and antidiscrimination policies) have overshot their mark, leaving outsiders at a distinct advantage and insiders at a loss. It is because of these "politically correct" policies that the insiders "cannot say anything" without the fear of a lawsuit or of being fired by the men in the trailer—or so the story goes.

Examples of this claim occur in various forms, including the subtitle of an article run in 1998 in the *Engineering News-Record,* a weekly publication of the construction industry: "As construction welcomes more women, sexual harassment is a growing liability worry." And farther down the first page the authors, Richard Korman and others, add, "The real test is just beginning as *women carve a bigger foothold* in construction's high-testosterone jobsites."[10] The women are coming and they are gaining control; the future of these high-testosterone, men-only milieus is threatened. More specifically, the two basic claims made in this article are that the numbers of women are going up and that they might reasonably be assumed to be staying up and thus changing the culture.

But the second claim does not necessarily follow from the first; in fact, it directly contradicts the statistical evidence offered by the industry itself. According to Jerry Jacobs, women enter nontraditional occupations at roughly the same frequency as other occupations but tend to leave them at a much higher rate.[11] Thus, although more women will enter the construction industry in the near future (the product of both industry recruiting and an increasing population), it also appears to be the case that more women will leave. This outcome is predicted not only by Jacobs's research on women in nontraditional employment but also by the fact that after more than several decades of federal affirmative action guidelines for construction, the proportion of women in the industry is almost identical to the proportion that existed when Jimmy Carter was president of the United States.

This observation is borne out by the statistics provided in the Korman article: "While 813,000 women are employed in construction, or 10% of the total workforce, only 2.5% hold production-related jobs."[12] According to the classic and much-validated research of Rosabeth Moss Kanter, it is the percentage of women or people of color and not their actual numbers which will determine their working conditions.[13] This is so because it is the percentage or proportion of the population held by a minority group that allows them to gain control of the way in which they are defined and treated.[14] Thus, even if the absolute numbers of white women and people of color increase as the industry expands, unless their *proportion* in the workforce grows, one will see neither the striking demographic shifts predicted by the Korman group nor the dramatic change in culture declared and decried by the traditional white male workers.

## "Not Enough White Guys"

As much as the men decry the allegedly increasing numbers of white women and people of color, though, they are also bemoaning an apparent shortage of white men. The fifth and final ideological tool that I examine in this chapter is embedded in (and revealed by) the industry's discussions of diversity: When we explore the way that company leaders, industry publications, and the workers talk about recruiting "diverse" workers, it is clear that even their pro-diversity campaigns have male and white preferencing at heart.

The industry reveals its true gender and race biases most dramatically (and most ironically) when it actually reaches out to white women and people of color, explaining its need to recruit outsiders as the result of a shortage of white male workers rather than any intrinsic benefit of diversifying or any moral obligation for equality. Although the individual authors selecting this language may of course have had different intents than the ones I impute to them (they might even have perceived this to be the most compelling argument for an apparently pro-male and pro-white audience) the use of this language is still significant. The extended reliance on such arguments by both persons in the industry and those writing about the industry reveals the ideological foundations existing behind the appeals for diversity.

### "We Don't Know Where to Find Them!"

In almost all meetings and publications dedicated to the increase of diversity in construction, one can observe that those who represent the industry as either employers or union representatives raise similar if not identical questions about the process through which this increase in diversity should take place. Specifically, they argue that nontraditional workers need to be *found* and *recruited*, not that the rules or practices of the industry need to be made more welcoming. In the national industry-based meetings that I was able to attend in 1999 and again in 2005, highly placed individuals framed the problem and proposed solutions by raising questions that echoed questions raised across the country—and across the years:

> "How do we get the word out?"
> "How do we let them [the Outsiders] know about how good these jobs are?"
> "How do we find and recruit them?"

As sincere as these comments may be, even a perfunctory review of the industry's history suggests that these questions are more the *product* of the true problem than a path to effective solutions. This distinction can be made clear by an analogy to a door or gate: questions ask how applicants might be convinced to knock upon the door, yet they do so while ignoring the loud knocking in the background. The historical record is clear on the fact that the gate has been and in fact is locked to those outside.[15] Therefore it is important to note that these questions identify the problems as the opposite of what they are: systematic and ongoing insider actions that perpetuate an industry-wide climate hostile to outsiders.

It is my assertion that these questions—ineffective in leading to strategies for increasing diversity—offer important insights into the ideological frameworks surrounding discrimination and segregation. This is made clear by further examination of the two subclaims implicit in the questions "How do we 'get the word out' about these occupations?" and "How do we recruit new workers?"

*Getting the Word Out About Job Benefits.*   The first assertion implied by these questions is that the "word" about the nature and value of construction work *needs* to be gotten out. That is, the public needs to be educated about the pay, skills, pride, and security offered by the construction trades. As I have demonstrated in previous chapters, however, it is at least as reasonable to argue that the public perception of these jobs overestimates rather than underestimates their "value." In most if not all published accounts of construction work—such as Studs Terkel's description of the mason who takes great pride in what he builds and LeMasters's 1975 descriptions of midwestern construction men in a tavern—the work is portrayed as good, satisfying, pride-inspiring.[16] The public consciousness is thus imbued with the image of the working-class, manual-laboring man as one who is strong, macho, proud, tough, and *satisfied*. Americans see construction workers as having more prestige than those in many other occupations.[17] And researchers follow mainstream stereotypes in describing construction workers as autonomous "craftworkers" able to set their own tasks, methods, pacing, and outcome.[18]

Additionally, in my own experiences, I found that people consistently *overestimated* the pay I received, the control I had over my work, and the amount of time I might be able to "stand around" while on the job. Although my position as an apprentice certainly weakened my access to these perceived privileges, I argue that the estimates were consistently (and sometimes dramatically) higher than the pay, control, and paid leisure time experienced even by the journeymen out in the field. Similarly, the people with whom I spoke consistently *underestimated* the physical risks and occupational hazards of construction, whether in the form of chemical and environmental dangers or the extent to which social norms and pressures militated against the use of safety procedures. Thus I argue that the public perceptions of the work are *unrealistically positive*, and not the converse. Perhaps the word that needs to get out is not about the benefits of the work but rather about its drawbacks.

*Finding Willing Recruits.* The second assertion implicit in these questions, that outsiders must be "found" and recruited to the industry, not only assumes that potential recruits are unaware of the jobs' worth (discussed above) but also ignores the fact that "new people" have been trying for years and decades to get in. Yet from the insiders' perspective the problem is not that outsiders have been denied entrance, work, or promotions within the industry but instead that there are *none ready or willing to apply.* Given the voluminous literature citing the discrimination and barriers faced by white women and people of color within—or denied entrance to—the construction industry, this hardly seems a credible claim.[19]

One *might* interpret the foregoing questions as asking either (1) how outsiders might be informed that the industry has changed to such an extent that discrimination no longer occurs, or (2) how to recruit sufficiently large numbers of them to change the nature of the culture that has allowed such discrimination and harassment to occur?[20] Perhaps—but it is important to realize that the core beliefs neither acknowledge previous discrimination (although individuals may acknowledge it) nor make any substantial claim to change. Instead, the widespread discrimination of the past and present are by and large denied. Not only is the playing field described as being open; it is interpreted as *having always been open.* Consequently, the solutions generated from such questions are doomed to only the most marginal of successes.

### Still "Not Enough White Men!"

Even as the industry purports to open its doors, then, it is highlighting the first-class entrance for white men and offering only a smaller side door for women and the men of color who would like to enter. Both in the industry's own writings about diversity and in the larger media publications about the construction workforce, even in the statements of need for diversity, the normative and preferential status of the white male worker is apparent. This is done by centering the recruiting dialogue on the notion of scarcity, the oft-used phrase that there are "not enough white men" entering the field. This claim is made in many forms, including the following from a *New York Times* article, "faced with a shortage of trades workers to meet the voracious demand for construction in the United States, *desperate builders and eager unions* have begun aggressive campaigns to court new workers, attracting women and members of racial minorities to the traditional bastion of white men."

And even more striking, perhaps, is the caption next to two accompanying photos of black apprentices: "*Faced with a shortage of trades workers* to meet an intense demand for construction in the United States, builders and unions are recruiting *people like* Simmie Hoskins, above left, Steven Wilson, above right, and Alesia Cherry, left, as carpenter apprentices."[21]

The phrase "people like" makes it clear that the author wishes to indicate that the unions and builders are now hiring *blacks* as the obvious result of the shortage of "trades workers"—a term apparently synonymous in this case with "white workers." The need to diversify the workforce beyond the prototypical white males does not appear to rise from any moral ground, any historical corrective, or even an imperative of kindness. Instead, the discourses surrounding diversity generally declare that the industry is simply running out of its first choice of worker, the white working-class male. Thus, even as the trades reach out to the outsiders, they simultaneously reinforce their occupational identity as being both male and white: "Already, some unions and businesses . . . are finding themselves looking for women and minorities to replace skilled white males who are retiring—and whose sons are going to college instead of following their fathers into a trade."[22]

It is important to recognize that the sense of urgency in this economic and skill-driven recruitment of outsiders is uttered primarily by management, union officials, and the media—and all in public forums. It is not a sentiment that has come from the ground up, nor has it found its way into the field to be embraced by the average worker. In fact, as I have outlined in previous chapters, larger structural changes in both the industry and the economy have created conditions in which the average worker in the field does not feel secure or "scarce" but rather is likely to feel insecure in his economic location. As a result, he sees these newly recruited outsiders not as meeting the needs of the industry and its workers but rather as taking what little security exists and ruining the potential of a just hiring system. The outsiders are seen as violating the workspace of the "real" construction workers, taking their jobs, and subverting the American values of hard work and fair play. These outsiders—and not a shortage of workers—are the *visible* problem.

## Power, Structure, and Commonsense Knowledge

Karen Pyke has argued, "The main mechanisms that link macrostructural relations of power and micropractices are cultural ideologies woven into the fabric of 'commonsense' knowledge. Thus, it is necessary to examine dominant cultural ideologies to understand interpersonal power dynamics."[23] In this way, then, we can understand that ideologies often described by workers as "just a joke" or irrelevant are not only important parts of the culture but also the foundations of industry practices and ultimately the political and economic relations of the construction industry itself. Because they shape the way that persons are perceived, interpreted, and thus treated, such beliefs reproduce the *hierarchies of worker desirability* and shape the queues of hiring, firing, training, and promotion. These beliefs don't just shape the ways that workers are talked about; they shape the ways that workers are allowed to exist.

# 4

# BODIES AT WORK

The Social and Physiological Production of Gender

**R**egardless of how far construction wages have declined in recent years, it is likely that these jobs will continue to be appealing to men because of the very specific social wages that they pay. By this I mean that the jobs not only provide the opportunity to earn more than a living wage but also provide elements of social status and prestige that are potentially absent from other, financially equivalent positions. In chapter 2, I described the social wages of masculinity and whiteness as they are created through the workplace negotiation of "good" and "bad" worker labels. In these negotiations, workers are deemed more valuable and skilled if they are white or male. Simultaneously, the identity of being white and male is made more valuable, too, through its increased association with good workers and quality men.

Next, I look at the *microsocial* processes of masculinity production—the ways in which workers are made masculine through the physical and the *physiological* effects of work—and illustrate how they serve to reproduce as dominant the culturally and contextually specific masculinities. By reproducing the individual workers' masculinities as well as the industry's sense of itself as masculine, these processes affect the industry at both individual and collective levels. And because they are also tied to the larger cultural and economic performance rules that exist out in the field, these microsocial processes must be understood as having structural as well as cultural effects.

## Socially Desirable Men and Undesirable Women

To discuss the body's effect upon the construction industry's rules and culture, I draw upon my own experiences and observations as well as focus-group data gathered by other researchers. I do so to illuminate two very distinct ways in which workers are made into and celebrated as men. First, workers' bodies are physically altered in ways that are considered to be appropriate and even desirable evidence of working masculinities; these include the weathering of skin and the building of physical strength. Looking at how the men respond to and talk about these changes leads me to argue that the changes themselves can be understood as a form of social, public, and psychological wage.

Second, workers are made into men by *how doing the work feels* and how these feelings are interpreted. The physiological responses of the body to work (such as an elevated heart rate) are coupled with cultural "feeling rules" to produce sensations that can best be thought of as the *physiology of masculinity*—the processes through which men in construction are able to *feel* that they are naturally and truly masculine.[1] By exploring the social and cultural cues that guide the men's interpretation of their feelings, I am able to show that these physiological feelings can best be understood as a psychological and a *physiological* wage.

Like all social exchanges, however, the acquisition of the social and physiological wages of masculinity has its price. A closer look at the interpretive cues provided to the men reveals not only that the male workers are constructed *as men* through their work but also that this public masculinity is tied to their location in the market economy and thus to their successful production of profit. These men become bound not only to their ongoing public performances of masculinity but also to the need to prove their value as workers through the production of profit for the employer. This fusion of gender with market relations has detrimental and even dangerous effects for the men and their co-workers.

## Weathered Men and "Craggly" Women

Although the physical processes and experiences of work tend to be taken for granted, they are in reality socially meaningful—in part because they forge physical bodies that look the way working-class men are supposed to look. The bodies get bigger and stronger—visibly stronger—but also worn and weathered, often scarred, with parts broken, torn, and scraped. These changes, although undesirable on one level because they can represent damage and deterioration of the physical self, nevertheless create bodies that approach the iconic masculinity of the American worker and the American West. As the skin is tanned and leathered by the sun, wind, and cold, as it is calloused and scarred by the many tools and surfaces with which it comes into repeated contact, it is not only aged but *masculinized*.

This is the skin on one side of the binary gender world, where men are seen as rough and hardened by family-supporting and city-building labor; women, as an important contrast, are portrayed as desirably soft, supple, nurturing, and receptive. Construction work thus offers men a public and psychological wage of masculinity, because it helps to convert its male job entrants into the rugged and life-experienced sorts of men that they know they are supposed to be.

This masculine benefit of work is not outwardly or explicitly addressed by the workers, for as Anthony Easthope has argued, for men to publicly acknowledge the underpinnings of masculinity would be to weaken its power.[2] The power of binary male/female imagery and the binary structures is that they are put forth as natural—men simply are this way and women simply are not. Thus the production of this sort of masculinity is also made to seem "natural." It can be recognized primarily in its practice of nonavoidance, such as the nonuse of sunscreen and the almost universal refusal to treat smaller cuts and scrapes in ways that could prevent scarring. Some of these practices, of course, are tied into the larger structures of employment, such as the lack of protection from arbitrary firing and the pressures for profit that tend to see each trip to the trailer for a Band-Aid as wasted work time. Were it not for the masculine pressures—and the masculine payoffs—though, workers could find ways to meet both the pressures of time and the pressures of cosmetic self-protection. Workers *could* carry sunscreen, Band-Aids, and antibiotic gel in their lunchboxes, for example. But of course, they do not.

One can also see the wage of this physically produced masculinity in the ways that these men talk about the work. When they speak of the wear and tear on their bodies, they do not do so to agitate for greater protections or even to note it as a problem for men as a whole but rather to make clear that this job is *bad for women* and women's bodies. I heard men complain individually about their aches and pains—the bad back, the bad knee— but not collectively. The pain was simply put forth as the problem of the individual man, not a problem for men as a class. Bad knees and backs might be bad for individual men, but they seemed to be fine—or at least neutral—for working-class masculinities.[3]

Paying attention to the ways that men talk about their bodies can also reveal an additional benefit of this approach: justifying occupational segregation. In contrast to the way the changes are interpreted for men's bodies, such changes were seen as real and serious problems for women—not only for individual women but also for women as a class. Bodily wear and weathering were used to warn women away from the work. No similar blanket warnings were ever raised in my presence for the younger apprenticed males.

These warnings for women occurred in a variety of settings. On one occasion that I noted in my journal, a worker pointed out alleged signs of deterioration in one of the journey-level women and warned that I, too, would one day look so (allegedly) haggard:

> I get in a discussion with Lon (a journey-level carpenter) at lunch about . . .
> why I am working construction. . . . He tells me that I'll feel differently later.
> *"You'll be all bent over, too,"* he adds, saying how much Jane has aged since
> she first started. "She stood all straight on her first job, but now has rounded
> shoulders. And look at Ben . . ." He adds, laughing in a way that seems to
> indicate that it isn't as serious a concern for men as it is for women. Jane
> certainly looks fine to me, and I make a mental note to ask him why it is
> that *he* does this job, if one is at risk for such changes.

Another version of this gendered argument emerged in focus groups conducted in Minnesota in 1997 by a consortium of governmental and nongovernmental agencies. When a number of the men there challenged the training that women had received prior to entering the industry, strikingly, their argument was not that the women they work with are insufficiently trained (a complaint that one might expect in such arguments) but rather that *someone should have told the women what they would look like* after working in the industry. Thus their concerns were not about women's physical or economic performance, or even their skill-based training, but about making sure the women knew that this work could make them *less attractive as women:*

> "Are you preparing them mentally? Do they also understand what they're
> going to look like after . . . when they're 50 years old?
> "We can look wrinkled and craggly and humped up, and at 37, when
> they're wrinkled up and crippled up . . ." Another carpenter interjects,
> "they're old." And the first carpenter agrees, ". . . they're old."
> The moderator of the focus groups asks, "Yeah? Does it bother them or
> does it bother you?"
> "I think it bothers them. Well, it bothers me, too. I just don't, I'm still from
> the old school, I don't think a woman has to look old just because of
> work. . . ."[4]

Thus it is clear that to be "from the old school" not only means that women should not look "wrinkled and craggly and humped up" but also that men *can* and perhaps even that they should.

Although such conversations took place in many settings and forms, my personal favorite occurred in a discussion with some ironworkers about whether or not being an ironworker is too difficult for women. The men expressed varying degrees of doubt that a woman could "take it"—meaning, of course, the physical work rather than harassment or discrimination. The foundation for their claim was challenged at least somewhat by my working next to them; we were doing different work, but they were *not* doing harder work than I was on this occasion. In fact, I was hauling and placing steel-framed plywood, and they were twisting pieces of medium-gauge wire, used to connect the pieces of reinforcing bar (rebar) that would become the backbone of the concrete wall I was forming. Their most likely injury from that job would have been carpal tunnel to the wrist, similar to what troubles clerical office workers.

This is not either to suggest that ironworkers' work is undemanding or to downplay the risks of office-based work; I am certainly not using the sexist routine of insulting the ironworkers by comparing them to women. Rather, I want to make clear that ironwork is sometimes but not always dangerous and sometimes but not always reasonable and mundane. Ironworkers *do* have a physically demanding and often dangerous job, but it is not a job that *no* woman can do, any more than it is a job that *all* men can do.

It is important to note that among construction trades, ironworkers are most likely to travel long distances for work, spending days and even weeks living on the road. These traveling requirements are undoubtedly problematic for mothers and can also create a 24/7 male-dominated work environment, allowing women little to no respite from often-hostile settings. As a result, the social and logistical aspects of being an ironworker are likely to be at least as responsible as the physical requirements for the lack of women in the trade.

In this conversation, however, what was most interesting was not that we were discussing gender segregation—that topic of debate was as common as air on this and other sites—but rather the succinct explanation given by an older man as to why women shouldn't be ironworkers. As I wrote in my journal, he didn't just argue that they *couldn't* but rather that they *shouldn't*, because it hurts their bodies in ways particular to their female physique:

> "We had a number who've started out, but they drop out because they can't take it. Don't have any upper body strength," said a white ironworker in his early 30s, working as he spoke.

I laughed and said that I thought the term "*any*" was a little harsh, imagining all women lined up with rubbery, useless arms hanging at their sides.

The guy next to me laughed and said, "Yeah, she's got some, do you want to be an ironworker?"

"No," I say with a smile, "I'm happy doing what I'm doing," and begin to say that I know that their union is working to recruit women across the state. I am interrupted by an older ironworker who asserts that:

"*. . . all of the lifting is hard on their boobs.*"

I laugh again (out of surprise as much as at the humor of his comment, [humor] which, at least to me, seems obvious) and respond,

"But you don't lift with your *boobs,* you lift with your *arms.* How can it hurt their boobs?"

He didn't respond in a manner to clarify; he simply repeated insistently while nodding,

"It's hard on their *boobs*" (emphasis his).

Even if interpreted literally, this ironworker's comment is both humorous and false. Outside of a direct hit to her "boobs," or that she might accidentally catch and pinch her "boobs" between the beams she is lifting, a woman is likely to find that her "boobs" are improved rather than damaged by the lifting. Toned pectoral muscles, located roughly behind and above the breasts, would tend to give a woman the appearance of larger and more youthful breasts. If being an ironworker did anything to a woman's "boobs," then, it should improve them.

Regardless of the actual effect upon "boobs," though, this worker's point was clear: the changes that take place in working bodies are not to be regarded as the same for men and women. Instead, these changes should be seen as making men into bigger, stronger, and even more desirable (if weathered and worn) men, but they should not be so interpreted for women.

## Desirable Men and Scandalously Sporty Women

The second way in which construction workers' bodies are shaped to look like culturally desirable working-class men is through the building of strength and muscle. One could argue that the benefits of functional strength are shared by men and women. We all gained the greater sense of well-being that comes from physical activity and the building of physical strength. And certainly, the strength of the body was celebrated in unspoken but obvious ways. We were, after all, using our most basic selves to construct the world around us. It was as if our strength was calling the world into being.

But it was not the case that the strength of men and the strength of women were celebrated similarly. It hardly needs to be said that to be working, to be producing, and to be strong are all positive parts of the masculine-American role. The strong man is almost by definition the better man, regardless of other qualities or social standing. Thus, for male bodies, the development of a more muscular physique and greater functional strength was seen as a clear advantage in the social status game.

The same relationship of strength to social status did not exist for women, in my experience. Instead, women's physical strength was often downplayed or ignored, such as when male workers either offered to help or insisted upon helping female workers. Additionally, women's strength was often problematized in larger sense, by depicting it as masculinizing the women or by associating it with lesbianism.[5]

It is important to note, of course, that these bodily processes are not gendered in themselves; they are simply processes (such as getting weathered by the sun or the building of muscle) that happen in a certain manner. A sunburn is a sunburn, a muscle is a muscle, and a scar is a scar. The bodily changes, however, are clearly gendered because they become gendered in their interpretation by others. Although the development of physical strength and muscle is natural and even necessary for both male and female workers, in many settings it is seen as positively masculine but decidedly unfeminine. That is, construction workers who develop physical and functional strength are likely to be seen as becoming more desirable and more masculine men, but less desirable and less feminine women, at least within mainstream (and certainly work-related) contexts.[6]

Although one could certainly argue that there is increasing social appreciation for women's physical strength—citing, for example, the increased recognition of female athletes—the physical power of women is often framed as something that reinforces rather than undermines the distinction between genders: that is, stronger female bodies are interpreted as becoming more powerful in ways that are neither competitive with nor comparable to men's strength.

In general, when portrayed favorably, physically strong women are seen as bending gender norms in a way that still maintains or even amplifies a definition of them as sexy and acceptable in a very heterosexual way. This is evident, for example, in the media's treatment of female athletes, who tend to be celebrated most when they fulfill the mainstream values of attractiveness and femininity. These include skaters such as Katharina Witt, Ekaterina Gordeeva, and Michelle Kwan; soccer star Mia Hamm; volleyball player Logan Tom; swimmers Amanda Beard and Haley Cope; and track stars Amy Acuff, Suzy Favor Hamilton, and Florence Griffith "Flo-

Jo" Joyner.[7] Women athletes who do not fit these norms are much less frequently covered by the media and are certainly less likely to become press darlings. In this case, then, the mainstream celebration of women's strength can initially appear to be inverting traditional gender roles but is in reality simply a more muscular version of the "beauty quotient."[8] Women are still expected to be physically attractive and to be using their bodies primarily for obtaining the approval of society.[9]

This is not to claim, of course, that women become strong only in ways that reinforce the current gender structures. Women certainly can and do lift weights and develop muscle; they build bridges and high-rises and, in another area of the economy, corporations. Women drive pickups and race cars and fighter planes. And women who become strong sometimes pose real challenges to the ways that these activities are seen and understood by mainstream culture. It seems clear, however, that mainstream society at the present time is still focused on the reproduction of gender difference to the extent that women whose behavior truly challenges the gendered status quo do not get the same sort of social support as women whose behavior can be used to reinforce it.

## Locating Gender in Class and Race

As much as these distinctions serve to reproduce gender, of course, they also highlight and re-create the social divisions of race, ethnicity, and social class within each of the gender categories. For example, although women "in general" have been argued to be too weak to be skilled or competent in physical labor, this restriction is one that was often enforced only for white middle- and upper-middle-class women; poor white women and women of color were often expected, if not required, to work alongside men in fields and factories.[10]

Gender distinctions are also inseparable from the socioeconomic locations of the men who voice them. Although it is certainly an aspect of mainstream popular culture than men *in general* are seen as rugged and weathered, it is not the case that middle- and upper-middle-class men embrace—or even accept—this sort of wear and tear. To the contrary, though I am unaware whether they wore sunscreen, the men who worked in the supervisors' trailers—job superintendent, engineers, architects—did not appear to be at all unusually tanned or prematurely aging. If I were a gambler, I would wager significant amounts of money that they were significantly less likely to have multiple broken bones in their past or damaged knees and backs. And it is a truism of this and other manual fields that the guy with the unmarred hardhat is either a supervisor or a visitor on site.[11]

At the same time and in the same way that the term "women" is used to refer largely to white middle- and upper-class women, then, these physical characteristics of masculinity must be interpreted as both a characteristic and a *cost* of performing working-class masculinities. And to the extent that they are culturally and contextually desirable, and even the extent to which they are seen as reflecting what might be considered the core elements of "universal masculinities," they also clearly reflect circumscription as much as power for the men who experience these changes.

## The Physiological Production of Masculinity: When Work Makes You Feel Like A Man

The social wages enjoyed by men in construction as a result of *external* bodily changes are, however, not nearly so striking as the wages enjoyed by the men as a result of *internal* bodily changes: the *physiological production of masculinity*. By this I mean that men are not only made to look like manly and contextually dominant men but are also made to *feel* like men, in the physical, the heterosexual, and even the marketbound ideals of the industry.

I term this the *physiological* wage of construction because it is both created and experienced within the body. It includes the physiological (bodily) experience of doing the work and the cognitive label that is placed on these bodily sensations. Although the cognitive label is created by the social cues and rules of the environment, the fact that the label is applied to feelings in-the-body (literally *embodied* feelings) means that these socially defined feelings are experienced as "natural." Because these embodied feelings are also tied to gender dominance and sexuality, they provide a physiological wage not only of feeling *good* but also of feeling *right* and *naturally right*. The body internalizes these sensations and understandings in a way that underscores the naturalness of the feelings (and the "naturalness" of gender) at the same time that it obscures the sensations' cultural and structural foundations.

### Gender as an Embodied Emotion

In this argument I am putting forth a reconceptualization of gender as a physiologically experienced emotion. This understanding of gender (and thus also of emotion) is grounded in the work of cognitive social psychologists who study emotion, such as Stanley Schachter and Jerome Singer; Rolf Zillman, Rolland R. Johnson, and Kenneth D. Day; and Theodore

Kemper.[12] According to this view, what one's body feels is not an absolute or given response to one's circumstances but rather an interpretation of somewhat general feelings to fit the specific circumstances. The cognitive approach to emotions recognizes that there are a number of different forms of arousal, each of which can serve as the basis for a variety of specific emotions; which emotion we "feel" is the product of both the arousal and the interpretation or label we put on it.

The classic studies of cognitive approaches to emotion reveal that emotions comprise a physical base of arousal and a cognitive label that informs us what the feeling *means*. Although subsequent work modified the most original models to include more than one type of base arousal, it is still the case that emotions must be *felt and known*.[13] Emotions are thus are a complex combination of arousal and socially bound interpretations.

I build on the cognitive theories of emotion to describe how the men working out in the field of construction experience a fairly general physical arousal as the product of physical labors and then draw upon the cultural cues that are present (the images and language, for example) to determine what they are feeling and what these feelings *mean*. Essentially, then, the men experience a physical feeling tied to the elevated heart rate and other conditions that are the result of a low-level, work-induced physiological arousal. They then turn to their cultural surroundings to decide why and what it is that they are feeling. This joint product of feeling and cognition (or feeling and the label placed upon the feeling) is emotion, an emotion tied to larger understandings of sexuality, dominance, and marketbound rules about men's economic performances.

The specific meanings attributed to the arousal are important not only for the reproduction of gendered employment (the processes of which will become clear) but also for the reproduction of class inequality, whereby the men themselves are subordinated. This latter outcome is the product of the fact that masculinity is not simply experienced but must also be proved: the workers not only experience a sense of masculinity as an emotion but also experience an embodied masculinity tied to the labor process. This means that the men must then prove themselves as men and workers. To fail to fulfill the emotional script is thus to fail to prove oneself either as a worker or as a man.

### Discovering My "Inner Masculinity"

It is important to begin my explanation of all this with an acknowledgment of how I first began to realize that there *was* a physiological component to gender, a way in which the body itself bridges the theoretical chasm between bodily "sex" and the social "gender." This recognition came, of course, from my own recognition of how my experiences were shaping the ways that I saw and understood myself. More specifically, as odd as I am sure this might sound, it was my recognition that I had begun to *feel* like "one of the boys." In a manner going beyond the simple worksite cama- raderie, I began to see and *feel* myself as being "masculine" in a way that felt both positive and, more important, *natural.*

It is not the case that I actually developed any confusion about my sex/gender or even that I developed a sense that I should be or would like to be male. But I did come to "see" myself and experience myself as male in a manner of social identity. I began to use the language that marked me and the "other" men as male (in spite of my ideological predilections against it). I adopted the use of sexual language to define my work, and I came to see myself, oddly, as somewhat flexibly identified with each side of the gender we-they divide. I was also aware of a "vitality," a very physical joie de vivre that emerged from the collective interactions and implicit cultural celebra- tions of what it meant to be a working man among other working men. Put most simply, I began to realize that I had "sensations" of being masculine, manly, and a man among men, and that these sensations were *positive,* an internalized social wage in themselves. They were also "convincing," of course, because they were embodied. At the same time, I was happily aware that I was female, socially and biologically. Thus in spite of the fact that feelings-from-the-body are generally seen as being more "natural" than the things that we think (thoughts-from-the-head), this experience highlighted the ways in which thoughts and feelings, gut reactions and sensations might only *seem* to be distinct. In reality, thoughts and feelings might actually draw upon each other in a conflation of bodily and cognitive forces. "Well," I said to myself, "I certainly understand why men think that gender is biological! It certainly *feels* real in a way that makes, well, *sense.*"

In a most simple way, then, it was this embodiment of knowledge *that could not be true* that highlighted the *embodiment of gender.* By this I mean the way that socially learned gender performances can become internalized in a manner *fused with physiological responses.* Such responses would generally not be visible or notable, of course, since they would largely *confirm* the ex- pectations and feelings that we are supposed to have. That is, feeling like a man is likely to happen more often to men (the result of social and occu- pational segregation, social feeling rules, and other aspects of social life) and thus would not be noteworthy or surprising. Men are probably not surprised by—nor do they feel a need to question—masculine feelings. It is my opinion that such physiological confirmations of social realities happen constantly and that they are generally made invisible by their re-flection of the status quo. The complex nature of these processes became apparent for me only because my feelings of masculinity were *disconfirm-ing* my reality—that my body was telling me something that I intellectu-ally knew could not be true. The larger theoretical arguments about what this means for gender as a concept are beyond the scope of the project at hand, so I return to the production of masculinity in construction work.

### The Production of Arousal

The now classic research on the misattribution of arousal has made clear that the conditions for misattribution are best when the arousal level is low enough to be unrecognizable by the body's owner. For, if the body is able to recognize that it is aroused because of riding a bicycle in a laboratory or because of crossing a rickety bridge spanning a deep gorge (the methods by which arousal was created in some of the early excitation transfer stud-ies) then the mind is able to attribute the arousal to the riding of the bike or to the adrenaline rush of fear, rather than looking for an explanation out-side of the body.[14] If, however, the level of arousal is low enough that the body is aroused but does not recognize itself as aroused, then it is consid-ered to be primed for taking the cues of the environment as the actual source of the arousal itself.

It is significant that the physiological arousal created by ongoing work in the construction industry is both constant and generally at a low enough level to meet exactly the criteria for excitation transfer. Because of the in-formal industry rules that one must always be moving and at least look as if one is working, bodies in construction are subjected to *chronic activity* and *chronic arousal.* Bodily activity must be generally kept at a level that is sus-tainable for an eight- or ten- or twelve-hour period. Arousal is therefore likely to be present at a level low enough that it is difficult for the body's owner to recognize as it "arousal" per se. And it is these low and barely per-ceptible (or even taken-for-granted) levels of arousal that are the most fer-tile for excitation transfer. The high levels of sexual banter (discussed below) certainly also contribute to this arousal as much as the sexuality defines it.

The conditions of low-level arousal are exacerbated by the fact that con-struction workers (as workers and as men) are overwhelmingly encour-aged *not* to pay attention to the reactions of their bodies outside of their sexual responses and drives. Of course, to some extent this trained igno-rance is simply practical: When much of the work is "bull work" (hard physical labor), and many of the constant and ongoing physical feelings are likely to be pain, exhaustion, or excessive heat or cold, ignoring bodily sensations becomes a reasonable occupational practice.[15]

Ignoring one's body is also a gendered practice, coming from both the childhood socialization of males and the ongoing adult socialization that occurs in workplace norms and pressures.[16] For example, one construction supervisor in a focus group is quoted as saying with pride that—in contrast to the women who worked for him in construction—he had "never had a guy complain" about the physical conditions or dangers.[17] Though one would never suggest that there is no reason to complain, it is obvious that a badge of masculine pride is "never" to have complained or to have heard a man complain.

It is the combination of these three elements—the constant but barely detectable level of arousal, the tendency of the workers to ignore the physical messages of their bodies (and thus to be even less likely to identify ongoing physiological arousal), and the highly gendered and sexual cultures of work—that keep the construction workers' bodies not only available for excitation transfer but also *prepared, primed, and vulnerable* for it.[18]

### The Feeling Rules of Masculinity

Although men who work construction are certainly discouraged from focusing on their fear or discomfort, it is not the case that they are prohibited from feeling *anything*. In fact, there are abundant cultural and linguistic cues about how the workers *should* feel about themselves, their work, and their co-workers. Even a brief review of construction's culture reveals that these workers are to be seen as *men* (culturally understood and affirmed as the opposite of women), that they are to be seen as very sexual men, and that their sexuality is clearly limited to a form of publicly aggressive heterosexuality. More surprisingly, perhaps, it becomes clear that this masculinity is also tied to the successful completion of work and the production of work and profit. There are distinct and logically connected cultural cues to this mandated masculinity.

*"The Worker, He."* The first and most obvious cue in the culture of construction work is the use of language and graphics to signify the worker as male, to distinguish him from women, and to use this distinction as a threat of how he might be seen if he should fail to perform.[19] First and foremost is the use of the pronoun "he" to refer to everyone except when a particular woman is being discussed. Members of the industry are almost always referred to as men: the worker, he; the superintendent, he; the foreman, he;

or simply, "a guy could. . . ." It isn't that this usage is thought to be neutral; it is instead (as I suggested in my justification for retaining such language in my own writing) essential for reproducing an environment that clearly defines itself as male.

Only one time do I remember someone specifically amending his speech in this regard. In a discussion of bathroom remodeling where I was one of four workers, a fellow carpenter corrected himself by saying that "a guy could . . . I mean, a person could . . ." Most amusing about this anecdote is that the project was mine and the "guy" was *me*. Even when he corrected himself, of course, my co-worker referred to me not as a woman but simply as a "person." It was the case that a *person* could but not that a woman could; this might be work for a man, or maybe even for a person, but it was clearly not work that "a woman" could do. In this way the language of construction work identifies the male sex of the "generic worker" and reproduces the vision of the industry as an all-male enclave.

*To Fail Is to Be Female.*   To the extent that "women" are included in the language of construction work, they are portrayed not only as nonworkers but also as that which men become when they *fail to be men*. A poor performance, in construction, is a *female* performance. On days when the work was not going well, journey-level workers complained, "Aw, we're just a bunch of women out there." A man who didn't swing his hammer hard enough was told to "hit it with your purse," and anyone working too slowly was advised to "hike up your skirt and get it done." Women are equated with incompetence and weakness in language (similar to that used outside the construction industry); men are ridiculed simply by equating them with women, girls, and worse.[20]

The definition of "worker" in construction, then, is not only male but predicated on the definition of masculinity that posits men as the opposite of women and necessarily their superiors. Since bad male workers are redefined as female workers, it is not surprising that these beliefs provide the framework of hostility toward actual women workers. After all, if workers must be male and not female, and the condition of "female" is equated with failure, then the presence of females successfully completing the work is itself potential evidence of a collective male failure. As a result, the presence of women on site can "logically" be taken as a threat to the communal constructions of reality.

*"Paper Pussy" at Work.*   This demarcation of gender as men-over-women is highlighted also by the extraordinarily common—though illegal—

graphic displays of nude and seminude women in posters, calendars, and vehicle auto fresheners in the construction environment. Women are thus not regarded as employed or employable subjects but put forth as objects of desire and consumption. The most prominent example during my years in the industry was the "Makita Girl" promotions that hung in the workshops, company offices, and even the wholesale and retail outlets of the construction industry.

The "Makita Girl" is a long-running promotional project of the Makita tool company which features scantily clad women using power tools. In addition to totally neglecting safety equipment, the women are often shown provocatively straddling sawhorses or spread out suggestively on fiberglass insulation. Not only do these promotions add to the obscurely referenced connection between men, masculinity, and machinery mentioned by Robert Connell in his 1987 *Gender and Power,* but these posters and calendars also make clear how "ridiculous" the idea of female construction workers must really be. Women represented as an after-work reward for men appear more likely to masturbate with the tools than actually use them. There is no suggestion of women as legitimate or even potentially legitimate workers. Instead, these graphics reinforce construction work as a male domain and suggest not only what women cannot do but also what they are "really" good for. Put more simply, they place women in the sex trades but not the building trades. A woman is something to be "done" by men, not someone who can do the job.[21]

*Donkey Cocks and Humping the Forms.*   The language of construction is not only *sexed* as male; it is also sexualizing, meaning that the language of the construction site is peppered, more than liberally, with references to sexual behavior and body parts. Tools and accessories are given sexual names, and the verbs of work are sexual as well. Construction workers handle "donkey cocks" (connecting pins used to connect two or more pieces of scaffolding) and often spend their days "humping" (or carrying) concrete forms, 2×4s, and bundles of shingles. They drill, they nail, and they screw—all verbs commonly used also to refer to sexual penetration.

It is significant that in the cognitive approach to emotion, sexual arousal is considered to be one of the more easily misattributable emotions. This means that when a person is feeling *something* (perhaps fear, perhaps simply an elevated heart rate), sexual arousal is easily substituted for some equally plausible explanation for the feeling—including even the recognition of an elevated heart rate. Significantly, a core feature of the construction industry is this abundant and ubiquitous sexuality that can convert work arousal to a sexually interpreted emotion.

The combination of physiological arousal and sexual banter is also socially and economically significant because it both *adds* to the physiological arousal of the workers *and* allows the arousal of work to be recoded as a sense of sexual vitality and identity. This suggests an additional "sexual wage" for workers, since it potentially converts what might be fatigue and discomfort into a sense of heterosexual male joie de vivre. Work is thus made pleasant—or at least somewhat more pleasant and distracting. The sexual nature of this embodied masculinity, called forth and amplified by the work and work culture, gives a new and slightly humorous twist to the notion that one can "love" or even "get off on" doing one's job.

*"Getting Her Done."* The cultural cues provided to workers are not only sexual but heterosexual. According to the cultures of construction, to perform work is not only to be male and to produce sexuality but also to *perform heterosexuality,* and to do so in a traditional and male-dominant fashion. Work is thus male and heterosexual in its essence, because *whatever is done* is done to something female, and whatever has been done must be *or must be made to be* female. Male workers ask each other, "You got her done?" The shift is ended when you "call her a day." To finish putting concrete forms together is to "button her up." Thus to "do construction work" is to be a man performing sexually, performing heterosexuality, and getting her done.

Even more striking than the heterosexual imperative implicit in this language is the connection of violence with the act: the mandated verbal intersection of male agency, violence, and sexuality. To demolish a wall is to "knock her down." To attach sheetrock or gypsum to 2×4 studs is to "screw her down" or to "slap her up and nail her." A stubborn piece of wood that cannot be wedged into position is frequently a "bitch," and thus it is the bitch that gets nailed, gets screwed, gets done. In all these examples it is the male worker who exerts his action and his sexual agency upon the female object. The images of sexuality are both clear and violent.

## Caveats: Questions of Intent

It is important to recognize, of course, that these are not the explanations that the men themselves might offer for their language. In fact, whenever I asked about the alternative meanings of their terminology, they tended to shrug off the question and roll their eyes—clearly they thought that I was making something out of nothing (or looking for a lawsuit). But that response doesn't necessarily mean that the men disagreed, only perhaps that this language loses its power if discussed—like much of the social production of masculinity.[22]

*Evidence of Intent: Anecdotes that Suggest the Sexual Meanings Are Recognized.* There are, however, signs that these meanings were known—even consciously known—to the men. Once when I was forming concrete on a small crew with two other men, the working foreman, standing in the center, turned to the man at his side and said, "Got her done?" Roughly a minute later, he turned to me and said instead, "Got it done?" Since the former was almost always a replacement for the latter, it was notable that he had used these two different phrases so closely together. The time span was short enough to suggest both awareness and intentionality on the part of the foreman. The double entendre of sexual production, it appears, was more appropriate for the man at work than it was for me.

A more dramatic example of such "unveiling" occurred when I had been in the industry for roughly six months and was attempting to pick up the "lingo" as seemed appropriate. I was working on a small roof with Silver (another apprentice) and Vinnie, the supportive and energetic foreman at Remodel Co. I needed some more shingles to complete my section of roof. I knew that the term applied to moving shingles (and other large objects) was "to hump." It seemed to me at the time that one ought to be able to treat it like other verbs and use the ordering of the verb, object, and indirect object to suggest who is doing what for whom (the astute reader may see, uncomfortably, where this is going). When one is having a birthday, for example, one can say either, "Please bake a birthday cake *for me*" or "Please bake *me* a birthday cake."—in either case clearly requesting that the cake, not the person, be baked.

It is also significant, of course, that I had already been informed repeatedly that terms appearing to be sexual were really not; they were simply the terminology of work; it was irrelevant that most ten-year-olds are likely to know the sexual connotation of "humping." Nevertheless, when I looked up from my work and said in a loud and confident voice, "Hey Silver, would you hump me over a bundle of shingles?"—*clearly* requesting that he bring some roofing materials over to me—it was the alternative and slightly more sexual interpretation that hung in the air. Both men were in fact speechless and motionless for a short while. And the previously denied sexual meaning was in fact so apparent that when Silver, roughly six months later, sat in our classroom full of apprentices and said loudly, "Hey, you guys should hear what Kris said on the job. . . ." I knew what he was going to say before he said it. Despite assertions that the language of work is not actually sexual, these two examples make clear that the alternative interpretations are both knowable and known.

*Homoeroticism and Homophobia.* Even though the sexual climate is both clearly and mandatorily heterosexual, it is not the case that all of the sexual language is unambiguously so. Since the men appear unwilling to acknowledge conventionally heterosexual meanings, however, one can imagine that the phrases suggestive of homoeroticism or homosexuality are entirely barred from interrogation. This matters, of course, because potentially homoerotic phrases, like the heterosexual ones, add a layer of sexual charge to an already physical, sexual, and virtually all-male environment. Though I am sure that my male co-workers would disagree if asked, in my opinion there is an undeniable element of both the homosocial and the homoerotic in the largely male, physical and sexual construction environment—similar to those of other virtually all-male venues such as athletic locker rooms, the military, and fraternities, to name a few. Although the culture of construction (like these other virtually all-male environments) is permeated with homophobia, it is also filled with men, physically working and physiologically aroused, who talk incessantly about sex and even engage in nonsexual acts that they describe sexually.[23]

This is not to suggest that the majority of men working construction are actually homosexual; that would make as much sense as asserting the opposite—that the heterosexual language of work might mean that the men of construction are all heterosexual. Instead, I assume that the sexual demography of the construction industry is roughly the same as it is elsewhere, with potentially fewer gay men choosing to work in an industry that is verbally, at least, more than moderately homophobic (and, of course, that has a history marked with violence).

The men's arousal, in spite of its inability to mark them as heterosexual or homosexual, performs a number of significant social functions. As suggested earlier, it adds a sexual charge—and thus a sexual wage—to an occupation that could otherwise be simply at times tedious and painful.

Additionally, this sexual wage is part of a larger wage of social masculinity, through which the men are able to mark themselves as possessing a sort of omnipresent, omnivirile, and almost unstoppable sexuality. Because this "emerges" (as if naturally) in an all-male environment of work, the emergence in what is considered to be a "nonsexual" environment is itself taken as further proof of the constancy and the power of this working-class male sexuality. In spite of what one might consider to be fairly obvious cues and practices, the constructed and enacted nature of male sexuality is neither acknowledged nor addressed, instead, it is denied and made invisible through cultural practices, and the beliefs in biologically determined behaviors are reaffirmed.

Because this sexuality is seen as less refined than middle- and upper-class male sexualities, it is heralded as the more natural and the more real sexuality. Thus these men earn a respectable social wage of being more masculine, more sexual, more powerful than men of other classes. Not only does work feel good, then, by producing a physiological arousal that identifies the men as real men, it also allows them to recode physiological responses to work as sexual arousal, making what could feel tiring feel sexual and aggressive. More important perhaps, the collective creation of sexuality serves to bolster their identities in real individual and collective ways. These men are in this way, the sort of men that all men are supposed to be and all women are supposed to long for. At the end of the day, one has not only produced a tangible product of work, one has also reproduced embodied ideologies of gender, sexuality, and power.

There are also other, less obvious, and more economic functions of this sexual charge. Because they work in an almost exclusively male environment filled with sexual banter, slang, and physical activity, it is significant that the arousal created among men is strictly prohibited (on the surface at least) from being interpreted as occurring *between* men. The overt rules and sanctions of the culture prohibit the recognition of any meanings beyond the very heterosexual interpretation "we're men, they're women, we're getting them done." As a result, the erotic charge in construction work appears to perform a function similar to what occurs in other male-dominated settings, where arousal combined with sexuality and homophobia intensifies the arousal. This arousal must then be sublimated into a proper channel—for example, work or sports or war. Arousal becomes consent, the heightened sexual response of the construction workplace becomes a valuable method for eliciting men's consent to and participation in tasks they might not "rationally" consider desirable.

*The Importance of the Asshole.*   This interpretation of a sublimated homoerotic sexuality is supported and highlighted by the use of another term I encountered when working on the large job for Concrete, Inc. The workers used the term "asshole" to denote little squares of plywood—roughly 4" by 4" with 3/4" holes drilled approximately in the center. Assholes serve as large destructible washers; in attaching plywood forms to concrete, they are used to hold the head of the anchor (a very large and thick nail of sorts) away from the steel and plywood form that will shape the concrete. The asshole is placed on the plywood form and the anchor is then driven through the hole and into the form. One cannot think too much about the asshole without realizing that this is essentially a hole through which a thick metal shaft is to be driven and destructively removed once the concrete has hardened. Even the most unimaginative reader will likely be able to see other, less heterosexual interpretations.

That this language, in spite of its homoerotic overtones, is seen as reproducing a *heterosexual* version of the workforce is contradictory but not entirely surprising. When men produce sexually and/or produce sexuality in American society, it is not a neutral or value-free exercise but a clearly value-laden one, heavily constricted by norms and sanctions. John Stoltenberg, in his 1990 piece "How Men Have (a) Sex," suggests that sexuality is so essential to male public definition—and its failure so threatening—that men learn as boys and adolescents to identify as sexual only those situations that support the proving of their masculinity.[24] Thus it should not be surprising that a culture such as construction, both highly sexualized and almost entirely male, would also be structured so as to preclude any interpretations other than heterosexual. It does also suggest however, that there are alternative explanations for these cultural performances beyond the more obvious and "straight"-forward interpretations.

### Men, Women . . . and Dogs?

At this point, the production of a physiological wage of masculinity might appear to have only benefits for the men who receive it: they are able to feel not only more manly through their work but also more manly in the way that men are supposed to be—sexual, aggressive, and aggressively heterosexual. When the language of working and production is compared with the language of misspent energy, however, this achieved masculinity is revealed to be closely tied to, if not fused with, the economic production of work. Proving oneself as a man becomes dangerously tied to the proving of oneself as a worker.

The connection of masculinity with the production of profit is revealed most gracefully through the common use of a single phrase: "fucking the dog." I first learned this terminology on a roofing job when it was 96 degrees Fahrenheit with no clouds, no wind, a company requirement for wearing hardhats, and a prohibition on wearing shorts—and we were working on the black tarpaper that serves as a water barrier under the shingles. This means that we were standing on a black roof, under a hot sun, with no wind. We could not have been much hotter if we'd been standing in a frying pan. Though we had water on the job and were encouraged to take breaks, the day was not "called," and we didn't leave early. Instead, we stayed and continued working, although we were slightly slower and less focused than usual.

To compensate for the fact that most sensible people (or those with any choice) would not have been working under these conditions—and, of course, to prevent the very real possibility of heat-related illness—we slowed down the pace. No one was running, and in the conversations that took place as we worked, the men were more likely than usual to stop moving to make their point or to even to pause for a few minutes to share a conversation with others. Such a deliberate slowdown was called, as I was told, "fucking the dog." That is, to loaf, in construction (and, I believe, the military), is to "fuck the dog," and to describe someone as loafing is to describe him as doing the same.

Although it was at first almost too obvious to seem plausible, the meaning of this was revealed matter-of-factly by a social psychologist with whom I had previously taught and liked to visit on campus. This was not a person I would have expected to be offering up a fairly feminist interpretation, and thus I was surprised when he explained in an almost off-hand manner that what this phrase made clear was that men "fucking the dog" were seen as wasting their life's energy.[25] Thus it is through the comparison of the language of work with the language of loafing that the rules for production-related behavior—as well as the connection of sexuality to production—become clear. To work well is to nail, to screw, to drill or "do" a female. To waste one's time and energy (to waste one's life force, perhaps) is to fuck the dog.

The focused interpretation of this phrase is underscored by the lack of tolerance for synonyms or word play when using such expressions, no matter how clever they might have appeared to be to the instigator. After I learned to say "fucking the dog" (and I was explicitly taught this phrase by my co-workers, in exchange, humorously enough, for my agreeing to stop saying "excuse me" when I passed them on the roof's edge), I became comfortable enough to vary my wording of it. I played with a number of equivalents such as "copulating with the canine" and "mounting the hound." Yet despite the endless possible variation and great word game potential (a great thing, I thought, on a long, hot, and monotonous roofing job), *all phrases other than "fucking the dog" were stonily rejected.* Because I am humble—or perhaps humorously pathetic—enough to resuscitate a joke when possible, I tried this word game on more than one occasion and was able to observe this same reaction on more than one job. Therefore, I believe that this insistence on terminology does not simply reflect a distaste for word games but instead suggests the importance of the signifier "fucking" as a means and a method for sex and domination, as well as the intersection of the two. "Screwing the pooch" one of the few acceptable variants I have heard on this phrase (more common in the military, it seems) clearly maintains this sensibility.

The importance of "fucking" in this phrase is again suggested by Stoltenberg, who explains how men's social understandings of sex are shaped by what men are socially allowed to do and feel, as well as how they must identify and comply with their referent male peers.[26] Men thus generally interact sexually with or in front of their peers only in ways that are action-oriented and non-emotional and that present man as the dominator, not the dominated. From this perspective we can see that although it is not socially *preferable* to be "fucking the dog" if one's peers are working, at least "fucking" the dog provides a public affirmation of *a* form of sexual manhood. To fail both in the production arena (by not working) and the sexual arena (by not fucking) would leave the male worker with no socially available safety net at all.

## Compulsory Masculinity, Heterosexuality, and Production

These ways of talking about work, working, and tools clearly do more than *connect* productivity with sexuality—they equate them. To produce well is to do her; not to produce is to "fuck the dog," to waste one's energy in an inappropriate and shameful way. As important as the production—no production ("do her"—"fuck the dog") comparison, perhaps, is the good worker–bad worker parallel: to do work well is to *do her*, and to do work poorly is to *be her*. Thus a good worker (who makes profit) is a good man, and a better man makes better profits. Masculinity is effectively tied to the process of profit production in capitalism.

Contrary, then, to the image of men who simply *choose* to prove their masculinity continuously (although this is certainly a part of the culture for some men), an image emerges of a masculinity so tightly connected to other forms of social structure that it can be ignored or "failed" only with great risk. To step outside the cycle of proving one's masculinity is to step outside the proving of one's worth in production, a key component of "doing capitalism." And this cycle of masculine-economic "proving" cannot be easily be separated from the lack of job security in the union construction industry: to fail to prove oneself as a worker is not only to be a woman but also to be at risk of unemployment.

Although it might seem a perfectly reasonable aspect of capitalism that workers either produce or leave, the fusion of masculinity and capitalism serves not only to elevate the standards for "good work" but also to redefine basic concepts such as "reasonable" and "safe" in ways that circumvent extant safety and labor laws. Because these laws are often the products of long and contentious labor struggles (during which and for which men and women literally lost their lives), this is no small point. Yet men in construction work appear to be rolling back the gains of the labor movement in their public push for sex and gender politics, and they are doing so at great cost to themselves and their peers. Chapters 5 and 6 deal with this issue and its ramifications for worker culture and worker safety.

# 5

## "WE'RE ANIMALS . . . AND WE'RE PROUD OF IT"

### Strategic Enactments of White Working-Class Masculinities

It is a hot, muggy day in late August, and Frank and I are working at the bottom of a dirt and gravel pit, shoveling and leveling out the ground where a large concrete foundation block is to be poured. We place the steel and plywood forms as we go along, and we are soon as covered in the form oil (sprayed on the plywood to prevent the concrete from sticking to it) as in dirt and our own sweat. What little wind there is does not make it down into the pit, and we work without relief from the strong glow of the sun. Over time, the heat of the day takes an additional toll, adding to the stress and exhaustion that come from the work itself. With each hour, it seems, the work grows harder and my own arms heavier—by midafternoon, almost as heavy as the forms themselves, forms that are already about as big as I am.

As usual, Frank and I are talking about a lot of nothing as we work—some general comments on family, some remarks about this or that person with the company, some story about people's off-site activities. Then, as if it were relevant to what we were saying, Frank tells me I've been given the nickname "BT" for "Big Tits" and that Sara, a long-time and successful carpenter, is now known as "LT" for "Little Tits." These names, he explains, are used in the supervisor's trailer at lunch and on breaks by the various men who gather there—the job superintendent, the foremen, and a handful of the supervisors. In short, all the men with any influence among the roughly five hundred "men" on this job are in on the joke. In spite of all of my work, in spite of all of the hot-summer-sun-and-no-wind days, I'm not a worker; I'm not an apprentice; I'm just a pair of "tits" ranked and evaluated by those in charge. And everyone else knows it, just in case I should forget.

Though I tell myself that I'm not going to let this get to me, his words hit me like another ten hours of labor in the sun. My limbs grow even heavier with the disappointment. I try to work through it by simply working harder, by throwing the heavy form pieces a little farther, and by swinging my hammer as if I could break the steel and plywood. At some point, though, my sublimation fails, and hot, unwanted tears of frustration roll silently out from under my sunglasses. Unable to stop the tears and unable to pretend it doesn't matter, I bend my head a little more and just keep working.

At some point, Frank catches on that I'm upset and attempts to convince me that I shouldn't be. He doesn't try to convince me that "Tits" is a good nickname or one that I should be proud of, but rather that my being upset is an inappropriate response to the events, given the environment that I am in. This is, he suggests, just how construction work *is*.

> "It's been that way as long as I've been in construction. That's just how it is . . .
>
> "We're animals," he said, and he laughed. "We're animals, we yell at women . . .
>
> "We're *construction workers* [emphasis his], *that's just how we are*."

On the surface, of course, Frank is claiming that this is just a little playful banter between men, passed on somewhat innocently (if unadvisedly) to the woman at the heart of the joke. And he might be right if this were an unusual or a one-time event in the industry. But it isn't. The explanation that Frank offers here is meaningful far beyond this incident, far beyond this worksite, and far beyond this contractor. In fact, this is essentially the same explanation I heard in entirely different circumstances offered up by apprentices, journey-level workers, union representatives, and, in at least one instance, a company president. This is also the sort of occurrence and explanation that most, if not all, women in the industry (and many men of color) are likely to be familiar with.

When set in the context of the larger construction culture, it is clear that this "joke" is just one variant of an oft-repeated practice and, as such, can better be understood as a strategic part of the work culture. By claiming that this is just how these guys are and that these are just the things that these guys will do and say, Frank communicates that this is the nature of the men—as if naming women "Tits" is part of a biologically determined set of working-class male behaviors. This assertion matters, of course, because biologically based behaviors are not likely to be easily changeable, if at all. And if the behaviors are natural and not to be changed, then the pigs' co-workers must know that it is useless to complain or push for change. Not only should other workers save their energy and just "let it go" (i.e., ignore the offending behaviors), but the managers as well are freed from any expectation that they would attempt to correct their men.

The assertion that the men are "pigs" and "animals" would appear on the surface to be an insult levied against the working men, but it is not. "Pigness" is a term used by the working men to describe themselves, and it is strategic. The assertion that men are pigs and animals is strategic because it communicates who belongs in the industry, the appropriate forms of workplace conduct, the nature of the men who do the work, and the reasonable managerial responses to violations of both cultural codes and the law. In this way, then, anecdotes about the piggish and animal behaviors of white male construction workers are best interpreted as part of the larger cultural practices that illuminate—and reproduce—the gendered, racialized, and economic structures of the industry. I believe the central contradiction of the social, political, and economic worlds of construction is that the workers' justifications for their social and economic power are exactly those reasons used to justify the workers' further subordination. The positive aspects of these relations are first visible in what I call the workers' "wage of masculinity," the social wage that white male construction workers gain as cultural icons of the "real" and core masculinities to which all other men refer (and defer) and against which all other masculinities are measured. This strategic assertion of dominance is, however, simultaneously turned against the men and becomes part of the rationale through which they are both subordinated and devalued. Because the subordination is predicated on the same arguments as the social wage, the ability for the workers to free themselves from further subordination would require a sacrifice of this largely nonmonetary wage.

## Men as Pigs and Animals: Strategic Claims and Contradictory Outcomes

### Pigness as Turf Protection

Although the anecdote at the beginning of the chapter focuses on an incident of sexual harassment, it would be a mistake to interpret "pigness" (the patterned assertions that these men are animals) as simply outlining the relations between women and working-class men, for the claim to pigness is also a declaration about hierarchies of race and sexuality within the context of work. Pigness makes clear that white working-class men will not be held to externally imposed standards of "political correctness," standards that they often dismiss as simply pandering to liberals or "special interests." Because political correctness is seen within the culture as mandating overly polite language that prevents an accurate description of reality (by forbidding, for example, negative generalizations about the occupational capacities of women and men of color). Political correctness—and thus liberals—are seen as less able than the men who are pigs to state what they believe or to "call it like it is." Pigness is put forth simultaneously as a form of authentic expression and also a "license" to use racial and ethnic slurs, to make generalizations about who can and cannot do the work, and to display overt hostility and animosity toward others as the pigs deem appropriate.

The significance of pigness as an appreciably durable and obstructive workplace ideology was explained to me on my first job by a Latino laborer. He pulled me aside after a jobsite lunch where I had objected to the conversations about "niggers, spics, jews, and Ay-rabs." José, the laborer, and I were both running loads of debris out to the dumpster, and once we were beyond the earshot and sight of the other workers, he asked, "Are you Hispanic?" I replied, slightly puzzled, that I was not. He then wondered aloud why I was upset, since I wasn't personally addressed by the line of slurs. He suggested that I adopt his personal strategy for survival: "I have learned to not react unless they touch me"—that is, he went on to explain, he had learned over time to ignore all verbal comments and to respond only to physical threats as necessary. In this way he could get by without trying to change the larger realities of work. It wasn't that he didn't *want* to change these realities, of course, but he knew that attempting to alter the environment was not a way to "make it" at work or to keep one's job as an outsider in the industry.

*Pigness as a Public Assertion of Sexuality.*    The identity of pigness is also an assertion of a bold heterosexuality, one that is not likely to be tolerant of effeminate or homosexual men. As explained in the previous chapter, these assertions do not necessarily mean that all the men actually possess heterosexuality but rather that heterosexuality is a mandatory public performance. After all, the environment is virtually all male, it is physical in a way that keeps workers' bodies in a state of arousal, and the jobsite is constructed around a language of work that is focused on sex and male workers "doing" female objects. When defined as a heterosexual-only environment, construction work is a physiological affirmation of manhood and heterosexuality. To acknowledge and accept homosexuality would likely call into question whether these cultural practices involving public sexualities are potentially masking elements of a virile homosexuality. And of course all masculinities retain their power best when they are not called into public view. Therefore, although I have no doubt that there are gay men working union construction or that there are heterosexual men who engage in homosexual encounters along the line of the "tearoom trade,"[1] it is significant that the public and acknowledged culture of construction work is both heterosexual and anti-gay. Pigness is a justification and an affirmation of overtly sexist, racist, and homophobic behaviors.

*Pigness as Class Status.* Pigness also reveals the relationships between the white men of different socioeconomic strata, between the men who work on the jobsite and the men who own and manage the companies. The claim that "these men are pigs" is a statement about the men who do the physical work of the industry and the ways in which they are distinct from the men who are not or cannot be construction workers. Pigness does this in part by highlighting what might be considered deficits in other subcultures and revealing them as strengths. For example, to call a man a pig is to suggest that he might not know what fork is to be used for salad but that he knows which drill bit is used for different forms of masonry under different and varying conditions. He might not know what sort of wine goes best with salmon, but he knows what grade of motor oil is needed for each piece of workplace machinery. He can get a machine running that is clearly past its usable life, and he is the man—in all meanings of the phrase—"to get the job done." It is thus no mere coincidence that an article in *Redbook* magazine used exactly this phrase ("to get the job done") to describe the sexual proclivities of men by occupation.[2] To call the men animals is to make clear that they might not know the right words to use in polite company, but they're the ones that women should turn to when they're looking for task-specific satisfaction.

By indicating that construction workers are rougher and less politically correct than the more socialized men of the middle and upper classes, pigness also implies that construction workers should be seen as *less refined* men and thus as possessing a more natural form of masculinity. This distinction is significant in understanding their relationship with other men, of course, because it is this raw masculinity that is seen as "real." And it is this raw masculinity that is at the heart of construction workers' role as one of the primary icons of manhood in American popular culture. These men refer to themselves as pigs in part because this marks them as the men that all men, in at least some ways, are supposed to be. Put another way, this identity of raw masculinity and real manhood is clearly a nonmonetary job benefit that the men can cash in on when they claim that they are "pigs" and "animals."

*Pigness as Conscription.*   The interpretations and implications of animal identities are complex, however, and a full analysis of pigness reveals that as a strategy it has, like all strategic actions, unpredictable and often unplanned negative consequences. On one hand, for example, male construction workers' equation of themselves with animals protects the otherwise illegal behaviors that maintain the workplace as a white- and male-dominated environment; in this way, pigness is empowering for white working-class men. Yet on the other hand, the use of animal identities reveals and exacerbates the class, economic, and power inequalities between the men who physically do the work and the men who supervise and profit from it. Asserting pigness exposes the workers as lesser men in society at large, where women are supposed to be treated (at least in theory) as equals and are not supposed to be called "Tits" in mixed company. In the "real world," of course, construction workers are readily recognized as being less wealthy, less educated, less sophisticated, less powerful, and thus less desirable in general than white-collar and managerial men. Pigness, therefore—as a claim to a specific masculinity recognizable within the general hierarchies of gender, race, and class—gives these men privilege over people of color and white women in some circumstances, yet in others it cannot prevent them from being made subordinate to the managerial classes (including the white women and people of color who manage).

Claims of pigness also have effects beyond the gates of the construction site and even beyond the boundaries of the industry. The use of animal imagery to celebrate workers calls up what David Nibert and others have called a "hierarchy of value," in which thinking animals (generally humans) are placed above those who are seen as existing to serve.[3] It is clearly the latter category that is represented by "pigs." Certainly, part of what is celebrated about this raw, animal masculinity is working men's social inability to reflect on their own pain, vulnerability, or discomfort. The construction culture is founded on the ideal of "taking it like a man" and thus simultaneously "working like a bull" and working through pain; the idealized image of a man (or beast) who's too tough to let pain slow him down becomes the standard that workers try to meet. This effort makes it difficult, if not impossible, for the men to organize successfully around the traditional labor issues of working conditions, hours, and safety. The result is that the celebrated images of construction workers as pigs and animals ultimately conscript the workers as much as they elevate them: although these images are economically beneficial, because the desirable jobs are successfully protected as the turf of white, working-class men, the protections available to the men on the job are reduced, and the larger social and economic value of the jobs is decreased. Thus here again we see the contradictory outcomes of pigness.

### Pigness as Power: Asserting the Primacy of Physical Masculinities

As insulting as it might seem to folks outside of the industry, the claim to pigness and animal nature is at its heart a claim to pride, strength, and virility. After all, these are terms that the men have coined for themselves. The men use these terms to informally describe the culture (*"You've got to understand, we're all just a bunch of pigs"*; or *"Men are pigs, Krissy, didn't you know that?"*) and to denote various trades and specialties, such as "mudpigs" for the concrete carpenters and "sandhogs" for sewer and tunnel workers.[4] These terms are also used frequently when explaining the rules and nature of the building trades' environment. They may refer to a work crew, a specific construction trade or specialty, most men in construction, or even to men in general. As compliments, such as being as strong as a bull or an ox, they can of course refer to a specific individual.

The positive connotations of animal imagery are numerous and varied. On one hand, the strength of the image asserts the solidity of the men, that they are born to do this sort of work and, as many Americans believe about farm animals, that they are bred for it. Pigness is thus an economic claim through which white male workers attempt to maintain their control over a large set of desirable jobs. On the other hand, it is also an essentialist message about physicality and sexuality. Because the masculinities asserted by "pigness" are corporeal and not cerebral, they celebrate the "animal" physicality (including strength and raw sexuality) that is a core component of construction workers' concept of masculinity. And because this core is seen as central to all masculinities, and it is epitomized in American culture by the men of construction work, the claim to pigness is also an assertion that working-class masculinities have primacy over femininities, gay masculinities, and the more "effeminate" white-collar masculinities.

All of these are perhaps best summed up in a passage of semi-autobiographical fiction from Dagoberto Gilb, a former carpenter turned prizewinning author. It is most meaningful, perhaps, that this work has been ex-cerpted in *Carpenter*, the trade magazine for the United Brotherhood of Car-penters and Joiners. Thus it is a description made by a carpenter and celebrated by carpenters:

> None of us worked construction because we were rich, but neither did any let his body get this aching and exhausted and dirty for love of money. It was a need, and what we learned, physically and mentally, was that not just anybody could do it, not week after week, month after month, year in and year out. Our job was our pride. . . . It was the sex that women liked about us, the muscles our children admired. Employed, it was what we were never ashamed of.[5]

Within this quotation there are four intertwined claims about the men who are construction workers—they are natural workers, born to work; this work is real work; these men are real men; and their natural sexuality is a pure form of male heterosexuality in general—all part of the masculinity that is asserted and claimed by pigness.

*Construction Workers as Natural Workers.*   Animal imagery is used to make a claim about the sort of men who become construction workers and what it is that makes a good worker. The biological nature of the imagery suggests that these skills and talents are on some level innate. It isn't the case that just anyone can learn a trade; there are simply some (as Gilb sug-gests) for whom the work is in their bones and in their blood. To use this claim is to argue that these men are the ones who "naturally" belong in con-struction work and are likely to make the best and most competent trades-men. And as Gilb argues, they need the work as much as the work and the industry need them. These men want to work, and it is the work that makes them whole, even work that is dangerous, physical, and painful—and per-haps particularly the work that is dangerous. "Getting the job done" is the fulfillment these men require. Like the animals laboring on a farm, they should be understood as living to work.

By calling up the images of some animals but not others, the claims of pigness also allow the men to lay a racialized claim to the industry. They do so by highlighting the bread-and-butter animals of American farming while excluding more "exotic" animals that come from continents other than Europe. Although the usage appears casual—and, like all strategic ac-tions, need not be calculated by each individual user—it is significant that the claim to be animals clearly includes some animals and excludes others, even when alternative images might be closer to the actual work that is done. Most simply, these men are not lions or tigers, monkeys, apes, elephants, or hard-working and enduring camels. Even in instances where a monkey might be a more appropriate icon—with bridge workers, for example, or ironworkers on the high steel, where pigs and bulls would be less than successfully employed—I never heard that term applied to the white ethnic males laboring in construction. Perhaps monkeys are close enough to humans that the comparison might assign construction workers to an evolutionary place between monkeys and humans, rather than making clear the empowering nature of the imagery. It is certainly the case that the racialized connotation of "monkey," often used as a slur against black Americans, prohibits its widespread adaptation by white construction workers. Thus, by drawing only upon images of animals emerging from the European-American conquest of the United States—pigs, horses, bulls, bears—construction workers are able to reinforce their historical claim to the industry and to reproduce the racial and ethnic segregation that they have successfully maintained in both union and nonunion sectors.

Their imagery is also gendered: it makes clear that the desirable image of work and worker is male. The men are bulls (not cows) and pigs (but not sows), images speaking to aspects of masculine pride and particularly *excluding* the qualities believed to be associated with women. Women are cows (and not bulls), able to produce with their bodies but not with their strength. Women are cats, kittens, birds, and vixens in everyday discourse—and, of course, women are shrews. None of these animals evokes the image of strength and power needed for construction; all of them, in fact, imply the laughable nature of allowing a woman to attempt to do what has clearly been designated through history and culture as work in a man's domain. In this way, then, language that appears to be casually selected and thoughtlessly applied is able to designate these white working-class men as naturally belonging at the center of the occupation.

*Construction Work as Real Work.*    It is also the physical mode of work that is celebrated by the animal imagery: through the images of farm animals, of laboring beasts and their strength, construction work is connected to preindustrial times when men and their animals were the primary, if not exclusive, sources of energy for the work that was done. The men still use their bodies, and their bodies are used up, by time and by their physical effort. Theirs is thus the most basic form of work, irreducible to any more primary form.

This celebration of the physicality and the tangible nature of work is further revealed by a co-worker's response to a female bartender who had criticized a group of construction workers for being covered with dirt and oil and, in her opinion, smelling too bad to be sitting at her bar. His comment to her—and he was laughing as he retold the story to me—was that she needed to understand that they were "just animals. . . . We're just a bunch of animals *and we're proud of it*" (emphasis his). She accused him of violating the middle-class norm of clean work clothes. Recognizing and rejecting the class slur inherent in her comment, he laughed and told her that they transcend such norms.

It is clear that his claim to "being an animal" is at least partly a celebration of the physical strength and tangible achievement inherent in the production of construction work. It reveals the pride that a worker might reasonably have after a day of hard physical work in which he has become dirty (and apparently malodorous) simply by doing his job. After a full day of exhausting and productive work, he is able to sit back and celebrate his own strength and accomplishment. And, because of the tangible results of his work, others are likely to take notice of it as well.

This aspect of manual work stands in clear contrast to white-collar work with its stereotypes of the endless and unproductive paper shuffling of office workers. There is no need for construction workers to offer further proof that they can "get the job done." The tangibility of the result is not only a psychological benefit enjoyed by the workers themselves but also an aspect of construction work (and manual work in general) that is heralded in truck ads, in beer ads, and by society at large. As such, it is clear that manual work is the real work against which other forms of work (perhaps bartending or being an academic) can be compared. Several writers have suggested that it is this sense of the *realness* of their work which leads to manual workers' often-described disdain for the effeminate nature of office work and the men who do it.[6] Thus the physicality of the work, the tangible nature of the achievement, and even the corporeal effects (such as stinking up the local bar) are parts of this masculinity to be celebrated. They are part of what marks it as more valuable than those masculinities lived by other sorts of men.

*Manual-Work Manhood as the Real Manhood.*   The barroom anecdote also suggests that physical masculinity is pride-inspiring in part because it is the *real* masculinity and that it is real in part because construction men's work is real. Construction work and the pigness identity allow these men to prove their masculinity vis-à-vis not only women but also vis-à-vis middle-class and upper-class men. Although male construction workers are constantly held in check by the omnipresent threat of failing masculinity (such as when they're acting like a "girl" or a "bunch of women"), this claim allows them to thrust white-collar men between themselves and failure. They may be less economically powerful than the white-collar men who employ them (certainly an important component of masculinity), but they can rest assured that they are more *truly masculine,* and this assurance is an important form of power in itself.

The value of this wage should not be underestimated. Despite the clear and notable limits to the dominance of working-class masculinities, this wage maintains its currency far outside of the industry itself. In fact, the assertion that construction workers have "real manhood" is generally supported by men in other occupations and industries, thus validating the construction workers' identities as "real men." One powerful example comes from academia itself: in conversation with the chair of a large and prestigious department, when I mentioned that I was writing about "masculinity in the construction industry," he turned to me and said with a sincere smile, "Well, that's really the only place there's any *real* masculinity left, isn't it?" thus placing himself in the unusual position of acknowledging that his own masculinity, by comparison, was seen as lesser or at least less authentic. He went on to describe the amusement that construction workers, hired to work at his home, had expressed at his lack of knowledge about materials and procedures, as well as his inability to do the work himself. In this way, he acknowledged, he was clearly marked by the construction workers as less masculine in regard to traditionally male skills, knowledge, and bodily abilities.

The accusation of ineffectual or effeminate manhood is almost always wielded by working-class men against white-collar men and is rarely, if ever, lobbed in reverse. White-collar men might accuse construction workers of being less intelligent or less refined than they are, or even of being more like animals than men, but they do not accuse construction workers of being insufficiently manly. Social consensus suggests, then, that construction workers *are* the real men, and their work *is* the real work.

*Real Masculine Sexuality as a Raw and Uncontrollable Sexuality.*     In its portrayal of this authentic and primordial masculinity, pigness also makes claims about the sexuality of the men, asserting their sexuality as raw, genuine, and containable only with great effort and difficulty. As discussed by the men themselves, this claim is tied to the image of construction-worker masculinity as the real masculinity. All men are believed (according to conventional gender stereotypes) to have a potentially uncontrollable sexuality, but it is best exemplified by the bearers of true and "natural" masculinity—the physical laborers of the American unionized building trades.

This is perhaps best illuminated by one conversation at lunch with a handful of the guys from my apprenticeship class. Over our sodas and french fries the guys decided collectively to give me advice on handling the challenges of working as a woman in an all-male environment. Even though some of the hostilities I faced were similar to those experienced by male apprentices (such as being stuck with a less-than-energetic or less-than-helpful foreman or being given jobs that are tedious and relatively insignificant within the project), they framed the issues as sexual issues. In fact, they focused on the idea (which I would call a myth) that I was likely to spend my days having to fend off persistent and aggressive sexual solicitations, and their solutions, not surprisingly, reflected that view:

> "Be extremely clear, as in 'not in a million years,' and in front of their buddies if possible," one male apprentice suggested.
> "Yeah," another one chimed in, *"men are assholes, and we're proud of it"* (emphasis his).

Although they recognized the public element of the sexual interactions (for I was encouraged to deny the men publicly, so that the shame of refusal would curb their persistence), they saw the sexual drive as real and targeted. I must "be extremely clear," as they said, so that the men could hear my denials above what we can imagine as a roar of constant sexual arousal.

In my experience, however (as suggested earlier), virtually all of the public sexualizing actions I witnessed seemed less a matter of real sexuality than a compulsory form of masculine performance—*performances* of this supposedly raw masculinity and of the mythically and *mandatedly* uncontrollable sexuality. Women at work become a proving ground for this masculinity: the presence of women allows men to demonstrate to other men both that they both know the proper role of women (to be sexual and not in the paid labor force) and that they as individuals have the appropriately explosive masculine heterosexuality.

Similarly, in a different variation of the "deny publicly" advice, one of the apprentices suggested that I could negotiate problematic relationships with men by *asserting* my sexuality and insisting upon its being recognized as the source of power in the interaction. I was to remind my co-workers that I, a woman, was apparently in control of the situation, since I had the body they were supposed to be wanting. In fact, he recommended that I say to a foreman who was giving me grief, *"Hey, just remember who has the ultimate tool, pal!"*—as if the reminder that I was in possession of a vagina would bring the otherwise powerful and incorrigible man to his knees.

In short, the only thing more powerful than a construction worker is his uncontrollable heterosexuality and his compulsion to perform. Ironically, of course, it is this assertion of an uncontrollable sexuality that allows these men—through their alleged possession of the most authentic masculinities and sexualities—to justify their dominance over those around them over whom they can have only partial control.

Although it is certainly true that the apprentices in question were engaging in impression management among themselves and that they enjoyed creating this salacious image of their own masculine sexuality, it is significant that they did so not by discussing their own behaviors and actions but by describing the larger group of men to whom they belong. Perhaps putting forth these characteristics as characteristics of individuals could create very specific performance expectations to which no mortal could rise. To attribute such skills and drives to a collective of men, however, could diffuse both the responsibility and the actual need to deliver said performances. These men—and construction workers in general—are thus collectively framed as driven by sexuality, a powerful sexuality that is tied to the power of all men. Their collective masculinity is the real masculinity, and their collective sexuality, raw and barely controllable, is seen as the source of the true heterosexuality of men.

In all the meanings discussed thus far, it is clear that "pigness" and "animalness" distinguish the construction worker from white-collar and middle- or upper-class men and that they do so in a manner that asserts, not abdicates, power. Pigness is an assertion that the physical and traditional masculinity of construction is the true and desirable manhood. Pigness makes clear that all other men and masculinities must be measured (unsuccessfully, of course) against it. In this way construction workers are both tied to all other men and granted primacy over them.

## When Pigs Rule: The Culture of No Complaints

A second way in which the claim to being "a bunch of animals" is beneficial for the white working-class men in construction is the freedom it grants them in their worksite behaviors. In the same way that the assertion of pigness informs the listener of what she or he can expect from the pig in question (e.g., knowledge of motor oil and not fine wine, of NASCAR and not NASA, a presence of physicality and not finesse), it is also a declarative statement about the nature and culture of the men who do the work—and thus of the place of work itself. To say "these men are pigs" is to say that they will behave like pigs, and an informed listener should be neither disturbed nor surprised at the occurrence of such behavior. *Neither should she expect that others will be concerned.* These men are pigs; they will behave like pigs; and the people who choose to enter the environment are expected—and ultimately required—to deal with it.

The expectation of "pigness" from white working-class men must be recognized as affecting the experiences of these men themselves as much as it affects the experiences of other persons and groups who enter into construction. Because the environment mandates either conformity or acquiescence to "animal" conduct, those working men (and women) who choose to join or stay in the industry are likely to act, at least on occasion, like pigs. Thus, the self-selection pressures involved in who enters (and leaves) the workforce would appear to support, at least on the surface, the biological argument about the workers' true nature. It appears that these men choose to become construction workers because they "are" that way, rather than acknowledging that the rules and expectations of the worksite create pigs, even where there might have been none.

By shaping the way that the industry thinks about and responds to worker conduct, the culture of pigness has meaningful effects upon the ways that race, gender, and sexuality are negotiated in the workforce. Because working-class men, like animals (according to this ideology), cannot be expected to act differently from what their "nature" requires, the claim that men in construction are pigs becomes a way of not only excusing but also protecting and preserving their behaviors. Pigness provides companies a justification for failing to enforce some supposedly mandated policies—after all, how can foremen be expected to discipline or control a *pig*? Because this animalistic nature is seen as endemic to and systemic within the industry, punishing or removing a worker is regarded as futile: the next worker will be identical. Companies cannot and should not be expected to waste their energy challenging the men's allegedly biologically determined problem behaviors.

This approach to worker conduct is significant because it allows the rules of pigness to supersede the formal harassment policies that companies are required to have in place. By doing so, pigness redefines harassment as something *outside of management control*. According to sexual harassment policies—and sexual harassment law—the definition of problem behavior is clear: harassing behavior is behavior *determined by the recipient to be ha-*

*rassing.* If a person considers herself or himself to be harassed by behaviors, those behaviors are *by definition* harassing. In the more complex cases, the standards "a reasonable person" and, more particularly, "a reasonable woman" are used to verify a recipient's claim. This means that harassing conduct is defined as any behavior (or set of behaviors) that a reasonable woman would find problematic. According to pigness rules, however, *intent* is taken as paramount. If a co-worker didn't mean anything by calling you "Tits," or if we can assume that he really didn't know any better (after all, he *is* a pig!), then it isn't a problem and it certainly isn't harassment. It is at worst a case of poor judgment, a bad joke; as such, it is simply to be ignored.

It is clear that if women or men of color or gay men want to remain in the industry, it is they who must adjust to the environment and not the reverse. The result is the creation of what I call a Culture of No Complaints in construction: for women (or nonpigs) to make it, they must put up (with) *and* shut up . . . or get out. To complain about harassment and mistreatment—and certainly to complain about something as innocuous as titty posters and sexual graffiti are perceived to be—is to violate the widespread code of the industry. Such persons, clearly, do not belong.

It is not the case, however, that union representatives and company men are unsympathetic to the conditions of harassment and hostile environments. On the contrary, they are often as sympathetic as they are aware of the rough, competitive, and hierarchical nature of the field culture. It is, after all, their business to be aware, and most of them have come through the ranks themselves. To say that they are sympathetic is not the same, however, as saying that they are proactive or engaged on the issue. They do not generally act aggressively—or in some cases even act—on their sympathetic concerns, even if required both by law and by the union and company policies to do so. Instead, the responses, formal and informal, are generally focused on how the person who is *offended* should act.

Take an example of sexual harassment: women who complain about the sexualization of the environment—perhaps the posters and calendars referred to as "paper pussy" and outlawed by a federal court in 1991—are often given fatherly or brotherly explanations from an "insider" who knows the rules. The union rep or the company man is likely to say something like, "Yeah, its tough and certainly disturbing. Those guys are really pigs," and then shift his attention to the ways in which the *woman* (not the union or company) should best respond. The most common forms of this advice include the following:

"You should just learn to let it roll off."

"Women need to have big shoulders in this business so that you can let this stuff just roll off."

"Don't let it bother you!"

"You just need to learn to ignore them!"

The problem, although acknowledged, is deemed unfixable, and the only suggested remedies offered *by the men legally responsible* for preventing and punishing infractions are modification of the *women's*—and not the pigs'—behaviors. Not only is placing the responsibility for the proper handling of harassment on the women who experience it clearly similar to the pattern of blaming rape victims for their own victimization (by suggesting that women simply not dress "that way" or put themselves in such situations), but it is also bad legal advice for the woman. By contrast, for the male workers, the companies, and the unions that serve them both, telling women to ignore sexual harassment is almost brilliant (if old-fashioned) advice.

The strategy of ignoring harassment is bad for women because it does not prepare them for the problems that they are likely to face should any of the conditions worsen. Although the advice to "let it roll off!" might be interpreted as a friendly and well-meaning suggestion for "getting along" in the industry, it dismisses the very real possibility that the harassment will continue and even get worse—especially where (and perhaps because) it is clear that the men in charge are not willing to intervene. In attempting to let issues or unpleasant conditions "roll off," women are unlikely to report or record promptly any offending occurrences and communications that take place, and they are likely to find (as I found) that a later attempt to address what has since gotten worse is met with a resigned admission from the management that they *could have* done something "had they known earlier." In fact, the woman herself is likely to be held responsible for failing to address the issue promptly and directly, and thus any escalation and detrimental effects are likely to be seen as her "fault."

A second set of recommendations often offered by co-workers, supervisors, and union officials includes the allegedly humorous, "just give it back to them!" or, put another way, "Bring in your own calendar and put it up right next to theirs! That'll bug 'em!" But for a woman to "give it back to them" or to respond to female pornography with male pornography clearly makes the woman vulnerable to the accusation that she "wanted it" or, at the very least that she publicly appeared to welcome sexual behaviors on the part of her co-workers. Such a "solution" to workplace sexual harassment is thus likely not only to exacerbate the conditions but also to remove from the complainant the legal protections of redress.

Most research indicates that women just want the harassment to stop; they are not "looking for a lawsuit," as the cultural stereotypes suggest. But if (or when) the problem behaviors escalate, a woman who follows the industry's advice is likely to find herself with no choice but to put up with the harassment, to leave the employer or industry, or to steel herself for a formal legal intervention using an outside channel such as a city or county agency or regional working women's organization. Women who choose the third option are likely to find that they are so increasingly unwelcome after their actions become known that leaving the industry becomes necessary. Fighting harassment or discrimination in a formal venue, then, can be interpreted as the first step toward ending one's construction career.

Thus, the protections afforded the men by pigness are dramatic. It is not simply that pigness protects illegal behaviors and those who engage in them, or that the formal complaint procedures are ignored—although both situations are very often the case; it is that the rules of pigness reverse the direction of the social constraints and sanctions—it is those who complain, and not those who are complained about, who are most likely to be sanctioned by and even isolated from their peers. In this way it quickly becomes clear that the Culture of No Complaints is also a Structure of No Complaints, where pigness and the prohibition of protest are among the industry's formal responses to harassment and discrimination.

## The Structures of No Complaints

Not surprisingly, perhaps, given its effects upon workplace culture and conduct, pigness also has important implications for diversity in the workforce. Because the Culture of No Complaints makes clear that "this is just how it is," and that those who don't like "how it is" should just get out, there is little room for protecting one's own rights, regardless of existing laws and formal policy; if you think the behavior of your co-workers is a problem, maybe you're the problem. A woman who finds that she doesn't like to be called "Tits," or to be asked for "hand jobs" at lunch, or to have the foreman tell the other workers he's sleeping with her (to use three examples from my own experience) might decide to try another kind of work. Gay men unwilling to tolerate overt and omnipresent homophobia are likely to look elsewhere. Similarly, men of color who don't choose to be called "spic" or "boy" or to be accused of stealing, drug use, or other "immoral" behavior might choose to leave the industry as well.

However obvious it might seem, it is worth stating to those outside the industry that full-time work is hard in general, and full-time construction work is demanding and exhausting enough without having to put up with the additional stress, anxiety, and harm that sexual or racial harassment and discrimination bring. Thus, for women and men facing this sort of situation, leaving the industry becomes a reasonable response and, I believe, a good part of the reason behind the "revolving door" of women in construction work. As Jerry Jacobs argued in a book by that name, it is the rate of women *leaving* nontraditional work, and not a lack of women *entering* nontraditional work, that is at the root of ongoing occupational segregation in many industries.[7] His diagnosis certainly appears to be true for the construction industry. The cultural and structural practices of pigness, codified in the responses of management, serve to discourage nontraditional entrants from joining the trades and often encourage the exits of the white women and people of color who have applied.

By imposing a Structure of No Complaints upon the construction workforce, then, pigness is able to protect the jobs for people who can "handle" the environment—most often and most likely, people who look like or are related to the men working in the jobs already. In this manner, the culture of pigness is able to do informally what exclusionary laws and rules, discriminatory practices, and systematic violence did for many years but are no longer formally allowed to do.[8] It is not that women (or gay men or men of color) aren't *formally and legally* welcomed, it is simply that the men who chose to be construction workers are "pigs" and that under the right conditions most women (and nonpig men) will choose to do something else somewhere else. Thus pigness serves companies as an *occupational gatekeeping* mechanism for women (and men who are offended or targeted as undesirable and deserving of harassment) without their having to hire or fire explicitly on these lines.

### Pigness as Performance: The Strategic Use of the Animal Claims

At this point, perhaps, it is easy to see these men as actually *being* pigs and therefore a lesser and less sophisticated sort of man. It is essential to remember, however, that pigness is not a physiological condition but a very specific code of conduct determining the rules of behavior and responses within the industry. This fact is revealed in part by the way that the men conform to the codes of pigness and the situations in which they are able to set them aside. Similarly, the contradictory ways in which the men do—

and don't—talk about themselves as pigs highlight the strategic nature of this public identity.

*"We" Are Pigs, But "I" Never Is.*   The strategic and enacted nature of pigness is first revealed through the ways in which the men talk about themselves as pigs. Most simply, pigness is a group, but not an individual, characteristic. In the foregoing anecdotes the workers claimed that *"we're just a bunch of animals,"* referring (however erroneously) to all of the men who work in construction. Similarly, I was often warned by co-workers and supervisors, "You've got to understand *they're* just a bunch of pigs."

In contrast, I *never* heard a man in construction say specifically "*I* am a pig." Each individual man is clearly addressed by a statement that labels all men as pigs, yet no man is labeled individually as one. In fact, I am unable to recall a situation in which one man described another man *individually* as a pig. It appears that such phrasing crosses the line between asserting that a man is simply assuming a pig role (that is, that he fits into the workforce and environment) and stating that he truly is a pig. To label an individual as a pig would move beyond the realm of camaraderie and group cohesion and become instead what one might call "fighting words."

This strategic use of the term matters. The men can simultaneously assert a group-level animal status (that is, assert that they are part of a group of pigs) to justify and excuse problematic behaviors and still maintain enough distance from the label that they are freed from it as needed. Likewise, the strategy further diffuses the responsibility that pigness has already dispersed: pigness makes it impossible for harassing and discriminatory conduct to be placed upon any one person or set of persons. Instead, it is a characteristic of the group and the culture and, like the biology of farm animals, likely to continue unchanged.

*Public Pigs and Private People.*   That these men are only strategically "pigs" is further revealed by the fact that many of them behaved quite differently when they worked one-on-one with a woman (me) than they did in a larger group of men. This same experience is expressed by a tradeswoman interviewed by electrician and poet Susan Eisenberg: "You know how men can get—when they're alone, they're fine, they're actually brothers? And then they get in a group and they're just beasts?"[9] Put another way, pigness is a public project, and the men are simply persons (jerks or nice guys, harassing or kind) in private.

Most important, the overt sexual comments and aggressive come-ons that allegedly characterize male-female interactions in construction were almost all *public* interactions and thus were absent from one-on-one working situations. That is, virtually all the men who engaged in traditional sexualizing behaviors—making sexual reference or overt sexual invitations—did so in front of others. In private, even those men who were publicly suggestive were likely to set sexuality aside. Certainly, a few engaged in subtle side conversations that might or might not have been inquiring about my availability, but it is important to note that this happened largely in the same manner and with the same frequency as it did in nonconstruction environments.

The same difference between public and private appears also to be true for the racialized and homophobic aspects of pigness. As a white woman in a white-dominated environment, I was not able to access the sort of backstage racializing that I could observe for gender performances, but it was my strong sense that men who were overtly or complicitly racist or homophobic on the job were not necessarily so in their private lives. In fact, I was often surprised to learn about the men's off-site friendships and activities—their educated wives, their multiracial interactions, their gay acquaintances—because their performance of pigness on site was so complete.

Of course, it is not the case that *all* the men were kind in private, that no one used the one-on-one situation to try to "score" when the mating competition was out of range, or that racist or homophobic jokes always fell aside in these dyadic interactions. And certainly, some of the kindnesses I describe (such as the offers to give me little-known tricks of the trade or to help me get on steady with the boss) were done less out of goodwill than in an attempt to get "in with" (literally and figuratively) the "girl" on the site. For these men, interactions with me were just a smaller part of the proving of masculinity that they engaged in with other men.

Still, variation in the men's private behavior is significant because it reveals that pigness is not as dominant or as exclusive among the men as the biological claims might seem to imply. This is best explained by theories of dramaturgy and impression management.[10] As an apprentice in these situations, I almost always had less power than my co-workers, and thus the men should have felt largely free to behave as they wished. And according to the superficial claims of pigness, of course, I should have been harassed *more aggressively and more unrelentingly* in private interactions than in public. Yet the opposite often appeared to be true, and these private interactions—in which I could easily have been seen as highly vulnerable and the men freed from competition—often showed little of the supersized and "uncontrollable" sexuality that characterized public encounters. Instead, I often found that I was given less grief and more helpful hints: about how to get on steady with a company, which foremen to watch out for, and so forth. At the very least, then, it makes sense to recognize that construction men are not simply a certain, more animalistic type of man but rather that they, like other men, vary as individuals and by situation.

If one looks more closely at the variation between men's public and private conduct as well as the variation among men, it becomes clear that these behaviors reveal more about the rules of the work culture than they do about the men *as men*. More specifically, the variations make clear that there are recognizable expectations for pigness—perhaps even a contextual mandate for pigness—seen by the men as being reasonably binding in public situations. This also suggests, of course, that the public performances of pigness are strategic and even that they are recognized as such by these men themselves.

*When Pigness Is Prohibited.*  The value of pigness as an extralegal structure comes from the belief that pigness is a trait of the workers—enduring, omnipresent, and challenged only at great cost to their employers. In reality, however, it appears that pigness is better understood as a product of the work culture, a project of joint production by the workers *and* management. This was revealed to me by my experiences working at Family Builders, the name I have given to the small company run by two brothers and a sister. That harassment and discrimination were truly not tolerated there was seen in the informal as well as the formal policies. More important, it was seen in the total lack of such behaviors by the workers in the settings where I worked. This difference was first indicated by my being quickly warned by a white male journeyman not to tell "black jokes" to the boss because he didn't think they were funny. This same boss (one of three sibling owners) was described by his sister as a "feminist," and he made it clear that *any* evidence of harassment was grounds for immediate termination. As a result, such practices were virtually nonexistent at this company.

Although one might argue that Family Builders simply employed a different sort of man, they drew from the same union pool as the other employers. Indeed, though Family Builders tended to have less turnover than the other companies, some workers there were the same ones I had worked with at Concrete, Inc., or Remodel Co. Thus, it was the behaviors and not the worker pool that varied, and the settings and not the men that were the primary source of the variation. And this dramatic difference in worker performance suggests that it is not an *uncontrollable* pig nature of the workers at issue but rather a *highly controllable* culture subject to the wishes and regulations imposed by management.

This idea is further supported by an explanation that I received from Rocky, a skilled, savvy, yet intensely competitive and masculinist apprentice who was working for a smaller contractor in the area. Rocky's comment followed the assertion of another apprentice that men don't and can't "watch their mouths" on the job.

> "Well," Rocky responds, "We do a lot of work around homeowners, so we have to watch what we say. I can't be going around saying '*Last night I got a little . . .*'" [referring, of course, to sexual activity].
>
> I notice that this contradicted what he had said earlier, that colorful language and so forth is just part of the trade. So it is part of the trade, but it is a chosen element and one that can be turned on and off. I wait a few minutes and then I ask him why.
>
> "You just talk tough," he says, "*it's part of the job.*" And he goes on to describe a sort of gentleman's agreement to talk bullshit.

Thus it appears that white heterosexual men are just as likely to be *shaped into* acting like pigs as they are to be *prevented from* acting like pigs. As a result, since these behaviors could be controlled by management but are not, the question must be raised whether the pigness identity is not actually more strategic for the management and the industry than it is for the average white male worker.

*Pigness and the Risk of Strategic Claims.*    The complexity of pigness—an identity that is not only assumed and held at a distance but also taken on and shed contextually—makes clear that the workers are not simply "this sort of man." Neither are they adopting these rules unquestioningly. They are aware of the nuances of the culture and, to some extent, the drawbacks and the advantages of this identity. Thus it is a strategic claim. And, as Michel Foucault warns, such use of power in discourse is dangerous as a political strategy because a claim put forth to one end can easily be utilized by others toward the achievement of a different, even contrary, end.[11] And I argue that this is exactly what occurs. By strategically claiming pigness as both describing and not describing themselves, the men attempt to straddle the fence between a romanticized masculinity and a stigmatized class position. They attempt to walk the thin (and I believe untenable) line between pigness as an empowering identity and pigness as a weak and undesirable location. Although this collective identity enactment does allow the men to extralegally protect the construction industry as the turf of white and heterosexual men, it also reproduces them in the long run as the less valid and the less valuable sort of man—and thus ultimately weakens their position within a capitalist economy.

## The Value of Animals: Pigness and the Circumscription of Working-Class Power

It is perhaps not surprising, given the way animals are treated in human society, that the use of an animal identity by a cluster of men denigrates them as much as it is able to elevate and protect them. Although the pigness identity does have positive connotations that elevate the working-class men in relation to some women and also in relation to other men in some forms and contexts, a full investigation of pigness reveals that this strategic claim also lays the groundwork for working men's (and thus working people's) physical and economic exploitation. On one hand, this identity does elevate *all men* as men by reinforcing the idea of a natural masculinity that is the foundation of gender difference and inequalities. On the other hand, if we expand our perspective to include social class across races, it becomes immediately clear that the use of the pigness identity by working-class men does not elevate all men equally. The men's own language and actions demonstrate how that identity is ultimately one that widens rather than narrows the gap between the white men of construction and that it does so to the advantage of the middle and upper classes.

### Pigs as a Lesser Class of Men

From a middle-class or a female perspective, it is clear that describing the men as animals and as pigs marks them as distinct from and *clearly lower than* the men of more "dignified" classes. "Pigness" to the middle class is something that closes doors and something that marks a man as too uncouth to work with women, to be put in front of the public, or to fit in with the educated white-collar crowd. Although middle-class men may often choose to be pigs or piglike (when tailgating or at bachelor parties or at other all-male events such as cable TV's *The Man Show,* for example), *they do not claim it as a central identity.* In fact, middle-class men recognize their power in part by claiming themselves distinct from and socially above the men who are pigs. Pigness is something that they can return to and wallow in, thereby publicly verifying their masculinity as real and authentic—but they can exit and be freed from the label and the condition at will.

It is clear that by enacting and reifying the authentic primordial masculinity to which middle- and upper-class men can retreat, working-
class men promote the power and status that middle- and upper-class men
can experience as *men* (what we might describe as male power or patri-
archy) while being unable to diminish the class differences between them.
Whereas pigness is seen as contextual, optional, and ultimately a status-
enhancing identity for the middle- and upper-class man, it is a label that
sticks to and stigmatizes the working-class man. Working-class pigs aren't
seen as men who can *return* to the animal nature inherent in man; they *are*
the animal. They are the animal that cannot be trusted to be refined, re-
spectful, or respectable.

### Workplace Hierarchies and the Realities of Power

In spite of the fact that pigness is used to assert the pride, power, and real
masculinity of the workers, even the men in the field are unable to ignore
the real hierarchies of masculinity and power in force in the general world
outside the construction gates. Although the strongest man on the crew
might be seen by his peers and even his supervisors as the most masculine,
on larger sites the strongest man is governed by a foreman who no longer
wears his tools, for he has earned his way out of them through age, training, or patronage. The foreman, in turn, is governed by the job superintendent, a man who rules through his knowledge of budgets, blueprints,
and scheduling. And the superintendent is governed by the almost invisible men back at company headquarters who may or may not have spent
any time working in the field. More likely than not, these men are callus-
free, comfortable in neckties, and driving vehicles that cost more than the
annual take-home pay of the company's best carpenter. Even if they are
sport utility vehicles or trucks with four-wheel drive, those vehicles are
likely to be clean and free of tools. Thus the assertion of a physical masculinity is successful *contextually*, but it is bittersweet at best. Being a
stronger man doesn't move you into the office—in fact, it makes you more
valuable in the field. And economic decisions, too, are not made by physical strength: the mightiest man with the biggest hammer is still easily
struck down by the superintendent's pencil.

Given the clear and steep hierarchy of the construction workforce (since
a profit line requires that there are far fewer men in the trailer or office than
in the field), it is implausible to assert that the loudly celebrated camaraderie of manhood overwhelms the working-class men's ability to recognize their own location within the hierarchy. In spite of the widely reported

disdain of the blue-collar worker for his white-collar counterparts, it is clear that the blue-collar worker is not only the recipient of others' disdain but is aware of it. He is also aware of the compensation, power, and prestige of his own work relative to that of the managers and supervisors—and the attorneys, politicians, and professors that he allegedly disrespects. Everyday workplace discourse includes all sorts of self-deprecating jokes that make light of the situation and range from more to less bitter. I recorded some examples in my journal:

> "I knew I should have taken the job as a brain surgeon."
> "I just figure that I get paid from the shoulders down, if you know what I mean, Krissy."
> "Don't think; you'll weaken the team!"

Although I am unable to say that jokes like this were never told before the shifts in work organization that occurred in the late twentieth century, it seems clear that the decreasing respect for manual work—felt by the workers and even shown by the workers themselves—is exacerbated by the de-skilling that has defined the industry since the 1970s. This is not to say that men in de-skilled construction jobs don't think or solve challenging problems at work, because of course they do. The cognitive tasks of their work are far more limited than they might be, however, and the autonomy of the process greatly reduced from the working conditions described in the mid-twentieth century by previous writers on the industry.[12] Many workers in commercial construction *are* increasingly paid less to think less, and this is especially true on the larger and more heavily supervised jobs.[13] Although pride remains connected to construction competence, to interpret the expressed blue-collar disrespect for white-collar occupations literally is folly. It is also contradicted by the fact that many blue-collar workers encourage their own children, as they repeatedly told me, to go into something else and to "make something of themselves."[14] On at least some level, then, even for union construction workers, being a union construction worker isn't "something."

## The Paradoxical Strategy of Pigness

To the extent that pigness is a claim to power, then, it is also laden with the ironic recognition of where these men actually fit in the larger scale of social structures. Although working-class men may overtly reject the perceived effeminacy of middle- and upper-class masculinity, they also recognize that their self-claimed animal nature exists in a world where the physical power of man (and I use this word intentionally) has been surpassed and is outranked by education, wealth, and technology. Real wages and union membership have fallen, and unions' abilities to organize and protect their workers have been steadily weakened. These changes are, of course, widely recognized by the workers and the unions themselves.

The broader cultural awareness of such changes is illuminated by the comments of the faculty member mentioned earlier. When this man from the academic world described how the construction workers he employed were amused by his lack of knowledge concerning remodeling and repairs, he was not speaking from a place of powerlessness. Although he said directly that his masculinity was inauthentic in comparison with that of tradesmen, it was apparent that he in no way was or felt emasculated by the revelation. In fact, it was clear that although they were on some levels more manly than he, he had hired these men, was also in control of them as workers, and thus more manly than they. To the extent, then, that he recognized construction workers as more masculine than he was in the *traditional and physical* sense, one might argue that he also realized that this is no longer the sense that *matters*. Piggish and animalistic masculinity may be culturally celebrated as the real and powerful masculinity, but it is clearly not the most powerful in practice.

Therefore, for construction workers to assert that they are pigs is to assert a positive identity and a more powerful social location, but this is not a blind assertion. It is made with at least one eye focused on and aware of the changing cultural contexts of men, masculinities, and power. Even as piggish and physical masculinity is elevated to quasi-mythical status as the *authentic* masculinity, the men who embody it are increasingly scorned, challenged, and constrained by mainstream society. For example, one might argue that these men are challenged and even attacked not only by contemporary rollbacks in pro-union legislation but also by affirmative action policies that challenge their claimed turf and by harassment policies that allegedly curtail and even prohibit the enactment of piggish behaviors. Thus, even though pigness protects these men *as pigs* in their specific context, it does so within a world increasingly intolerant of such behavior. What they claim for themselves is an increasingly devalued entitlement.

And piggish imagery has corporeal consequences as well as psychological ones. By using the animal comparison, these workers unwittingly place themselves within a historical tradition which justifies the subordination of—rather than the domination by—an animal-identified group. To attribute animal status to a group is to remove them from the moral responsibility and consciousness of the nation. It is to mark them as a group whose interests, pain, and suffering are to be seen as bearing little relation to those of the general public. And under conditions of increasingly globalized market pressures, ongoing if not rising drives for profit, and increasingly tight production schedules in the construction industry, this sort of cultural posturing might be all that the industry—and the public— needs to turn its attention and concerns elsewhere. The conditions of occupational safety and risk illuminate some of the ultimate costs borne by the workers as a result of these strategies.

# 6

# THE BODILY COSTS OF THIS
# SOCIAL WAGE

Occupational Safety in the Construction Industry

**C**oncrete, Inc., like the other companies for which I worked, had formal safety policies, weekly safety meetings, and full-time, paid staff to "enforce" the rules. All company employees were given the company safety manual at the time of hire and told that we were expected to read it and follow it.

> We at [Concrete, Inc.] consider you, our employees, to be our most valuable assets. We will take every practical action to make your working conditions as free as possible from physical hazards. . . . Each superintendent and fore-man is required to conduct all operations under his/her jurisdiction in such a manner as to afford maximum protection for employees, equipment, materials, and property. Your safety is one of their primary responsibilities. . . . It is important that . . . you take no unnecessary chances, that you use all safety equipment and safe-guards provided. (From the safety manual at Concrete, Inc.)

In our weekly safety meetings, usually Wednesday mornings just before we headed out to work, portions of the OSHA regulations on construction were read out loud and explained. All workers were then required to sign the form that was circulated, indicating their attendance and, one assumes, their comprehension and agreement.

All of this, of course, would suggest to an outside observer that Concrete, Inc., placed a premium on worker safety and truly wished that each worker would strive to remain safe. In my experience, however, the "premium" placed on worker safety appeared a lot less significant to the company than the actual "premiums" paid to insurance companies. By this I mean that the formal safety policies at Concrete, Inc., as well as at Remodel Co. (and, to a lesser extent, at Family Builders) seemed to be more geared to the off-site interests that determine the companies' political and financial standing—such as insurance companies and government regulators—than to actual worker well-being.

Off site, formal policies appeared to allow Concrete, Inc., to emphasize its self-presentation as a safety-focused company. On site, however, the company's actual focus seemed to be on maintaining an *appearance of safety* (similar to the maintenance of an *apparently* harassment-free environment) while getting the job done as quickly and cheaply as possible. In reality, then, workers were not expected simply to follow the formal safety regulations; they were instead required to make ongoing determinations about when and if the rules mattered, and when shortcuts could "reasonably" be taken to *get the job done.*

The dual realities of occupational safety in construction are revealed in the following excerpt from my personal notes written while working for Concrete, Inc.:

> Harry the foreman and I have moved across the site and are going up in the "cherry picker" . . . to begin work on forming up the grade beam, a horizontal concrete support beam. Since this beam will sit on top of a roughly 25 foot high post, all of our work will be done from inside of the cherry picker, a machine that looks like a small version of a crane with a rectangular "manbasket" at the end of the arm. Once we've climbed into the basket, there is a small control panel that allows us to raise and lower the basket, to turn the basket and to pivot it in relation to the base. Using a cherry picker allows us to work more safely and easily than if we had to use a ladder, especially since most of our materials will fit in the basket with us. Using a cherry picker isn't without risks, though, as a fall from the manbasket of the cherry picker would have at least as much chance of being injurious or fatal as a fall from a ladder.
>
> As we climb in the basket of the cherry picker and get ready to start the engine up, Harry hands me a webbed safety belt that I am to put around my waist and clip to the side of the basket. He tells me that I need to wear it in case OSHA . . . drives past. As I put the belt on, he comments on how loosely it hangs around my waist, and tells me that it "won't do any good" if I fall out:
>
> "It'll just slide up, dislocate your shoulders, and then drop you on the ground."
>
> "Oh," I said, reflecting upon the information. "Could I get a smaller one?"
>
> "No," Harry says in response, "there aren't any on the site."

This and the excerpt from the safety manual highlight the two different versions of occupational safety rules in the construction industry: the official version and the actual operating procedures (or what I call the AOPs). The recognition that there *are* two different sets of rules is theoretically significant because it challenges a common assumption of much safety-related research in construction—that worker behaviors and worker cultures are the most common causes of policy violations.[1] In contrast to this assumption, much of what is often construed as "worker culture" is actually at least in part a *structurally determined response* to the unwritten rules of the construction industry. Put another way, when workers appear to be breaking the rules, they may actually be following a *second set* of rules less visible to outsiders.

This recognition of often contradictory sets of safety rules is also theoretically significant because the assumption that workers "choose" to forgo occupational safety protections as part of their cultural performance (usually of masculinity or pigness) is then used to assume or prove the workers' ideological consent to the larger capitalist exchange of wages-for-work.[2] Although I am not arguing that there is an overlooked lack of consent to this exchange, this view of safety does suggest that the nature and processes of consent are complex and themselves likely contradictory. I consider it to be a combined process of *consent* (for which we can use a shorthand of "culture") and *compulsion,* illuminated through the relationship of construction cultures to layoff structures.

On an individual and lived level, of course, this distinction between "official" and actual safety is important because workers are significantly less protected and significantly less able to utilize protections than the industry and mainstream stereotypes about construction workers would suggest. I draw on my own experiences as well as fatal conditions from another worksite (analyzed in the regional media) to demonstrate that the foregrounding of worker masculinities is often little more than a smokescreen for the safety-related coercion and compulsion that are made to masquerade as consent. Additionally, I argue that this relationship is complicated by the gendered and class-based compulsion of workers not only to reject occupational safety protections but also to *explain and understand* their actions as representing their gendered and class-based cultural preferences. Thus the relationship between coercion and consent is complicated at least in part by what might be referred to in shorthand as the "coercion to consent," the *pressure to provide* ideological support for the nature and forms of economic relations between the men of different classes in the construction industry.

## The Realities of Worker Safety

As the example of the webbed safety belt at Concrete, Inc., reveals, the realities of occupational safety in the construction industry are contradictory, partly because of the two distinct sets of safety rules: the official version and the AOPs. The official version includes straightforward regulations about what workers should and should not do, and, as well, the sanctions that exist for rule violations. It is this official version that is given to workers at the initial hire and in safety training. Similar to affirmative action goals, then, the official safety policies are used to represent the employers to outside agencies, such as insurance companies and OSHA. Derived largely from OSHA regulations, the official version of safety is virtually always a conservative one in which worker safety is paramount.

The actual operating procedures, by contrast, follow rules that are in place out in the field. In my experience the AOPs were communicated by workers and supervisors in informal, unwritten, and often unspoken ways. The AOPs are far more complex than the official safety regulations because they require on-the-spot decisions about whether to comply with the official procedures or simply set them aside to "get the job done."

In order to conform to the AOPs, workers must make continuous "guesstimates" about the potential extent, costs, and likelihood of the hazards they face and balance these estimates of injury against the real and constant "push" to complete their work as fast as possible. All these calculations also seem to be clearly affected by the workers' lack of protection from arbitrary firing, seasonal insecurity, weak unions, and the need to maintain the employers' goodwill. As a result, in the AOPs the balancing of speed against acceptable loss—and not worker safety—appears to be paramount. Although the AOPs place responsibility for enforcing safety upon the workers, they do so in a highly constrained setting.

### Promising the Official Version but Delivering the AOPs

I use the term "bait-and-switch" to describe the simultaneous (and ongoing) provision of the official safety regulations and the informal provision of the AOPs. This merchandising concept is useful because it highlights how occupational safety training and its related policies are the objects of exchange between construction contractors and the workers they employ.[3] In this exchange the employers offer one product (official rules) but deliver another, lesser product (the AOPs). As in a bait-and-switch tactic in the sale of merchandise, employers benefit through this exchange as if they were providing the official version of safety. For example, they often receive re-duced insurance premiums—and perhaps even contracts with clients—because they have and claim to use an official safety policy and training package.

In this exchange, management benefits because it is able to deliver a lesser product than the product for which it has received compensation (such as reduced premiums). (One might envision here a sale in which a 2004 Cadillac is paid for and a 1990 Ford Fiesta is delivered.) Workers, in contrast, are diminished by the bait-and-switch. Because workers often sign attendance and acknowledgment forms at company-run safety meetings, they not only lose the potential protections offered by the official version of safety, but also receive the responsibility for—and potentially the liability of—safety's enforcement. This transfer of liability, which occurred both in and beyond my personal experience, has been described in publications on training policies and promoted by the industry's lobbyists as a policy that should be formally encoded into law.[4] And (as I recount below) it has also been used as a strategy by at least one set of contractors attempting to absolve themselves of legal responsibility in the deaths of three workers.

Although they take place partially in the literatures of occupational safety, debates on these matters are not simply "academic." For example, in spite of the increased regulation of the construction industry since the creation of the Occupational Safety and Health Administration in the early 1970s, and in spite of the fact that virtually all companies now have safety programs and safety officers, it continues to be the case that proportionally more workers die in construction than in any other industry: construction workers are only 5 percent of the workforce but sustain almost 20 percent of fatal occupational injuries.[5] Construction laborers, those who provide support to other trades and perform much of the drudgework on sites, were only 1 percent of all workers in 1996 but accounted for approximately 5 percent of all work fatalities in this same period.[6]

### The Role of Working-Class Masculinities

Although I argue that violations of safety rules are often the product of industry rules rather than a cultural performance of working-class masculinities, this is not to say that the values and practices of working-class masculinity are irrelevant. In fact, I would argue that the AOPs appear to be an important part of the loyalty that is expected—and required—between the men in the field (the workers) and the men in the trailer (the foremen, supervisors, and superintendents). Workers use the AOPs rather than the official rules to demonstrate their commitment to the employer's need to complete the contracted work quickly and efficiently. These intentions were made clear to me verbally as well as through the men's patterned actions on the job.

The AOPs are also an important part of worker loyalty to other workers, insofar as it is important not to "slow down the team," and because doing the work fast and with risk can be considered appropriately masculine— and thus appropriate to the site shared with other men. This horizontal form of loyalty display occurs in part, of course, because the relations between the men in the field do not exist independent of the relations between the men in the field and the men in the trailer. That is, one cannot understand the relations between workers without situating them within the larger employment relations. Thus, even though the horizontal and vertical relations between men are analytically different, the larger economic structures of employment are likely to affect all the cultural and interpersonal relations. In this way, the AOPs reinforce both the cultural relations between men (shaped primarily, perhaps, by gender and class socialization) and the economic relations between men (by reproducing the economic and occupational hierarchies of the field).

To best describe the culture that surrounds occupational safety in construction, I have loosely organized the significant attitudes into four different elements or "rules." They are, however, only analytically separate; each is clearly supported by the others and reliant upon them. All these rules work to support the creation of the AOPs and ultimately, the bait-and-switch of the official policies for the AOPs. And again, although these rules are created by the stereotypically gendered culture, they are made obligatory by the occupational structures.

*Cultural Rule #1: Expect Pain and Take It Like a Man.*    As a largely physical occupation, construction work tends to be rife with discussions of injuries, risk, and great mistakes. For example, Rocky, a third-year apprentice, remarked with obvious disdain in a casual classroom discussion of worksite injuries, "Any guy who uses one of those [a pneumatic nail gun] should just know that he'll get one of them [a nail] through his foot." Statements such as this were made in any number of places. For my purposes, the most meaningful aspect of the comment is not the injury but the target of Rocky's disgust. He wasn't wincing at the prospect of a nail forcefully piercing the tissue of a human foot, nor was he alarmed by the individual's shooting his own foot. Rather, Rocky was expressing his disdain for the man who *com-*

*plained* about the injury, and for those of us in the conversation who expressed discomfort at the thought of its occurrence. According to Rocky, then, it was not a question of *if* the operator would accidentally get a nail through his foot (or hand or leg) but simply a matter of *when*. Such an injury was seen as a calculable risk of the day-to-day work that should be both anticipated and *taken like a man*. A corollary, of course, was that to fail to take it like a man was to fail to *be* a man. Construction, like many male-dominated fields, is full of terms indicating that a worker is not man enough: "Hit it with your purse"; "Hike up your skirt and get it done"; "Tackle it like you've got a pair"; or the simple but classic "Don't be a pussy." As in many other male-dominated domains, these men must prove that they are men and must do so by proving that they are not women.[7]

*Cultural Rule #2: Protect Others over Yourself.*   A second rule of the hypermasculine culture was that one may (and perhaps should) put oneself at risk but should not simultaneously put others at risk. In fact, one should be willing to put oneself at risk in order to protect others. One example was visible in the actions of a few men immediately after a crane fell over on a jobsite of Concrete, Inc., an episode documented in my journal at the time.

According to a young laborer:

> "From where we stood we thought he [the crane operator] was dead. We got to the cab and tried to pull him out. He said he was fine, but you never know."
>
> Randy had to crawl into the cab and get the operator's boot off in order to pull him free. . . . [T]hey were afraid that the cab would slip and be further crushed. *Randy was in fact afraid that this would happen when he was in the cab, but had gone in anyway.*

In this example, when the large crane had literally fallen over, the cab (where the operator sits) was crushed by the pile of rocks upon which it came to rest. When the laborers got to the crane, one of them quickly scrambled up the rocks and pulled the operator out to safety. He did so in spite of being aware that the rocks could shift and that the crane might continue to fall. As in the military logic of never leaving a man behind, he knew that putting himself at risk was acceptable and leaving the operating engineer at risk was not.

Although individual workers were, in my experience, supposed both to anticipate injuries (within reason) and to welcome them without complaint (again within reason), the same level of risk was clearly not to be extended to one's co-workers.[8] Though one might "opt" not to wear protective eye-gear when striking or grinding certain materials, one should not strike or grind in a manner likely to pose a risk to others' eyes. One might "choose" to work on a roof without fall protection but would not remove the option from others. Each man was to decide for himself—and all workers were bound by rule number one, to *take it like a man*. The interconnected nature of the rules is significant because it is through the combining of the rules with the cultural performances of loyalty and brotherhood that the foundation is laid for sacrificing oneself for others—allowing and accepting injury to oneself for others' gain.

*Cultural Rule #3: Doing "What the Job Requires" and "Getting the Job Done."* A 1998 article in *Redbook* magazine offers a pseudoscientific review of how men's lovemaking styles are correlated with their occupations. Blue-collar men, and especially truck drivers, are heralded for their ability to "get the job done."[9] This is amusing not only superficially but also because it uses a stock phrase of the industry—a phrase often used to justify the cutting of safety corners.

The importance of "getting the job done" (described as a "finish-the-project focus" by John Anderson) is illuminated by the on-site discussions that followed the crane accident.[10] The crane operator hurt in the accident was widely praised by the men on the site because he could have prevented the crane's fall (and thus his own injuries) had he immediately dropped the load of wet concrete he was swinging. But because there were crews working under the boom of the crane, he kept swinging the concrete until it was well past the workers. By the time he was able to drop the load, the crane had tipped over too far to be righted. Thus, in the talk of the jobsite, it was his desire to protect others that resulted in his own injuries.

Absent from these discussions, of course, was the question of why an experienced operating engineer would push the crane past its point of balance. The physics of crane operation are not made of "guesstimates" but rather use formal calculations of the weight of the load, the length and angle of the boom, and the base upon which the crane is stabilized. The calculations are done by the contractors as well as by the equipment manufacturers and should be common knowledge for any seasoned operator. In fact, the ingredients of the calculation, if not the actual numbers, should also be known by those coordinating with the crane, such as the foremen and site superintendents. Yet though there were some private grumblings from the other operating engineers that he should have known better, these conversations were not held openly.

More important, had one asked this operator (or perhaps any of the other operators) *before the accident* why he was swinging such a heavy load on an overextended boom, it is very likely that he would have responded that this was "what's required to get the job done." Clearly, though, the job does not *require* that the crane operator push his machine past its physical capacity—in fact, the official safety procedures call for exactly the opposite. This job *did* require that the wet concrete be put in place so that it could cure, but there were alternative ways for this to have been done: a crane with a larger boom could have been brought in; an alternative pathway could have been designated; or, at the very least, smaller amounts of concrete could have been loaded into the bucket on the end of the boom. All these alternatives, of course, would have cost more money in the form of labor, equipment, and time. Additional hours needed for the laborers (then billed at roughly $30 per hour) or crane operators (then billed at roughly $125 per hour with crane) add up quickly. As a result, it was probably decided by some collection of folks that this is what was required to get the job done. And once agreed upon, "what is required" is treated as objective and nonnegotiable, as if no other options exist.

In spite of the fact that the determination of "what is required to get the job done" is *treated* as an objective calculation, it is clearly a subjective determination of how work should be done. It is a set of decisions generally made by management and the upper levels of men in the field. It is my strong sense that these decisions are primarily determined not by what safety requires but rather by the contract negotiated with the customer— the date on which completion of the project has been promised, the fines for finishing late or bonuses for finishing early, and the difference in labor costs between doing the work quickly and somewhat more slowly—and perhaps more safely. It is also important that those making these calculations are able to rely upon the male workers' performances of the first two rules: the estimators can assume that the workers will be *taking it like a man,* and each one *protecting others and others' interests at the expense of himself.* As a result, doing "what the job requires" and simply "getting the job done" also serve to maintain the AOPs of circumventing the safety training and regulations.

*Cultural Rule #4: Carrying the Boss's Burden and Shouldering the Costs of Safety.* One reason the workers do not challenge the supervisors' determination of "what the job requires" is their tendency to identify with those men *as men*, rather than recognizing the fundamentally different economic interests at stake. In this way, the gendered culture of the industry obscures the difference in social class between the men (here, literally, their relations to the means of production). The economic interests of the employer are taken as the primary interests on the site. "Getting the job done" becomes everyone's top priority, and concerns for safety are left to those who aren't team players or who are insufficiently masculine.

An example of this tendency to make employer interests primary can be seen in a comment made by a journey-level carpenter at Family Builders. During an informal lunch discussion about safety (at which no supervisors were present), Rudy declared impatiently that if he were working on a roof for the company, he would not take the time to go get a harness or belt (fall protection) *because the company could not afford* to have him do so. The economic interests of the company were put in front of his own potential risk of injury, paralysis, or death. And since the risk of both death and paralysis begins at around six feet—far lower, of course, than most roofs—these are hardly hypothetical issues for commercial carpenters.

In reality, the question of what the company can afford is a complicated one. An additional thirty minutes per carpenter per day can easily add up: if one imagines a job with thirty carpenters, lasting thirty days, and wage-and-benefits packages sitting at roughly $35 per hour, the additional cost of safety would be more than $15,000 on this job alone, and multiple jobs over multiple months would cause this amount to skyrocket. However, one could certainly argue that the company could better afford the thirty minutes it might take to set up a harness system on the roof than the loss of a good carpenter plus OSHA fines and a liability lawsuit. Then again, when the OSHA fines after the death of a worker can be negotiated down to $2,000, and liability insurance can pick up some or all of the payout, the numbers on the employers' side of the ledger aren't entirely clear.[11]

Regardless of what the company can or cannot afford, or how the company can best manage its risks and profits, the interests of workers and employers must be recognized as diverging—at least in practice—around the costs and benefits of safety. At the most basic level, each party in the wages-for-labor exchange has to be concerned with his future ability to participate in the exchange. Employers need to remain solvent so that they can compete for future contracts, and workers need to remain physically able to sell their labor power to future employers or on different jobs. Expressed in this way, the calculations can be seen not even to use the same currency: what the company can afford is a financial question, and what the worker can afford is a physical one, involving the potential for injury, debilitation, and death. When the workers fail to pursue (or are prevented from pursuing) their interests in physical safety, the discussion becomes solely a financial one (framed by employers' interests), and the pressure is on to "get the job done."

## The Intersection of Masculinity and Structural Insecurity

It is clear that the hypermasculine culture creates a disinclination in the men—and thus also in their female co-workers—to express fears and concerns about the safety of their work and working environment.[12] And it this culture that is often blamed by employers (and researchers) for the workers' unsafe behaviors. Though the men may not want to be seen as unmanly or as sissies, however, it appears to be the risk of losing their jobs that truly prevents them from following the official procedures. To the extent that the AOPs represent homosocial displays of loyalty among men, they might fairly be considered gendered cultural phenomena. To the extent that the AOPs represent worker displays of loyalty to the employer, they are made obligatory by the insecure nature of employment in the industry.

A good example of how the insecure nature of employment might affect workers' ability to raise concerns on the worksite came about during a situation in which I spoke about safety and was repeatedly warned and verbally sanctioned by my employer. Particularly striking was the fact that I had spoken at an event off site, on my own time; it was unrelated to my employment, although I *was* identified as an apprentice with the union local (not as an apprentice of my employer). The fact that one might assume that such activities could or should be entirely irrelevant to an employer (especially the employer of an allegedly highly protected union worker), makes the company's response much more notable. Although one can only speculate about the company's possible response to an actual worker complaint, this incident does suggest that the employer would be far from delighted and that the company might waste little time in making its wrath known.

I had spoken briefly at a public forum on workplace safety and legislative reform: I lived in the district of a legislator who was working to reduce the funding for or to dismantle OSHA, and this event was to be a sort of town meeting where the legislator could share his views and goals and also hear from his constituents. One might have assumed that as a union member, I was *expected* to speak. To the contrary, though, it appears that I was expected to stay quiet and to save my thoughts about the actual processes of safety for myself.

The argument I made in my brief comments was, ironically enough, that the structural insecurities in the construction union contracts provide construction workers no protection from arbitrary firing and thus jeopardize their abilities to complain about and report safety violations. Again, I spoke as an individual apprentice and did not affiliate myself with any company. I was hardly revolutionary, although I did suggest, as I do here, that to reduce further the outside oversight that is already approaching zero is potentially to ask some workers to choose between their jobs and their lives.

Also ironically (given my emphasis on the costs of employer displeasure), my comments appeared to have angered my employer. Concrete, Inc., pulled few punches in letting me know: on the first business day after the forum I was immediately pulled aside by the job superintendent, who sputtered furiously, "You've made a lot of people very angry. Not on this job, but in the office. They were calling me already this morning." (This conversation, not surprisingly, is recorded in my journal. As an apprentice on a job with roughly five hundred workers, it was not terribly common to have the superintendent talk to an apprentice, to say nothing about searching one out and yelling at her.)

A few days later, the company's safety director made a trip out to the site specifically to take me aside and repeat the superintendent's comments. It is not irrelevant, of course, that this woman was also the company's equal employment opportunity officer and therefore the person accountable for ensuring a harassment- and discrimination-free environment. In spite of her broader responsibilities, she had *never* made an effort to speak with me previously, nor had she ever, as far as I am aware, been at all interested in my experiences or behaviors on site. Her interest in me was tied solely to informing me how angry my public comments about safety had apparently made the management. She made it clear that the anger was still "rippling through the office."

If I had had my wits about me (not an easy task when one can be fired at any time and is in the process of being told how wrathful one has just made the bosses), I might have asked how it was that the men in the office even knew that Kris Paap was one of their apprentices. I might also have asked why, if the equal employment officer/safety director had known that I existed, she hadn't said hello earlier—when Harry had his hand on my backside, for example, or when I was told that the men in the trailer regarded me as "BT." I didn't have my wits about me, though, and so I said little, if anything.

Unsure of what to do, I called the union after I left the worksite. According to the union representative, there was no doubt that the company's response was unjust and violated my rights to free speech, especially since the speech had occurred off site and on my own time. The representative said he would intervene; however, no one from the company *or* the union ever addressed the issue or rescinded the verbal reprimands I had received. Since it was November and the company was beginning to lay off workers, I decided that I had no desire to spend the winter playing a wait-and-worry game. A few weeks later, with the assistance of a journey-level worker, I was able to secure an interview with and an offer from Family Builders. I transferred immediately.

## Various Forms of the Bait-and-Switch

Although the threat of sanction and reprimand often remains unspoken and implied (unlike the foregoing example), it is the power of threatened displeasure in an insecure industry that allows the bait-and-switch of safety to take place. The concept of bait-and-switch—the promise of one object of exchange and the subsequent delivery of another, lesser object—is an accurate representation of the safety training in much of the construction industry: workers are promised concern for their safety with an *official* version of standard regulations but are subsequently given a set of actual operating procedures (AOPs) in which safety is often compromised in order to "get the job done." This occurs in three general ways. First, in the most benign form of the bait-and-switch, the content of informal training makes clear that meeting the technical requirements of safety is more important than keeping the worker safe. In a second, more egregious bait-and-switch, workers are given tasks than cannot be done without violating the official procedures, and they often receive these tasks from the same foreman who trained them in the official safety procedures. The third and final bait-and-switch adds insult to the ultimate injury: in a worst-case scenario, contractors argue that workers are knowledgeable about the risks and procedures (having been given the official procedures and training) and thus should be held responsible for their own injury or death.

### Bait-and-Switch #1: "In Case OSHA Drives By"

In the example of the cherry picker, I was handed a webbed safety belt that was—theoretically—to secure me to the machine in case something went wrong and I were to fall out. But as I was tightening the belt, my foreman told me that it wouldn't do me any good because the belt was too large: it would simply "slide up, dislocate your shoulders, and then drop you on the ground." Though I certainly recognized the morbid humor in that description, one look at the belt, my waist, and my shoulders made it clear that he wasn't kidding.

*Won't Do You Any Good If It's Too Big . . .*  To be given a safety belt as fall protection and then be told that it won't prevent you from falling seems on the surface to be absurd. And it is important to note that my waist was by no means smaller than all (or even most) of the men's on the site. Therefore, this should not be construed as a "once-in-a-great-while" sort of problem or even as an expense that would have been incurred just for me (though legally, of course, that consideration should have been irrelevant; the company was required to provide the necessary safety equipment for its workers). The fact is that I was not the only one too small for the belt; it is likely that many workers had encountered the same dilemma with the same or a similar belt.[13]

The *real* reason for my wearing the belt however—especially since we were working near a main thoroughfare—was made clear when Harry handed it to me, saying I was supposed to wear the belt *"in case OSHA drove past."* Since OSHA requires that anyone working at or above six feet from the ground be using fall protection (such as the belt), its inspectors would be looking to see that I had a belt on.

It is meaningful that OSHA is put forth as the reason for the belt. Both Remodel Co. and Concrete, Inc., and (to a lesser extent) Family Builders not only built their safety training around the OSHA standards but also "trained to" the policies and the fines. By this I mean that workers were told to do (or not to do) certain things "because it's $10,000 for OSHA if they see that" or "you'll be in a lot of trouble if OSHA drives by." Although warnings about the risk of actual injuries and deaths were also included in the training sessions, the frequency, consistency, and emphasis upon the OSHA warnings, in both formal and informal settings, rendered their significance unmistakable. It is also important to note that even though OSHA fines are levied against the employer, not the workers, this fact is obscured by language to the contrary. This use of language implying worker responsibility adds, I think, to the perception that the interests of workers and employers should be treated as aligned or identical.

The OSHA justification for safety is also important because it indicates some of what drives the design and implementation of official safety programs. The extent to which workers are trained to regulations—not to their safety *qua* safety—indicates that it is the employers' interests, not the workers', that are taking top priority. One might argue that this sort of training could make sense for regulations that require checking and marking equipment, if workers might underestimate the importance of the rule. However, when the training and regulations can be entirely explained by obvious and indisputable safety reasons (e.g., "The safety guards must be kept on the tool at all times to prevent injury"), the use of financial and legal justifications is meaningful. When workers are told to keep the safety guard on the saw because "*it will be a $10,000 fine if OSHA sees you*," rather than "*you could sever a finger, hand, or arm with tremendous effects upon your ability to function economically and physically, at home and on the job*," worker safety appears to be taking a back seat to employer finances.

*Won't Do You Any Good Even If It Fits . . .*   The cherry picker example is also noteworthy in that I was handed a belt and not a harness. Harnesses were not supplied for workers at that time because they were not then legally required, despite common knowledge that falling with a safety belt on simply snapped your back and gave you roughly ninety seconds before killing you—too little time for "live recovery." A law was already on the books to ban the belts after January 1, 1998, but they remained legal until that time.[14] Thus I was not really given "fall protection" but only the possibility for an open casket if I should fall. The belt was not for the purposes of my safety but for the legal and financial safety of the company.

*Won't Do You Any Good To Wait For OSHA . . .*   The fact that the companies train to OSHA regulations is rather odd, actually, since OSHA in reality has a sort of nonpresence in the daily life of workers. Since its creation in 1970, it has been rather consistently underfunded and the source of political attacks.[15] Because of political pressure from employers and employer groups, the work of the agency has in recent years shifted from enforcement of codes to cooperative and consultative work with businesses. In this latter form, OSHA provides safety consultations to businesses in order to reduce potential hazards—as well as workers' compensation premiums.

Even if the emphasis could be maintained on enforcement and inspections, however, there are not enough people or funds for OSHA to do the work mandated by the 1970 act. This is something widely acknowledged by both the agency and its most vocal opponents.[16] According to a report prepared by the secretary of labor's office in 1995 (in response to Senator Bob Dole's proposed legislation to restrict OSHA's enforcement activities and cut its overall budget more than 15 percent): "OSHA currently has only

2,000 federal and state inspectors to protect 93 million workers at over 6 milllion workplaces. Even with current resources, a firm can expect to be inspected only once in 60 years."[17]

Even if the agency did have adequate resources to make worksite visits more than once every sixty years, though, enforcement in the construction industry would be challenged by the dynamic nature of construction workplaces. Construction poses a unique challenge to governmental and other outside regulation because by definition, the locations and nature of the work change over time and often do so quite rapidly. This makes enforcement very difficult, as it is nearly impossible to gain an ongoing sense of jobs or jobsite risks. Even if inspectors were to focus on one contractor, that contractor would be likely to have multiple jobs in different locations, each job a changing scenery of tasks and challenges for workers and inspectors alike. Therefore, the risks of inspections and penalties at each individual site are quite reasonably perceived by workers and supervisors to be low. As a result, occupational safety practices and accident rates say more about workplace power and social relations than they do about government regulation.

### Bait-and-Switch #2: "Under No Circumstances . . . Except for These"

The second form of the bait-and-switch occurs in situations where workers are explicitly told not to do some risky thing, often in conjunction with the formal safety policies and often in writing, and then are explicitly or implicitly asked to do exactly that which was just proscribed. Because the formal policies often specify obtaining a signature from the workers present at any formal safety training, workers sign a form acknowledging their receipt of the formal safety program—and *then* receive the AOPs, the more nebulous and contextually contingent set of rules.

All three of the companies I worked for offered weekly safety meetings in which a one-page or paragraph-length excerpt was read from the formal policies. All workers would then sign the bottom or back of the form that was circulated, indicating that they were present and had been informed of the regulation. Although this procedure was always explained by the foremen as a way to take attendance, it is clear that a worker's signature on such a form has definite (if undetermined) impact on larger questions of liability. If I sign a form indicating that I have been told "never ever" to do something, and then am hurt shortly thereafter doing that very thing, who is to be held responsible? This question, of course, was not discussed at the safety meetings, nor did I hear it raised in work, union, or classroom settings.

An example of this second form of the bait-and-switch occurred at Concrete, Inc., in a safety meeting that focused on the proper use of ladders. We workers were specifically reminded that stepladders were to be used only when they are folded open and the cross-supports pushed down into the locked position. Under no circumstances, we were told, were they to be used when folded flat and leaned up against something, since they would then be dangerous and unstable. As the foreman passed around the attendance and acknowledgment form that we all signed, a couple of the laborers commented loudly in a half-joking manner that if the employer felt so strongly about this, they should send someone to the company's main boneyard (storage area) to get some different ladders. The straight ladders had been taken to another jobsite some time before, and the only ones left on our site were stepladders—which, as far as the speaker was concerned, weren't any good anyway.

Once we had all signed the form, we stood up, grabbed our hardhats, tool belts, and gloves, and headed out to the job. As I gathered my stuff, I heard the foreman behind me say "Danny, you'll be cleaning off the forms so that they're ready for this afternoon's pour, and Marvin, *you're going to be up filling the holes on the wall over there.*" I knew that to reach the holes on the wall Marvin was going to have to climb a ladder. The only ladder on site was a large stepladder, and the only way to climb it, given the narrow foundation base at the bottom of the wall, would be to keep it folded and lean it up against the wall.

Marvin did not complain, nor did he point out that he had just signed a form saying that he knew that "under no circumstances" should he do exactly this. Instead, he just grabbed his stuff and headed out to work. Marvin, like many of my coworkers, was smart and full of common sense. Thus one cannot assume that he did not understand what had just happened. To the contrary, I am confident that he understood the unspoken messages and their cultural and structural implications all too well.

## Bait-and-Switch #3: Death and Contributory Negligence

The third bait-and-switch pattern is the most dramatic, and—one would hope—the most unusual. This pattern occurs when a worker is asked or expected to perform a task that involves risk and then is subsequently held responsible for that risk. It might be the case that the risk is underestimated, or that its likelihood is miscalculated—or it might be that the supervisors simply choose to turn a blind eye to the exact methods by which the job will get done. The precise circumstances of the request are less significant than the fact that the worker takes on himself the risk associated with completing the task at hand, a task that will be completed in a manner outside of that described by the formal safety practices. Should the task at hand end in workers' injuries or deaths, the employer is then able to assert that the workers chose to conduct their work in this fashion and should therefore be held responsible for the outcome.

Given the lack of protection from arbitrary firing, it is difficult to know the extent to which any task in union construction can be construed as voluntarily undertaken. It is exactly this question, however, that is at the heart of litigation surrounding worker injuries and fatalities. In the example below (taken from the media accounts of the accident and the legal events that followed), a fatal crane accident occurred in which three workers died on a job. Although the conditions of risk on this job seemed to be fairly well known, and the actions taken had been on the edge of propriety at best, in the litigation after the workers' deaths the employer took the legal strategy of placing the blame upon the workers and suggesting that, since they "voluntarily put themselves in harm's way," they should be held responsible for their own deaths.[18]

*The Final Flight of "Big Blue."*    On July 14, 1999, the plan on the building site of Milwaukee's new baseball stadium was simple: a piece of roof would be "flown" into place by "Big Blue," a 567-foot crane. This procedure had been followed successfully for months: three ironworkers would be in a "manbasket," hanging by a cable from another crane. Because they would have radios, they could observe and guide the flight of the piece. They would be the eyes of the project for those on the ground and, in particular, for the operator of the first crane. Although OSHA regulations permit the use of "manbaskets" only when no other options are viable, this was apparently deemed by those present the most reasonable way to get the job done.[19]

The plan on this day was complicated by high winds, which have a tendency to catch a large load like a sail and pull it quickly and violently out of control. Because this is well-known, wind speed is generally an integral part of the calculation for how work is to be done. The crane itself had been rated to make lifts in wind speeds up to 20 miles per hour.[20] Project supervisors and the designer of the crane, however, had declared any wind above 10 mph to be "risky" for crane operations on this site.[21]

On July 14, wind speeds of 17–18 mph were recorded on the crane's own wind gauge, located roughly seventy-five feet below the roof piece.[22] And wind speeds of 27–32 mph were recorded at the site and at a nearby airport.[23] In fact, smaller lifts on the project had been canceled for the day because they were regarded as too dangerous, given the conditions, and a previous attempt to lift the large roof section, roughly five hours before the actual accident, had been called off after the load was pulled dramatically out of balance by the wind.

Nevertheless, though the crane was not scheduled to be used for roughly a week, and though completing this lift on that particular day was not essential for staying on schedule, after some debate the decision was made to go ahead.[24] At 5:00 p.m., Jerome Starr, Jeffrey Wischer, and William De-Grave put on the safety harnesses that tied them to the basket.[25] They climbed in, snapped their belts to the basket, and were raised far above the ground. As they hung above the site, and as their co-workers stood and watched, the 450-ton roof piece was caught by the wind and tilted wildly. Once it was no longer parallel to the ground, a greater portion of the surface was exposed to the wind, and the entire piece, thrown out of balance, slammed into the crane that held the men. Within 14 seconds, the boom of the crane broke, the cables snapped, and the manbasket and its three occupants plummeted to the ground. Starr, Wischer, and DeGrave were declared dead at the site.

### "Voluntarily Put Themselves in Harm's Way"

Owners of a 567-foot crane that collapsed over the Milwaukee Brewers' new ballpark, killing three ironworkers, deny any negligence and contend that the victims *voluntarily put themselves in harm's way* at the time of the crash. . . . The company . . . alleged that the ironworkers who died "*may have been contributorily negligent*" because they "voluntarily assumed the risks attendant to being lifted in a 'man basket' by a crane while being aware of the job-site conditions."

Lampson [the company that owned the crane and subcontracted its use] *denied that the workers had been required by the employer to be in the basket at the time of the accident.* Attorneys for the families could not immediately be reached for comment.[26]

The primary argument offered by the lead contractor in the case was that the decision to continue with the crane work was "a consensus decision, arrived at unanimously, and that if even a single ironworker had complained, the lift would have been stopped."[27] According to a number of the ironworkers and their family members, however, the concerns of the workers were ignored.[28] Even more important is the claim made by the prosecuting attorney that the *culture of the worksite made it clear that complaining about safety was not wise.*[29]

It is worth asking why the men widely considered the toughest in the industry, the self-proclaimed "cowboys of the skies" were unable or unwilling to push their concerns through the chain of the command. Though the most commonly given answer is that of the hypermasculine culture, it is irresponsible to ignore the role of job insecurity in making the calculations that are at the heart of the AOPs. Whereas masculinity might have made proceeding with the lift in winds of roughly 30 mph seem reasonable, masculinity and the lack of protection from arbitrary firing made it mandatory.

## Epilogue

After a lengthy investigation and a full courtroom trial, the primary contractors on the stadium were found liable for the deaths of the three workers and were fined roughly $99 million by the jury.[30] In this case, responsible parties off site did not accept the argument that workers should be held responsible for the conditions of work.

On one hand, this ought not to be surprising. Issues of safety are often recognized as matters in which employers' desires for cost savings are pitted against the risks to workers; this is why employers and not individual workers are required to establish formal safety programs. On the other hand, one cannot ignore that the workers themselves talk about the problems of masculine cultures as problems of individual behaviors and machismo foolishness. If the jurors had accepted the stereotypes of the construction workers as cowboys and hotdogs—images clearly perpetuated by the men themselves—the verdict might have been different. It is in such circumstances, then, that it becomes evident how dangerous and costly the wages of white working-class masculinities are for the men who pursue them.

The broader value of the men's performances is further clarified by the responses of employers and employer organizations: after the verdict was announced, it was immediately appealed. The 1st District Court of Appeals of Wisconsin threw out the $99 million penalty in 2003, arguing that it was "unconstitutionally excessive," and that such punitive damages should only be applied when *intent to harm* can be demonstrated.[31] The case then moved to the Wisconsin State Supreme Court in 2005 where the penalty was reinstated.[32] At the end of 2005, business leaders and employer organizations were visibly gearing up to fight this precedent both in and beyond the courts, arguing that this and similar rulings create a "hostile environment" for business in the state.[33]

The argument that employers should only be given such penalties when the complainant can demonstrate malice or clear intent to harm—although seemingly logical on its face—can appropriately be applied only to circumstances of street crime or other traditional forms of violence outside of the workplace. It might be just, for example, to treat a vehicular homicide (a fatal car accident) differently if the driver is believed to have hit the victim accidentally (i.e., an accident) or intentionally (murder). In the supervision of workplace safety, however, particularly where the employer both controls the conditions of work and has almost unlimited power to hire and fire without regard to traditional protections against arbitrary or punitive firing, the standard of demonstratable intent *can only be just if it is defined as the absence of safety itself.* When an employer can encourage risk-taking simply by failing to discourage it or by emphasizing the job's timeline or the coming winter, a standard of demonstrable intent is likely to be impossible for any attorney or complainant to meet. Setting a requirement for demonstrable intent is therefore potentially equivalent to legislating that workers always be found "contributorily negligent" (to borrow a term from the employer in this case) regardless of the circumstances. In the end, then, it becomes poignantly clear that the wages of white working-class masculinities will become a wage paid to the employer and not the workers.

# 7

# THE WAGES—AND COSTS—OF WHITE WORKING-CLASS MASCULINITIES

**W**henever I use the word "pigs" or "pigness" to talk about the culture of construction, I have to emphasize very carefully that this is not a term that I selected. In spite of that, people are often disturbed by it. Depending on the audience, I'm likely to get a look of horror ("how classist!" from middle-class folks) or dismissal ("old-school feminist!" from working-class men). It is assumed, of course, that I have chosen this term myself and that I am using it as an *insult*.

This response to "pigness" is important for highlighting the negative perceptions that most people have about men who are pigs. This is in fact the same response I had the first few times that I heard the term or its equivalent used on site. When a company president told me that the guys in the industry were just a bunch of pigs, I wondered, was he that disconnected from his men? Did he really have that little respect for them? When I first heard workers use this term to talk about themselves as a group, I asked myself erroneously if they could really have that little respect for themselves. From my middle-class perspective, I wondered, what could be done about such an ingrained self-esteem problem, apparently affecting these men *as a class*?

Once I was working in the industry, it still took me a while to recognize the ways in which this terminology empowered the men. Most simply, of course, the men who used this imagery were saying, This is how it's going to be: put up with what you see, hear, and experience, or give up and get out. Complaints are going to get you nowhere—but out. This was true for me, for the other women with whom I worked, and for the men of color. As discussed at length in earlier chapters, the collective assertion of the "pigness" identity permits and protects a wide range of harassing and discriminatory behaviors, all of which are clearly proscribed both by law and by the companies' (and the unions') formal policies.

To see pigness as only pejorative is also to miss the majority of its connotations about masculinity. Out in the field, pigness allows the men to celebrate what is physical and alive about the job. It highlights the enjoyable parts of getting dirty and spent by one's labor. As Livingstone and Luxton have pointed out in their research on steelworkers, such celebrations allow the workers to extract greater meaning from what might otherwise simply be arduous and monotonous work.[1] Pigness is at least on some levels, then, celebratory, empowering, and meaningful.

Pigness also ties into larger structures and ideologies about masculinity and allows these men to claim for themselves the core of masculinity. At their physical, vulgar, sexualized "best," these men are icons of what men are supposed to be in their most natural state. Construction workers are joked about, mimicked, and referred to in other performances of masculinity as a sort of reference point from which masculinity begins. It is not simply coincidence that the construction worker costume is one that frequently appears in venues of the sex trade, including male strippers' performances for heterosexual women and homosexual performances for men.[2]

Pigness also offers ideological and psychological protection. Even as it clearly serves to help maintain the construction industry as a male, white, and heterosexual domain, it functions in a manner that offers the industry's insiders the appearance (at least to themselves) of formally complying with the laws of equal opportunity. The social scripts and performances of pigness (described in chapter 3) are able to offer up a version of reality that removes from these men the responsibility of re-creating the inequalities from which they benefit. This is not to say, of course, that all workers require this protection: some of the workers in construction, as in any occupation, are clearly content with their participation in the maintenance of inequality. But for the men who do not wish to see themselves as discriminating or unfair—a quality that seems as common among these men as it is in the rest of mainstream America—the cultures of pigness offer a language and set of beliefs that *neutralize and make legitimate* these practices of dominance. These men can thus actively discriminate and harass without—at least in some circumstances and for some people—having to acknowledge that they are doing so. As a result, understanding the ideological practices of pigness provides some insight into how it is that well-intentioned individuals are able to participate comfortably in the subordination and exclusion of others.

## Social and Economic Costs of the Pigness Strategy

In the bigger picture, of course, the individual readers and listeners who express alarm at the expression of pigness are simply foreshadowing the larger story of this book. In securing the industry for white males, pigness constrains and subordinates the workers as much as—if not more than—it elevates them. It does so first in a social fashion by giving the workers privilege that is contextual to the industry and limited to it. Men who claim to be animals do gain the cachet of being more "real" and "manly" men, but their cachet is limited to settings in which "animal," "real," and "manly" are dominant male ideals. It is particularly ironic, given the relationship between pigness and affirmative action, that it is the success of affirmative action both in and outside of the industry that has further increased the instability of white working-class men's social dominance. Since affirmative action and nondiscrimination policies have made inroads in other occupations, white women and people of color—particularly those of the middle and upper classes—have made significant occupational and economic gains. As a result, even the most dominant tradesman is likely to find that he is not only subordinate to the white men who supervise him but also that he will be working for—or at least answering to—a white woman or person of color who represents a corporate client or serves as a regulator from an outside agency.

For persons dependent on pigness for social affirmation of their dominance and worth, such circumstances would have to be troubling. Even if individual workers are able to successfully compartmentalize these interactions and frame them as irrelevant to each other, it seems unlikely that such compartmentalization could remain effective across settings and contexts. Thus the very "safety net" of one's dominance (the categories of persons who are by definition lower than and subordinate to one's own group) is able to re-present itself as equal in some settings and dominant in others. The value of the social and psychological wages of masculinity and whiteness are therefore revealed as fragile in some settings and potentially bankrupt in others.

The identity of pigness also has very real *bodily* costs. It does more than simply mark the worker as a certain kind of man; it also requires a certain workplace performance of him. Because the performance of pigness involves a noted disinclination to avoid risk (and a willingness to *take it like a man*), pigness becomes part of the reason for high rates of worker accidents and injuries in the construction industry. Though these high rates are described as a collective cultural choice (i.e., these men simply choose to violate safety procedures because they are just "that sort of man"), a cultural explanation for the problem and the practices is clearly insufficient. In reality, as illustrated in chapter 6, pigness becomes inseparable from the structural insecurity of the industry: the fact that workers labor at the pleasure of their employers. Pigness, now linked to work cultures and structures, draws lines indicating when men can express fear and discomfort and when they cannot. Thus proving oneself as a man is simultaneously proving oneself as the right sort of worker. When combined with a lack of protection from firing and pressure to "get the job done," pigness moves from being a foolish public performance to a patterned and structurally bound form of subordination.

## Reconceptualizing Pigness as a Managerial Strategy

To the extent that pigness is a strategic performance of the white working-class men, it is clearly a strategy that is vulnerable to appropriation. And in the final evaluation, it has been partially, if not wholly, appropriated. As Akhil Gupta and James Ferguson have explained,

> Practices that are resistant to a particular strategy of power are thus never innocent of or outside power, for they are always capable of being tactically appropriated and redeployed within another strategy of power, always at risk of slipping from resistance against one strategy of power into complicity with another.[3]

Although pigness is clearly an empowerment strategy designed to piggyback on the power of the supervisors (that is, to borrow power from the white men who have it), this piggyback ride appears to have the worker as the *ridden,* not the rider. Management appears to have the reins. Pigness is revealed at this point as having "slipp[ed] from resistance . . . into complicity" with the economic and political powers that subordinate and weaken these men as a class. Thus a full understanding of pigness must include a reconceptualization of pigness as a strategy, however unintentional or passive, that directly benefits the men who *manage* the men who are pigs.

To focus on the actions and performances only of *workers*, or of workers and the unions, is to miss the obvious: these performances are successful when they are *condoned or permitted by management.* They are also practices that benefit management. For example, workers divided by race or gender animosity are unlikely to unify against an employer. When workers are trying to outwork or outpace other workers (whether because of the structural insecurity that fuels competition or the race and gender animosity that does the same), employers benefit from the increased production. Jeffrey Riemer actually warned against such a divided and conquered workforce of the future in his 1979 text, *Hard Hats*. He saw it as a likely hazard of the integration that was starting to occur and described emerging signs of these fault lines at the time.[4]

## The Power of Passive Complicity

This is not to assert that all employers support the behaviors and practices of pigness intentionally, or even that they are wholly aware of these inter-locking relations. I believe, however, that management is often at the very least, passively complicit in all these practices. I use the phrase "passive complicity" to emphasize that employers gain real fiscal and political ben-efits from the practices of pigness and appear to be doing little other than the mandatory minimum to prevent them. The mandatory minimum, in many cases, is the creation and presentation of a formal set of regulations about worker conduct on site, such as safety regulations and harassment and discrimination policies. By creating and presenting the formal policies, employers appear to have met the minimum legal obligation for address-ing on-site behaviors. Ironically, of course, these policies are often used as indicators of *presumed* additional efforts (i.e., one assumes that these poli-cies are enforced). However, in my experience, the existence of the policies was substituted for actual enforcement. Instead of aggressively enforcing the stated rules, the foremen and lower management in the field simply raised (or kept elevated) the bar that determined the sorts of behaviors that must be tolerated from these allegedly animalistic men.

It is important to note that I am arguing not for *greater* regulation: I am not suggesting that employers undertake any action that they are not at present required to do. I am simply suggesting that in matters of safety, dis-crimination, and harassment the Actual Operating Procedures be brought into line with the formal policies that are on the books. I am confident that such changes would not be as difficult as some employer groups might suggest. In my own experience, workers clearly responded to and followed rules that *were* enforced and taken seriously by management. When an employer made it clear that he did not tolerate harassment and discrimi-nation and did not appreciate black jokes, for example, the proscribed behaviors did not appear to take place, and the jokes lost their public per-formative status. When workers know that property owners (clients) are likely to be offended by some behaviors *and* that management does not wish them to be offended, the behaviors in question are reduced. This suggests at the very least that when undue risks are taken and when harassment and discrimination happen, the official message of safety and antidiscrimination has been either unheard or unclear. Thus, although pigness practices are most obviously a problem of workers and of the union, they are most certainly a problem that rests with the employers and the managers as well.

### Power and Consent: Getting Workers to Take— and Seek—the Blame

It is meaningful that these practices do not *appear* to be a management issue but appear instead to be the product of preferred worker behaviors. As Michel Foucault reminds us in his *Discipline and Punish:* The perfection of power should tend to render its actual exercise unnecessary; . . . creating and sustaining a power relation independent of the person who exercises it; in short, inmates should be caught up in a power situation of which they are themselves the bearers.[5]

It is a truism of power that power is most successful when it is made invisible by the acceptance and support by those who are subordinated to it. Foucault goes on to describe the Panopticon, a prison designed so that each prisoner would always be visible to authority but would have no way of knowing whether he was actually being observed. These conditions would have the effect of inducing the individuals to *police themselves* and thus make the actual observations largely unnecessary. This combination of constant potential oversight and uncertainty—a combination common on construction sites—causes the subordinated class to use their power in the situation to subordinate themselves.

It does not take much imagination to see how Foucault's ideas apply to the union construction industry. The jobsites are often in the open, and workers are generally but not always under direct supervision. One never knows when a foreman, superintendent, or union representative may walk around the corner. Given their lack of protection from arbitrary firing, workers cannot afford to be caught looking leisurely and thus are likely to be moving at a pace wholly in contrast with the stereotype from the 1970s.

Construction is equally enforcing of the performance of masculinities and of economic production. And it is the intersection of production with masculinity that gives the class relations of the industry both intensity and the workers' consent to their own subordination. Because of the standards for the public proving of masculinity, workers must constantly prove their value as men. Because of the structural insecurity of the employment, men must prove their value as workers *and* as men. Because their jobs and their social identities depend on it, these performances are often both mandated and bound up in risk. Thus the workers of construction, asserting themselves as pigs in a claim to power, find themselves bound, subordinated, and at risk.

## How Construction Workers' Behaviors Are Restructuring the Capitalist Exchange

Even if one remains wholly unconcerned about the fate of construction workers as people, the actions and practices of union construction workers have ramifications far beyond the boundaries of the individual job. In fact, union construction workers' willingness to sacrifice their economic security for the reproduction of white and male privilege has both theoretical and practical significance. It is significant in a theoretical sense because these workers can been seen as inverting the most basic assumption of capitalism: *self-interest* in their sale of labor power to an employer. It is significant in a practical sense because it dramatically weakens the position of construction workers, unions, and workers in general.

### Theoretical Implications of Construction Pigness

The performance of pigness in the construction industry has theoretical significance because it restructures the basic premises upon which each party to the sale of labor enters into the exchange. The traditional views of labor-management relations assume that the worker attempts to minimize his work and maximize his reward. The employer is assumed to attempt the opposite—to maximize the output and minimize the reward; this is referred to as the *extraction of labor* because it purchases labor not simply as an object but rather as *potential.* Union employers in construction don't pay workers by the wall or the yard of concrete but rather by the hour; thus it is assumed that workers will be trying to work as little as possible (still keeping their jobs) and that employers will try to extract or get as much work out of each worker as they can (without killing all workers or causing them to resign).

The sale of potential labor power is known as the *capitalist exchange,* and much contemporary and union contract language is built around it. There is, for example, across unions a contractual prohibition against workers' setting an upper limit for production. This means that workers cannot say that they'll put up three walls per day but not four, or that they will pour only so many yards of concrete. There is, however, no prohibition in reverse. This means that employers may have—are assumed to have—minimum expectations and limits as to what a worker must do. The workers are both allowed and required to work as fast and hard as they are able. Although the employers' minimums may fluctuate because of weather, collective skill, or other challenges, there is no dispute about employers' being allowed to set such limits. Regardless of the extent to which one considers these rules to be just, it is clear that they are based on the assumption that workers and employers *have and operate from* different if not opposing economic interests. It is also clear that the parties do not enter the exchange with equal levels of control.

When the construction workers' performances of pigness are culturally and structurally mandated, however, the assumptions of worker self-interest become erroneous. In contrast to the assumption that workers will *minimize* their efforts, we see that white male workers are striving to *maximize* their production—at least in comparison with other workers and potentially "less desirable" categories of workers. Certainly tied to the lack of occupational security, these performances help maintain occupational segregation by gender and race and, more important from a *production standpoint,* conflate the interests of the workers with those of the employer.

It is at this point, too, that the inseparability of gender, race, class, and the labor process becomes clear: the nature of work, and how it is done (and bought and sold), must clearly be defined as more than a financial or economic exchange. The social relations and the actual physical processes of work are closely tied to the racial, gendered, and socioeconomic identities of the workforces. Thus we see that the capitalist exchange is not only being *restructured* but that it is being restructured through the different interpretations of racialized, gendered, and class-based interests.

### The Practical Significance of Pigness: Workers and a Union Movement at Risk

The strategies of pigness also have clear practical significance for the white male workers who engage in them as well as the workers who must compete with them. These workers not only are theoretically altering the capitalist exchange of labor but are doing so in a real economic and physical sense. By this I mean that the workers are renegotiating their own employment contracts to their own and others' detriment, resulting in lower piecework or pay-for-effort remuneration, greater physical and fiscal risk, and a weaker if not disappearing union movement. These costs are most clearly seen in an examination of the parties who are most damaged by them: there are costs to workers (as individuals and as a group) and larger costs to the union movement as a whole.

*Costs to Individuals: Selling Labor at a Cheaper and Cheaper Price.* By creating performative expectations for a fearless and functional machismo, pigness causes those who claim it to work against their own individual physical and fiscal interests. White male workers are able to use pigness to create and maintain a hostile environment for outsiders in the industry, but in doing so, these workers must also engage in work practices that ultimately weaken their position within the employment market relationship.

Their positions are weakened first and foremost as individuals, as they work harder, faster, and more dangerously to prove their machismo and worth to their employer. By demonstrating their masculinity through their ability to risk and sustain injury (in spite of the legal and organizational structures intended to prevent or minimize such risks), these men commodify their bodies (that is, they sell their bodies along with their labor potential to the employer for an hourly wage). They do so in a manner that weakens their own negotiating power—and their long-term ability to sell their labor to an employer. For every self-sacrificing act of machismo, the surplus labor (or profit) extracted by the employer is likely to increase. The wage of the worker, by comparison, is *decreased* in the sense of a lower piecework or pay-for-effort rate, as workers are providing more labor than they are required to, given the current expectations.[6] Also, because the workers do not need to depreciate their bodies as fast as they do, the more rapid consumption or "using up" of the workers' bodies can be seen as a sort of "freebie" in the trade with the employer.

Even more important, though, is the recognition that employers and workers engage in fundamentally different forms of risk at work. By performing pigness, workers are taking not only situational or temporary but also longer-term risks, as they place their very means of production—the body through which they work—at risk as well. A workplace injury is often more than just an injury and may include long-term or even permanent partial or full disability. It is in essence damage to the worker's means of production: an injury incurred today could decrease one's wages for the day, the week, the calendar year, and beyond.

Ironically, too, it is through the racialized and gendering of performance that the bar is likely to be raised yet again for the workers—this time by those with whom they appear to be competing. Because the white women and people of color in construction must constantly strive to prove themselves the working equals of the white men (regardless of the obstacles placed before them), they too must claim and prove this machismo. Thus, the white men who attempt to work harder, faster, and riskier than is formally allowed, required, or tied to common sense also mandate these behaviors for others. Should the outsiders achieve equality in this regard (mediated, of course, by the extent to which their achievement is acknowledged by the insiders), their success raises the standard of how much white men must do to prove that they are still better than the other workers. By striving to keep these jobs to themselves, then, it appears that white working-class men have begun and are maintaining a cultural and economic cycle that will make these a less and less desirable cluster of occupations.

*Creating Injury for All: Renegotiating the Labor Contract One Worker at a Time.*   It used to be said that in a strong union, an injury to one was an injury to all. In the union under pigness, it might be more accurate to say that the striving of one—the individual's pursuit of social and psychological wages as well as the nonexistent occupational security—is creating an injury to all. By risking their health, safety, and well-being to prove their value as men, as whites, and as workers, the workers sell themselves both individually and as a group at a cheaper and cheaper price. Thus it makes sense to say that in the pursuit of social and psychological wages, as well as the partial economic security that dominance can provide, workers are individually renegotiating the labor contract under which they work.

Their renegotiation matters in a most basic sense because it affects the conditions of all workers by raising expectations and mandating risk. It also matters more broadly, though, as these practices clearly undercut the very foundation of a union for workers. The purpose of a union is to band together and use the strength of all to protect each one. Under the practices of pigness in construction, the opposite occurs. Wages, hours, and working conditions are still *formally negotiated* by the union and the employers, but when the workers ignore the policies and procedures to prove themselves as individuals (and as a gendered and racialized group), they are essentially *contracting independently* with the employers. Contracting independently with employers (to renegotiate considerations of safety or work pace) is not only in violation of all union rules but also erodes the entire premise and raison d'être of the union movement. The workers have just given away the union that has the potential to protect them.

## Pigness and the Future of Labor

Because the performances of pigness are in part a method of proving that one is distinct from and better than the white women and people of color who compete for construction jobs, the white male workers are unable to form political or social alliances with groups that have their same economic station and interests. The opportunity for real working-class conscious-ness, for class-based organizing, and even, ultimately, for economic power is lost. For this outcome to change, white male workers will have to be will-ing to give up the security of the social and psychological wage, as well as their economic control of the industry, in order to build coalitions. The like-lihood of this happening in the near future, however, does not look good.

The workers will also have to change their relations with unions and unionism in order to protect their own interests. And they will have to give up the social and psychological wages of masculinity that define collective action as the work of sissies unable to succeed in the industry on their own. Although their doing so seems unlikely, it is not entirely without hope. In a 2001 article, Karen Beckwith discusses the ways in which officials of the United Mine Workers of America (UMWA) reframed masculinity to allow for nonviolent demonstrations and protest activity. In spite of a highly masculinist culture and a deep tradition of patterned (and often violent) responses to labor-management difficulties, the UMWA, an almost exclu-sively male union, was able to seek out and achieve change. This occurred, of course, not on ideological grounds, but practical ones: when the mem-bers recognized that their practices were both causing them to lose battles and putting the union at risk for massive and unaffordable fines, they changed the way they used and talked about gender. The result makes it clear that gender ideologies, even historically and culturally embedded ones, are subject to change when the strategy is required.

Of course, construction workers are not suspicious of unions simply be-cause of their gender ideologies. Some of the wariness exists because the unions are currently unable to do much of what the workers require and because the unions have not always shown themselves willing to do what they are entrusted to do. Thus changes are needed that are beyond the agency of the individual worker, or at least beyond the actions of the indi-vidual workers and work crews. The transformation of union construction work will require transformations in national unions, labor laws, and employment regulation, along with the transformation of individual and collective worker identities. These are all possible, although they do not appear likely in the near future.

My picture of the union construction industry is undoubtedly bleak, but it is too socially, economically, and politically significant to be ignored. Because the construction industry is roughly one-tenth of the American economy, union construction workers represent a significant proportion of the nation's workforce and an even more significant component of the unionized workforce. Thus their actions matter both on the worksite and off. When union construction workers undercut themselves and their own union, they do far more than simply harm the individuals on their worksite. In a bigger picture, they are undercutting both unionism and workers as a whole.

# Appendix

## THE BENEFIT OF BEING "DUMB AS ROCKS"—AND OTHER METHODOLOGICAL TOPICS

**W**orking construction is tiring. Working construction and attempting simultaneously to observe, record, analyze, and triangulate is exhausting. However, it is also enlightening: taking an ethnographic approach to studying construction might be the only way to truly understand the complex intersections of social, economic, political, and physiological forces that comprise the nature of work. A participatory approach reveals the differences, for example, between the formal policies of safety and harassment and the way that things are actually done on the job. It reveals the bodily experiences of work and suggests ways in which these experiences might themselves be the foundation of social and cultural understandings. It reveals the choices workers make and the resources they have to make their choices.

Attempting both to work and to think about construction is also important, however, for all that it can reveal about the methodology itself and about the constraints, the costs, and the challenges of observing social life while operating within it. Although I have written in greater depth about these issues elsewhere, I review here two of the topics that I consider most important—the logistical challenges to traditional notetaking practices in applied work environments, and the risk to the self posed by hostile environments—before closing with a brief discussion of my coding and data analysis procedures.

# Challenges to Orthodox Research Practices

The processes of observing, reflecting, and taking notes while working construction are complicated by a number of factors of the environment. For example, in contrast to less dynamic settings, one is required in union construction work to be constantly moving and to be visibly "at work." There are also few if any places to which one can retreat (bathrooms on a construction site are often little more than undersized fiberglass boxes of urine and related matter, in which one cannot and should not attempt to collect one's thoughts). Additionally, the processes of work itself are demanding, and I often found that by the time I had completed the day (including an often-lengthy commute), I was too tired to write, if not too tired to think. All these challenges had notable effects on the ways that I was able to record and analyze the data I collected and thus are worthy of review in tandem with the data and explanations themselves.

## Methodological Challenge #1: The Requirement of Constant Movement

One aspect of the construction industry I had not expected (for it is certainly not included in the common stereotype of the construction worker) is that one must be moving at all times. Even if the tasks at hand are fairly stationary or if one is waiting for something to arrive, one is generally expected at least to *look* busy, to appear to be a valuable commodity to the employer. If a foreman walks by when you are standing still without the most legitimate of explanations, you're likely to be "down the road" (laid off) or at least placed high on the layoff list, to be let go when things begin to "slow down."

And these pressures are widely recognized. Both apprentices and long-time journeymen told me stories about foremen who would grab a tool or shovel out of another man's hands just so they themselves could look busy—in contrast, of course, to the poor sucker who stood there empty-handed—when the job superintendent walked around the corner. The pressures obviously exist across positions as much as they do across settings and trades.[1]

These pressures also seemed to be amplified for me as an outsider on the site, given my sense that my standing still—even for a minute—would have provided just one additional piece of "evidence" that "we shouldn't have to hire 'them'!" There were times when I would simply be told to "hold on" by a foreman who was too distracted or unsure to give me an actual assignment, yet I learned quickly that this did not mean I should dally or do little. Thus I had to struggle both to keep moving and to rush back and be available when the foreman wanted me to hand him something, make a cut, or hold a 2×4 in place. Sweeping was always a safe activity where it was justified, such as in a woodshop where sawdust accumulated and was a fire hazard. On a larger or outdoor site, however, sweeping rarely made sense, and thus visible inactivity could be harder to remedy. On one occasion I stacked a pile of 2×4s and then restacked them a few feet away to look as if I were engaged in a fruitful activity. It is important to note that these are "tricks" I learned from other experienced workers. Even a man who had a "gravy" job would want to look busy, since foremen and superintendents were likely to show up, walk by, or drive by at any time.

These incentives to move complicated and actually prevented my ability to write down my thoughts during the day. Not surprisingly, writing anything on a pad of paper is hard to disguise as construction work, especially for an apprentice, and was therefore not a reasonable option for recording observations. This challenge might have been reduced slightly if I had not been an apprentice: supervisors can (but do not often) walk around with a clipboard. Using a clipboard on the job is actually how Herbert Applebaum recorded information for his 1981 ethnography of construction work, since he was working as a supervisor at the time. This also meant, however, that he saw the environment from the position of a supervisor, from the top down. Though that perspective is certainly valid, it does prevent (or "free") the observer from understanding certain aspects of the daily life of workers. As a result, Applebaum's book is really a supervisor's view of the industry as much as my text presents the viewpoint of an apprentice. These different occupations gave us different sets of notes, different generalizations, and different interpretations of the industry.

### Methodological Challenge #2: Jobsite Bathrooms as a Place To Run *From*

A second major methodological challenge to ethnography in the construction industry is the lack of places to which one might reasonably escape for notetaking. At least one well-intentioned faculty member suggested at the beginning of my apprenticeship that I sneak off and take notes in the bathroom, but doing so was wholly impossible. To begin with, the amount of time that one spends in the bathroom (and thus not actively working) is monitored by other workers as well as supervisors. Social sanctions for "excessive time" in the facilities range from private and public comments that one "goes" too often or for too long to a broader sense of evaluation that marks one as a less serious worker or as someone who avoids work. There are companies that allow workers to take one bathroom break on company time and allegedly fine those who use the facilities more than once a day or for a length of time considered "excessive" by the employer. This management attitude was explained to me by other workers on more than one occasion and is also described in studies of other industries.[2]

Additionally, the term "facilities" is often a euphemism for what is available in the construction industry. On many sites, there are no bathrooms but only portable toilets or "Port-a-johns" in which one can barely turn around. And they are not only small but often nauseatingly unhygienic. In winter I struggled to unzip and pull down my coveralls without letting the collar touch the sides of the cubicle or the snow, dirt, and urine on the floor (all in record time, of course). In July and August the sun beats down on the hard plastic exterior of the Port-a-johns, and releases the already pungent scent of the human-waste sludge. In addition to the unpleasant smell (and this is of course a euphemism), the toilet tanks are only infrequently emptied, and the sludge can reach the bottom of the toilet seat—something potentially acceptable *only* if one could remain standing up to use it. Needless to say, construction site bathrooms are certainly *not* someplace one would or could choose to sit a few moments and write, even if one weren't being watched and timed.

### Methodological Challenge #3: Trying To Write or Think When beyond Exhausted and in Pain

Entries in my journal:

> Cracking and bleeding fingers from the cold and the wet....
> ... it is hard to sit down and write notes when I am so tired and *everything* hurts. My hands ache not only from using muscles one might not know one had, also from hitting them repeatedly with hammers, sledgehammers, (etc.) and getting them wedged into tiny places unintended for and unfriendly to hands...
> I am not ony exhausted formmy first day [on this job], but it is also raining ... proudness on teh way home ... all fo the subs are ahhpu saying hi ... [errors reproduced from the original].

Maintaining orthodox notetaking procedures (such as the fifteen pages of notes per contact hour suggested by John Lofland),[3] was difficult not only because of the requirement to stay moving and visible but also because of the way in which the physical demands of the work tended to seep into or block out the remainder of my waking hours. In addition to the eight and a half hours spent on site each day, I often had a commute to and from work. I tried talking notes into a tape recorder during the roughly ninety-minute drive I had to and from a number of sites but found that I was often too distracted to process information effectively—to say nothing about driving safely. On some days it was all I could do to stay awake on the road, and that was virtually impossible once I got home. The hottest and coldest days were the worst, when it seemed as if my physical strength was used primarily to adjust to the dramatic temperatures. The notes I did manage to scrawl in a notebook were often illegible by the time I returned to them, or I found that in my haste I had abbreviated my comments beyond my comprehension.

As Sherryl Kleinman and Martha Copp argue in their monograph *Emotions and Fieldwork*, decisions about the time spent taking and analyzing notes are not governed by right and wrong so much as they are governed by—or at least tied to—theory.[4] It is perhaps more accurate to say that the ways in which research attempts to deal with logistical and time constraints should draw upon the available theory. Care should be taken to balance the degree to which one records and analyzes data. It was in this manner that I made logistical decisions and attempted to meet my methodological goals as best I could within the existing constraints. Although I came nowhere near the minimum notes that Lofland would have ethnographers make, I created a focused yet varied set of notes based on the things that initially seemed interesting or striking to me, as well as the issues that were raised (or highlighted for me) in discussion with others.

### Methodological Challenge #4: Emotional Exhaustion

The fourth methodological challenge involved the exhaustion that came from the challenges of harassment, discrimination, and hostility on top of the challenges of work. There were times when my hands and arms were functional, but I simply could not bear to *think* about my day, my experiences, or my observations. Sometimes I could not face recording what I had experienced. The up-close-and-personal aspects of some events made it more difficult to see that what I experienced was not simply a phenomenon specific to me but was tied to larger processes of power, gender, race, groups, meanings, and structures. It was here that the process of *verbal coding* (a process I discuss below) proved to be both intellectually and perceptually invaluable.

It allowed me to talk about my experiences with those outside of the work-site in a manner that helped me sort "me" from the data.

The most obvious way in which my experiences in construction were made more difficult to dwell upon involves the sexual harassment I have described. As the reader is no doubt by now aware, this was something I experienced on a frequent if not daily basis while employed by the first two of the three companies. Rarely (but not never) of the direct quid-pro-quo nature, this harassment consisted of an almost constant sexualizing of my environment, my work, and of *me*. Regardless of the form, these behaviors had an ongoing and dramatic effect on my experiences in the construction industry. They were sometimes irritating, sometimes nauseating, some-times horrific, and not infrequently humiliating.

To the extent that I was trying to observe the environment, the interac-tions, and the culture objectively or from a distance, then, sexual harass-ment posed a significant methodological and perceptual challenge. And this fact raises quite effectively the question of what an objective or dis-passionate observation of such an environment entails. "Objective" and "dispassionate" are often treated as synonyms. Can they be? Should they be? These are questions essential to the boundary maintenance of ethnog-raphy; the answers should reveal whether it is, for example, possible for a woman to observe objectively an environment that is hostile to women. If a woman can't, can a man? Can a man (or woman) who does observe such environments dispassionately really have any meaningful sense of the experience itself? The answers to these questions determine the limits of social science: if persons are not able to observe "objectively" any envi-ronments hostile to them as individuals or members of a group, it seems unlikely that we will we gain firsthand knowledge and experiential knowl-edge of the nature and effects of hostility, of discrimination, of aggression, and of violence—topics essential, of course, to an understanding of social life. Thus these questions are essential, too, to the understandings of social research. To ask and attempt to answer them is to engage some of the most fundamental assumptions of power relations between the observer and the observed, as well as the role of power in defining objectivity and knowl-edge. Attempting to work in and think about the construction industry provides at least some data with which to approach these issues.

## Hostile Environments and the Loss of the Self

Another important issue raised by fieldwork in construction is the risk that hostile environments pose to the physical and emotional self of the researcher. Although one might assume that a research identity could provide me with some distance from the workplace and thus some additional emotional armor, it did so in a manner that proved over time to be insufficient. Simultaneously, of course, my attempts to observe, record, evaluate, and analyze the environment meant that I could rarely, if ever, walk away from my work. Incidents that might have been only aggravating or insulting under different circumstances would roll around in my head, posing questions about their larger social significance and the myriad of potential interpretations. As a result, of course, all sorts of unpleasantries claimed my attention during times when I might otherwise have been able to disconnect, rejuvenate, and recover.

Because I was trying to observe the environment in the most neutral way possible, I tried to influence it as little as possible, to blend in, to go with the flow. On one hand, this was good methodological practice. I attempted to observe the situation in itself and have as little impact as possible on the men and their interactions with each other. I was observing—or so I thought—construction in itself, and not construction with Kris Paap in it. On one hand, my attempts at doing so were admirable. On the other hand, they were folly. I was never able to see the environment without me in it (an obvious logistical issue), but the fact that my presence appears to have changed it does serve to reveal the forces of gender and of race that had been largely taken for granted by some of the social scientists who had written about construction in the past. So there was real intellectual value in what I had been led to fear.

My attempt to lie low and not affect the landscape was also foolish because of its ultimate effects on me. It meant that in addition to trying to navigate a tremendously challenging social environment, I was also trying to evaluate my own behaviors against potentially unrealistic standards of "objectivity." I not only had to struggle with what I believe is an unwinnable battle of public gendering and sexualization (what I have earlier called my job-in-a-job of representing the Anti-Masculinity), but was also attempting to do so in a manner that created no waves. I cannot remember how this initially made sense to me.

I put these challenges forth as a danger of fieldwork in hostile settings because they ultimately led to the erasure of my boundaries of self-protection and, in a sense, to a loss of my self. This occurred in part through my attempts to conform to what R. W. Connell and Mike Donaldson have described as the working-class rules that see the *consumption of the body through work* as a proof of desirable masculinity. These were pressures that I, as someone who needed to be seen as equal to men, also needed to conform to. Additionally, of course, my boundaries were constrained and encroached upon by common occurrences of harassment and the social rules that prohibited my complaining about or preventing them.

As I have argued earlier in the text, learning how to cope with sexualized interactions is one of the primary social challenges for women entering the construction industry. Part of this coping involves learning where to draw the line: learning how to figure out and make clear what is okay, what is intolerable, and what is funny. The placement of the line, however, like the categories in which women are placed, can and does shift over time. Thus for many women, myself included, these lines must be drawn and drawn again. By the time I left construction, I found that I had moved far beyond what I ideologically or theoretically supported. Having entered the industry as a woman who did not want to be called "girl" or to hear jokes about women, jokes about gays and lesbians, or racial and ethnic slurs, I found that over time—and on the advice of Insiders—I slid into the "get-by" mode, and learned to "go along to get along." In short, then, I learned (or chose) to ignore as much as I could. I ignored absolutely as much as I could. And perhaps then some.

By the time I left construction, I no longer drew the line at being touched; I drew the line at being touched *only if I could not ignore it*. It is a position that is hard to defend when talking to others, but it was shaped by the fact that in my experience complaints had done little to improve the situation; I found that the men's behaviors remained roughly the same or, if anything, worsened after it became clear that no action would be taken on my complaints; instead, I (or any other woman) would be labeled as "troublemaker" or "looking for a lawsuit" (categories and conditions discussed in chapters 2 and 3).

## My Strategic Yet Dangerous Policy for Responding to Jobsite Trouble

My overall "policy" for handling sexualized interactions came to include roughly two points. First, occurrences that were public and addressed directly to me had to be handled immediately. These did not by then include jokes about women in general, or about the men's wives or girlfriends, or even about other women on the site. Whether verbal or physical, public occurrences directed at me (to me or about me) were clearly challenges to my position within the hierarchy and a statement about my right to be on the job. The few times I declined to follow this rule of immediacy, in the hope that what was ignored would go away, it was enforced by male allies who took me to task for not attempting to put the perpetrator in his place. These allies were men who were friendly and even somewhat protective, but they neither stood up for me nor condoned my desire simply to step outside of the interaction. Although their opinion was generally beneficial insofar as it effectively communicated the cultural rules to me, it also kept me locked in the "bitch-dyke-whore" cycle illustrated in chapter 3.

The second and undoubtedly more disturbing point of my policy involved my increasing recognition of "viable exceptions" to my first rule, meaning that I would on occasion allow myself *not* to address the situation—generally when I felt as if I could not handle the reality behind it. For example, I chose to ignore a number of things on a job where I believed I was clearly at risk of being labeled as "looking for a lawsuit" (again) or for long-term or permanent layoff.

It was on this job that Harry the foreman began to give me directions for the day by standing very close to me and placing his hand on my lower back, meaning on my lower, *lower* back. Rather than addressing his hand directly or overtly, I would sometimes rotate my body away from him as I leaned my head in, hoping to look as if I was just getting my ear closer to him in order to hear him better. At other times I would simply shift my body away from him as I nodded in response, trying to look "deep in thought." As I realized when I looked back after leaving the industry, I had moved from a position of not being called "girl" to one of letting people put their hands on my backside repeatedly, provided I could come up with some semiplausible way of ignoring it.

In my own defense, I did not ignore such events because I was lazy; I ignored them because I felt it was truly the best—and perhaps the only—option. Harry was in an ideal position to do what he did: he knew I didn't like it; I knew he knew; and we both knew that I could do little to nothing about it. I knew it was clear to him that wasn't welcome because, since he was next in my chain of command, he was the person with whom I had discussed ways to get another journey-level worker to stop touching me, to get the laborers' foreman to stop making comments about my breasts, and so on.

It may seem ridiculous that I shared such concerns with Harry, since he was often a part of the problem. But it is essential to realize that he was always a *potential ally*, sometimes my only potential ally, even as much as he was a potential harasser or a potential humiliator. By letting him know when I had difficulty, I could sometimes earn a measure of protection or distance from the individual in question, particularly someone Harry was not friendly with. It also allowed Harry to assume a level of patronage with me, however paternal, that could provide some protection—or at least the potential that he would be more protective than aggressive in his relations with me. If this, too, seems a silly and disingenuous way to negotiate the culture, I would suggest that such comments are easily made by persons outside the industry. Out on the jobsite, a physical space well insulated from external social worlds, getting by was something that in my experience was to be accomplished and not taken for granted.

I knew then that Harry's placing his hand on my backside was a strategic action, for he could count on my being unable to react in a meaningfully defensive way. My physical and mental contortions to ignore his actions were also strategic: I counted on his not having the clout or courage to push the issue further. I assumed that my ignoring his hand meant that he couldn't denounce me publicly as looking for a lawsuit and that he was also unlikely to risk a more aggressive or patterned invasion that might actually mark him as causing trouble for the company.

### The Costs of Decreasing Boundaries: Letting Myself Go to Get Along

As much as I can explain the strategic ways in which Harry and I might have thought about his ability to touch my backside at work, there is a voice in my head that tells me this explanation is inadequate. On one level, of course, it is sufficient: he did what he could, and I did what I could—which in this situation was fairly close to nothing. But this explanation suggests that the interaction ended when I rotated my body away beyond his reach. In reality, of course, his hand left a psychological handprint similar to the mark of a branding iron or of a particularly aggressive slap. Regardless of what we negotiated strategically, the reality was that I had become a woman whose co-workers could touch. They could talk publicly about my body parts, joke about my sex life, and make references to vulnerable and vulgar situations. I was, without any doubt, a second-class citizen with unsubstantial personal boundaries.

Though one might suggest that a stronger self-concept would have allowed me to leave all of this at the worksite gate, if so, then sexual and racial harassments in general could be seen as simple psychological problems rather than social or structural ones. Societal-level data might reveal that harassment and discrimination are caused by inferiority (a claim rejected vociferously and convincingly by Frantz Fanon in 1967) rather than the reverse. But this is not what the data suggest. Instead, contemporary evidence suggests that this sort of discrimination and erosion of the social self can have real and even potentially fatal physical effects.[5] Thus the problems of harassment and discrimination go far beyond what might be construed as my own personal weakness; they highlight instead the importance of utilizing ethnographic methods to reveal the nature and lived effects of various social forms of inequality. This is to say not that the study of experienced inequality must use ethnographic methods, but that it must be informed by an ethnographic approach.

## Power and Informed Consent

One of the first questions that I am asked when talking about my experiences in construction is whether the men with whom I worked knew that I was observing them in some formal sense—that is, beyond the most basic way in which these men were clearly watching and analyzing me. This question needs a variety of answers. First, I have to be clear that no, they did not, because I wasn't. I entered the construction industry for several reasons, two of which were to find a decent job that offered a bulk of its own training and to get out of graduate school and academics. For a large part of the time during which I was working as an apprentice, I was doing just that—working as an apprentice.

I kept a journal during this time, which I had done since my early adolescence as a way of figuring out the world around me and the nature of my presence in it. I observed and wrote about my co-workers to document my own experiences. My thoughts were at that time largely about *me,* about my thoughts and experiences. I also wrote about my experiences in a secondary sort of way, building on my writings about working-class women's reluctance to take on male-dominated work. To whatever extent I regarded these thoughts as having any generalizability, my focus was on the experiences of women and not men in construction. Men were initially on my sociological or psychological radar, then, only as agents and actors-upon, rather than subjective beings caught up in their own sorts of social, political, and economic turmoil.

As I mention in the text, it took me a bit of time to recognize the central contradiction in my social experiences: that even the things that seemed to be most personally about me (comments about my "tits," suggestions that I get lubed up with K-Y for the fun of my co-workers) had little to do with me-as-me; they were rather about me-as-category, as a representative of "woman" or "white woman" in a way that was socially meaningful for the identities of those around me. The public comments about my body, my behavior, and my intentions at work really had nothing to do with Kris Paap per se, or even Kris Paap as a performance. Instead, I came to realize, my presence simply altered the environment in a manner that made the contestations between the groups of men more salient and more significant. This is a point that a number of scholars have made about male-dominated environments into which women have entered.[6]

Thus, the men did *not* know that I was writing about them or even particularly thinking about them, because I was not. Over time, as I realized that my experiences were actually significant in their revelations about *men,* I also found that my commitments, for a variety of reasons, began to shift away from pursuing a lifetime career in construction and toward at least considering a return to academe. Once having decided that I was in fact writing about men created a different sort of relation to the persons with whom I was working—although it is neither as straightforward or as simple as much contemporary scholarship on social research might suggest. In fact, as I have written elsewhere, much of what I saw and experienced suggests the need for at least partially covert ethnographic projects, particularly in the realms of work, exploitation, and violence.

In any case, I did attempt to tell my co-workers, albeit selectively, that I was also working on my Ph.D. I even stated specifically that it had "something to do with construction." Oddly enough—especially given the concerns one might have anticipated from male co-workers—my comments were shrugged off and dismissed. In fact, on the job with Concrete, Inc., I prefaced my comments with a significant amount of explanation about the hierarchies of degrees so that my foreman would be clear that I was working on a doctoral rather than an associate degree level. In spite of all this, his only comment to me was simply "Well, everyone here thinks you're dumb as rocks." Needless to say, I did not offer to outline the greater particulars of my emergent ideas.

Ironically, of course, this was an environment (particularly with Concrete, Inc.) where I was publicly constructed as "very threatening" because I had previously made the "mistake" of trying to object to what was essentially quid pro quo harassment (among other things). And yet my declaration to my foreman—a man who reported directly to the superintendent of the site—that I was working on formal academic research concerning construction, something that I assumed would be *more* threatening than my simple existence as an apprentice, was disregarded.

Of course, several explanations for this are possible. First, as the foreman suggests, it is possible that some of the men with whom I worked may have seen me as globally incompetent because of my lesser experience in construction. Second, it might be that my academic work allowed them to discount me further as a worker and to assume that I was there only temporarily at best. Third, perhaps they simply didn't believe me. There is a feature of construction culture that I have come to call the "liar's effect," in which honesty with one's peers is greatly subordinated to the fast and cost-effective production of built objects. As a result, "working on my Ph.D." may have been roughly equated with claims made by my co-workers that they had "dry-humped" the boss's wife at the Christmas party, made a million dollars in side work during the previous year, or wrestled with a wild bear discovered accidentally in the woods (all versions of claims I heard). Because honesty was not necessary or highly valued, untruths ran rampant, and "bullshitting" at lunch or at coffee was often an art in itself.

Regardless of the reason for this apparent lack of concern, I cannot help but reflect on the various ironies in these relations. On one hand, the ongoing rejection of my identity as a "real" construction worker by the male construction workers certainly played a role in my eventually deciding to leave the industry prior to completing my apprenticeship. Yet it was the subsequent rejection of my researcher identity (also by the male construction workers) that gave me the ongoing access to the field and allowed me to remain and observe what I did. Remaining in the field as a semiprofessional observer has proved to be valuable not only for the information it provides about construction but also for the data it provides about qualitative research methods and data analysis.

## Coding and Data Analysis

As noted in the foregoing discussions of the methodological challenges of this project, the constraints of the worksites had significant effects upon the ways that I could gather, review, analyze, and write about the many patterns I observed. Rather than reviewing all the technical details of the project, I will simply touch on some key pressures and the necessary adaptations upon which I relied in conducting and completing this work.

### Initial Coding and Theoretical Sampling

The methods used for the initial processing and interpreting the data include the techniques of "Grounded Theory" laid out by Anselm Strauss and Juliet Corbin, meaning that I began interpreting and questioning the data at the same time that I was collecting them.[7] That is, as soon as I began considering my experiences as potential data, I started to question the meaning and the depth of what I was seeing and experiencing. As a result, my fieldnotes and analytic memos were often tightly interwoven.

My use and understanding of Grounded Theory as described by Strauss and others is modified in part by the work of Robert Emerson, Rachel Fretz and Linda Shaw, Harry Wolcott, and Robert Weiss, who stress the connection of the theoretical perspective with the data.[8] In contrast to Strauss's earliest formulations, Emerson and others argue that the theory emerges not purely and simply from the data but rather from the theoretical perspective with which the researcher enters the researched environment and therefore frames the data initially. When I entered, I did so with concerns about power and control, gender and race, privilege and discrimination. Even though my assumptions about who was powerful, who was "doing gender,"[9] and who was experiencing privilege became more and more complex the more I observed, what I was able to see was certainly shaped by the theories with which I began. Thus my practices certainly also follow the maxim of Michael Burawoy to use the available data to modify theory once its limits have become clear, and once observations have produced events and understandings that go beyond the ability of current theory to explain.[10]

This ongoing analysis of the data was important for two logistical and methodological reasons. First, the process shaped my *theoretical sampling*, meaning that it helped me identify the social events and activities to which I should most closely attend.[11] Because of the constraints of the worksite, this ability to focus was essential.

A second reason for the importance of this analysis was that it helped balance the perspective of an observer who had not simply *gone native* but whose presence on the site was premised on the condition of *being native*. Because I needed to survive as a worker, I found myself struggling to process the environment on two levels (and often in two contradictory manners): I needed not only to understand and react to events in a way that allowed me to negotiate the often highly contested terrain in my role as a worker (that is, as a white female carpenter's apprentice) but also to understand the events in a sense somewhat detached from my own experience, as an observer.

## Verbal Coding as a Response to Methodological and Logistical Constraints

It is important to emphasize that much of my initial coding took place verbally and was the product of dyadic and larger-group discussions. Verbal coding not only gave me the breadth and insight of viewpoints and literatures beyond my own contemporary knowledge and grasp but also helped me to identify what I was sometimes too close to recognize on my own. I ran my ideas by other people whenever and wherever possible, hashing them out not only with faculty advisers and graduate students but also with union workers in other trades, individuals in my Quaker social circles, and a construction supervisor and his spouse who lived next door to me during much of my work on this project and who have remained close personal friends. Many of these individuals repeatedly served as a kind ear and a sounding board for my ideas, questions, and interpretations. These interactions allowed me to supplement and verify what might otherwise have been simply a highly personalized set of observations (a possibility that remained a central concern throughout the project). The verbal coding both permitted and required a form of in situ data reduction, which allowed me to focus my attentions on the aspects of work and social life that appeared meaningful or problematic and to give less of my time to matters that appeared taken-for-granted, and reasonably so. Though the verbal coding might suggest that the method lacks the "purity" of data and theorizing suggested by Grounded Theory's tabula-rasa approach, verbal coding did provide the progressive focusing that is central to systematic observations across settings.

## Data Analysis

Because of the verbal nature of much of my data processing (as well as the built-in constraints to taking excessive notes, discussed below), I ultimately found that I did not need to utilize the qualitative analysis software that I had acquired for this purpose. Through the ongoing nature of the coding, memos, and analysis I found that the "block and copy" function of my word processor was sufficient for the analysis, organization, and later writing of the individual chapters.

# NOTES

## Introduction

1. Herbert A. Applebaum, *Royal Blue: The Culture of Construction Workers*, Case Studies in Cultural Anthropology (New York: Holt, Rienhart and Winston, 1981); Jeffrey W. Riemer, *Hard Hats: The Work World of Construction Workers* (Beverly Hills, CA: Sage, 1979); Marc L. Silver, *Under Construction: Work and Alienation in the Building Trades*, SUNY Series in the Sociology of Work (Albany: State University of New York Press, 1986).

2. On women in the trades, see Trudi C. Ferguson and Madeline Sharples, *Blue Collar Women: Trailblazing Women Take On Men-Only Jobs* (Liberty Corner, NJ: New Horizon, 1994); Molly Martin, ed., *Hard Hatted Women: Stories of Struggle and Success in the Trades* (Seattle, WA: Seal, 1988); Jean Reith Schroedel, *Alone in a Crowd: Women in the Trades Tell Their Stories* (Philadelphia: Temple University Press, 1985). Novels and autobiographical accounts include Mike Cherry, *On High Steel: The Education of an Ironworker* (New York: Quadrangle/New York Times Book Company, 1974); Dagoberto Gilb, *The Magic of Blood* (New York: Grove, 1994); Thomas Kelly, *Payback* (New York: Knopf, 1997).

3. Paul A. Brinker, "Violence by U.S. Labor Unions," *Journal of Labor Research* 6, no. 4 (1985): 417–27; James A. Craft, "Union Violence: A Review and Critical Discussion," *Journal of Labor Research* 22, no. 3 (2001): 679–88; Armand J. Thieblot Jr. and Thomas R. Haggard, *Union Violence: The Record and the Response by Courts, Legislatures, and the NLRB*, Labor Relations and Public Policy Series No. 25. (Philadelphia: Industrial Research Institute, Wharton School, 1983).

4. On white-collar crime and violence, see Gilbert Geis, Robert Meier, and Laurence M. Salinger, *White-Collar Crime: Classic and Contemporary Views* (New York: Free Press, 1995); Stephen H. Norwood, *Strikebreaking and Intimidation: Mercenaries and Masculinity in 20th Century America* (Chapel Hill: University of North Carolina Press, 2002); Jeffrey Reiman, *The Rich Get Richer and the Poor Get Prison: Ideology, Class, and Criminal Justice* (Boston: Allyn and Bacon, 1998).

5. Similar language and interactions are described in D. W. Livingstone and Meg Luxton, "Gender Consciousness at Work: Modification of the Male Breadwinner Norm among Steelworkers and Their Spouses," *Canadian Review of Sociology and Anthropology* 26, no. 2 (May 1989): 240–75.

6. Although there are certainly overlapping interests in terms of the ability of companies to stay afloat (that is, to be economically successful and survive), how each party ap-

proaches the employment transaction is dramatically distinct. As I demonstrate later, the interests of workers and companies diverge in significant ways that tend to be downplayed or ignored.

7. See, e.g., Lillian B. Rubin, *Families on the Fault Line: America's Working Class Speaks about the Family, the Economy, Race, and Ethnicity* (New York: Harper/Perennial, 1994).

8. A hallmark of this argument is seen in David R. Roediger, *The Wages of Whiteness: Race and the Making of the American Working Class* (1991; repr., New York: Verso, 1999).

9. This argument has also been used successfully in other male-dominated industries. See, e.g., Cynthia Cockburn, *Brothers: Male Dominance and Technological Change* (1983; repr., Concord, MA: Pluto, 1991); Livingstone and Luxton, "Gender Consciousness"; Leela Fernandes, "Beyond Public Spaces and Private Spheres: Gender, Family, and Working-Class Politics in India," *Feminist Studies* 23, no. 3 (Fall 1997): 525–47; and Rosanna Hertz, "Guarding against Women? Responses of Military Men and Their Wives to Gender Integration," *Journal of Contemporary Ethnography* 25, no. 2 (July 1996): 251–84.

10. Michael Burawoy, *Manufacturing Consent: Changes in the Labor Process under Monopoly Capitalism* (Chicago: University of Chicago Press, 1979).

11. Candace West and Sarah Fenstermaker, "Doing Difference," *Gender and Society* 9, no. 1 (1995): 8–37; Candace West and Don Zimmerman, "Doing Gender," *Gender and Society* 1 (1987): 125–51.

12. Burawoy, *Manufacturing Consent*.

13. One formal articulation of this work is Kirsten (Kris) Paap, "Working-Class Women, Occupational Realism, and Occupational Choice: Beliefs and Knowledge of Working-class Women at First Workforce Entrance" (paper presented at American Sociological Association annual meetings, 1995, Washington, DC).

14. Vivian Price, "Race, Affirmative Action, and Women's Employment in US Highway Construction," *Feminist Economics* 8, no. 2 (2002): 87–113.

15. See, among many others, Herbert Hill, "No End of Pledges: Continuing Discrimination in the Construction Unions," *Commonweal*, March 15, 1968: 709–12; Hill, "Evading the Law: Apprenticeship Outreach and Hometown Plans in the Construction Industry," *Civil Rights Digest*, Summer 1974; Hill, *Labor Union Control of Job Training: A Critical Analysis of Apprenticeship Outreach Programs and the Hometown Plans*, Occasional Paper (Washington D.C.: Institute for Urban Affairs and Research, Howard University 1974); Hill, *Black Labor and the American Legal System*, (1977; repr., Madison: University of Wisconsin Press, 1985); Jacqueline Jones, *American Work: Four Centuries of Black and White Labor* (New York: Norton, 1998); and Roediger, *Wages of Whiteness*.

16. Burawoy, *Manufacturing Consent*.

17. For example, John Lofland is quoted in Maurice Punch, *The Politics and Ethics of Fieldwork*, Qualitative Research Methods Series, vol. 3. (Thousand Oaks, CA: Sage, 1986), 27.

18. Applebaum, *Royal Blue*.

19. I am grateful to I. J. Cakrane of Washington Group International for pointing this out in a larger discussion of skill shortages, May 2005.

20. Herbert Hill (labor and race scholar), in discussion with the author, Spring 1999.

21. Center to Protect Workers' Rights, informal presentation at the May 2005 meeting of the Construction Economics Research Network, Silver Spring, MD.

22. Herman Benson, for example, argues that workers in some union jurisdictions can "criticize the president [of the U.S.], but not the business agent" for fear of being blacklisted (personal communication, Spring 2005). Although unions do not have the structural ability to actually put a worker to work (this is what employers do), the hiring hall procedures make it possible for unions to keep individuals on the bench and *out* of work. Informal practices, of course, are also likely to have difficult-to-measure effects on who gets work and how they get it. For more information on—and contradictory descriptions of—this process, see chapter 1; see also Cherry, *On High Steel*; Silver, *Under Construction*; and Herman Benson, *Rebels, Reformers, and Racketeers: How Insurgents Transformed the Labor Movement* (New York: Authorhouse, 2004).

23. Center to Protect Workers' Rights, *The Construction Chart Book: The U.S. Construction Industry and Its Workers* (Washington, DC: Center to Protect Workers' Rights, 1998).

24. I am grateful to Michele Ochsner at the Occupational and Training Education Consortium (OTEC) in the School of Management and Labor Relations at Rutgers University for this insight.

25. The concept of the public and psychological wage is one expressed first by W. E. B. Du Bois and later by David Roediger to discuss the social wages gained by whites who intentionally distanced themselves from and defined themselves as not "black." See W. E. B. Du Bois, *Black Reconstruction in America, 1860–1880*, Studies in American Negro Life (1935; repr., New York: Atheneum/Macmillan, 1962); and Roediger, *Wages of Whiteness*. I use this concept in the same way here and also extend it to include a public and psychological wage of masculinity.

26. Livingstone and Luxton, "Gender Consciousness," 253.

27. Sharon R. Bird, "Welcome to the Men's Club: Homosociality and the Maintenance of Hegemonic Masculinity," *Gender and Society* 10, no. 2 (April 1996): 120–32.

28. Cynthia Fuchs Epstein, "Tinkerbells and Pinups: The Construction and Reconstruction of Gender Boundaries at Work," in *Cultivating Differences: Symbolic Boundaries and the Making of Inequality*, ed. Michèle Lamont and Marcel Fournier, 232–56 (Chicago, IL: Chicago University Press, 1992).

29. Du Bois, *Black Reconstruction*; Roediger, *Wages of Whiteness*; and Eduardo Bonilla-Silva, *Racism without Racists: Color-Blind Racism and the Persistence of Racial Inequality in the United States* (Lanham, MD: Rowman and Littlefield, 2003).

30. In brief, the argument is that the North American usage removes from the term the sense of masculine responsibility, commitment, and pride that is present in Central and South American uses. In North America, "macho" tends to be callous and unfeeling, insensitive to the needs and emotions of the self as well as of the other. For more information, see, e.g., Rose Del Castillo Guilbault, "Americanization Is Tough on Macho," in *American Voices*, ed. Dolores La Guardia and Hans Guth (Mountain View, CA: Mayfield, 1993).

31. Rosabeth Moss Kanter, *Men and Women of the Corporation* (1977; repr., New York: Basic Books, 1993); Jennifer L. Pierce, *Gender Trials: Emotional Lives in Contemporary Law Firms* (Berkeley: University of California Press, 1995); Robin Leidner, *Fast Food, Fast Talk: Service Work and the Routinization of Everyday Life* (Berkeley: University of California Press, 1993); Judith Hicks Stiehm, *Arms and the Enlisted Woman* (Philadelphia: Temple University Press, 1989); and Cockburn, *Brothers*.

## Political and Economic Relations

1. E. E. LeMasters, *Blue-Collar Aristocrats: Life Styles at a Working-Class Tavern* (Madison: University of Wisconsin Press, 1975).

2. Riemer, *Hard Hats*.

3. Applebaum, *Royal Blue*.

4. Riemer, *Hard Hats*, 51.

5. Benson, *Rebels, Reformers, and Racketeers*.

6. Seymour M. Lipset and Ivan Katchanovski, "The Future of Private Sector Labor Unions in the U.S.," *Journal of Labor Research* 22, no. 2 (2001): 229–44.

7. United States Department of Labor, *Bureau of Labor Statistics News: Median Weekly Earnings of Full-Time Wage and Salary Workers by Union Affiliation, Occupation, and Industry* (Washington, DC, 2002). http://www.bls.gov/news.release/union2.to4.htm.

8. See, e.g., Nicole Dedobbeleer, Françoise Champagne, and Pearl German, "Safety Performance among Union and Nonunion Workers in the Construction Industry," *Journal of Occupational Medicine* 32, no. 11 (1990): 1099–1103.

9. Center to Protect Workers' Rights, *Construction Chart Book*; David B. Oppedahl, "Understanding the (Relative) Fall and Rise of Construction Wages," *Chicago Fed Letter*, 2002,

155, http://www.frbchi.org; United States Department of Labor, *Bureau of Labor Statistics Data: National Employment, Hours, and Earnings* (Washington, DC, 2002), http://data.bls.gov/servlit/.

10. See, e.g., Eileen Appelbaum, Annette Bernhardt, and Richard J. Murnane, eds., *Low-Wage America: How Employers Are Reshaping Opportunity in the Workplace* (New York: Russell Sage Foundation, 2003).

11. It should be noted that this was actually the *cancellation of an earlier reduction* in apprentice wages, not an increase per se. The starting wage scale for apprentices had been dropped from 60 percent to 40 percent; what I describe here was therefore a simple reversion to the earlier position.

12. See, e.g., Michael Schuster and Susan Rhodes, "The Impact of Overtime Work on Industrial Accident Rates," *Industrial Relations* 24, no. 2 (1985): 234–46; Evan E. Anderson and Rogene A. Buchholz, "Economic Instability and Occupational Injuries: The Impact of Overtime Hours and Turnover Rates," *Labor Studies Journal* 13, no. 4 (1988): 33–49.

13. Linda M. Goldenhar, Steven Hecker, Susan Moir, and John Rosecrance, "Developing a Model for Overtime in Construction: Not Too Much, Not Too Little, Just Right," *Journal of Safety Research* 34 (2003): 215–26; Steven Kinn, Sadik A. Khuder, Michael S. Bisesi, and Sandra Woolley, "Evaluation of Safety Orientation and Training Programs for Reducing Injuries in the Plumbing and Pipefitting Industry," *Journal of Occupational and Environmental Medicine* 42, no. 12 (2000): 1142–47; Center to Protect Workers' Rights, *Construction Chart Book*, 1998.

14. Riemer, *Hard Hats*, 163–66.

15. Marc L. Silver, "The Structure of Craft Work: The Construction Industry," in *The Varieties of Work*, ed. Phyliss Stewart and Muriel Cantor, 235–52 (Beverly Hills, CA: Sage, 1982); Silver, *Under Construction*. See also Bob Reckman, "Carpentry: The Craft and Trade," in *Case Studies on the Labor Process*, ed. Andrew Zimbalist, 73–102 (New York: Monthly Review Press, 1979).

16. It is important to note here that Benson (*Rebels, Reformers, and Racketeers*, esp. chap. 10) offers a very different vision of the union's inability to protect the average worker from arbitrary firing and other inequities. Although he argues, as I do, that structural insecurity is at the heart of many of the industry's larger labor problems, his work also ties this issue to problems of union corruption, collusion with employers, and mafia connections in many areas. As an apprentice, I was aware of rumors of collusion between union business agents and the employers' association, but I was not in a position to observe or verify them. And, although I would certainly argue that the union reps (with individual variation) seemed to be somewhat "in the pocket" of the contractors, it is impossible for me to say what part of this was simply a good working relationship; what part was born out of necessity, given the larger structural weaknesses of the union; and what part might actually have been corruption or collusion.

17. Marc Linder and Ingrid Nygaard, *Void Where Prohibited: Rest Breaks and the Right to Urinate on Company Time* (Ithaca, NY: ILR Press, 1998); Center to Protect Workers' Rights, *Patterns of Deaths among Construction Workers: California, 1979–81,* (Washington, DC: Center to Protect Workers' Rights, 1993).

## Social Relations of Production

1. This is an argument that David Roediger also makes about the history of the white labor movement; see his *Wages of Whiteness*.

2. See ibid. for a similar historical argument.

3. See, e.g., Hill, *Black Labor*; Martin, *Hard Hatted Women*; Stanley Aronowitz, *False Promises: The Shaping of American Class Consciousness* (Durham, NC: Duke University Press, 1992); Ferguson and Sharples, *Blue Collar Women*; Susan Eisenberg, *Pioneering: Poems from the Construction Site* (Ithaca, NY: ILR Press, 1998); Susan Eisenberg, *We'll Call You If We Need*

*You: Experiences of Women Working Construction* (Ithaca, NY: ILR Press, 1998); Roediger, *Wages of Whiteness;* and Deirdre A. Royster, *Race and the Invisible Hand: How White Networks Exclude Black Men from Blue-Collar Jobs,* (Berkeley: University of California Press, 2003).

4. See, e.g., Riemer, *Hard Hats;* Applebaum, *Royal Blue;* Silver, *Under Construction;* and Royster, *Race and the Invisible Hand.*

5. In fact, I was aware of many journey-level workers and apprentices who had switched jobs through contacts and informal information, but I rarely if ever heard of workers actually going through the union to get their work. It may be, of course, either that this pattern occurred frequently but was not considered noteworthy (and thus was not discussed during lunch and coffee breaks), or that the use of the union to find work was considered a stigmatizing form of individual weakness, given the desirability of getting on steady with a company. In any case, it is clear that the formal practices designed to equalize the field were not in fact the only path to a job.

6. Similar findings are reported in Price, "Race, Affirmative Action, and Women's Employment."

7. Of course, this in itself could hardly be construed as unusual for the construction industry. During my time in the industry, I met only one man who had a reputation for liking women (in a nonsexual way), and it didn't seem to serve him well with his co-workers or to make his own identity negotiation easier.

8. Although one might argue that the remark about carrying too much should qualify as a fourth example, it was really a very gendered comment and not one likely to be made to a male apprentice, who instead would probably be labeled a "hotdog" and given the appropriate proportions of esteem and competitive derision.

9. Arlie Russell Hochschild, *The Managed Heart: Commercialization of Human Feeling* (Berkeley, CA: University of California Press, 1983).

10. Pierce, *Gender Trials,* 177 (original emphasis).

11. Du Bois, *Black Reconstruction,* 700; Roediger, *Wages of Whiteness,* 12, passim.

12. Bonilla-Silva, *Racism without Racists.*

13. See, e.g., Elizabeth Janeway, *Between Myth and Morning: Women Awakening* (New York: William Morrow, 1974).

14. Similar observations are made in a more humorous fashion in Paul Fussell's disturbingly funny monograph *Class: A Guide through the American Status System* (1989; repr., New York: Simon and Schuster, 1992).

## "A Bitch, a Dyke, or a Whore"

1. See, e.g., James R. Kluegel and Eliot R. Smith, *Beliefs about Inequality: Americans' Views of What Is and What Ought to Be* (New York: Aldine De Gruyter, 1986).

2. Erving Goffman, *The Presentation of Self in Everday Life* (New York: Anchor/Doubleday, 1959).

3. Bonilla-Silva, *Racism without Racists.*

4. Ann Swidler, "Culture in Action: Symbols and Strategies," *American Sociological Review* 51 (1986): 273–86.

5. Kluegel and Smith, *Beliefs about Inequality,* chap.1.

6. Kanter, *Men and Women of the Corporation.*

7. For a related argument about the taxicab industry, see Elizabeth A. Hoffmann, "Selective Sexual Harassment: Differential Treatment of Similar Groups of Women," *Journal of Law and Human Behavior* 28, no. 1 (2004): 29–45.

8. Leora Tanenbaum, *Slut! Growing Up Female with a Bad Reputation* (New York: Seven Stories, 1999).

9. This label can also be used to dismiss and alienate people of color, since "looking for a lawsuit" implies resistance to sex/gender discrimination, sexual harassment, or racial discrimination; I discuss this below.

10. Richard Korman et al., "The Jokes Aren't Very Funny Anymore," *Engineering News Report*, September 7, 1998, 26 (emphasis added).

11. Jerry A. Jacobs, *Revolving Doors: Sex Segregation and Women's Careers* (Stanford: Stanford University Press, 1989).

12. Korman et al. "Jokes Aren't Very Funny," 26.

13. Kanter, *Men and Women of the Corporation.*

14. This distinction may be obscured somewhat by the fact that Kanter herself has used the term "number" to refer to the proportion of a minority population within a larger organization (ibid., chap. 8).

15. For a more recent review of race-based hiring practices in the industry, please see Royster, *Race and the Invisible Hand.*

16. Studs Terkel, *Working* (New York: New Press, 1974, xlv–xlix); LeMasters, *Blue-Collar Aristocrats.*

17. Keiko Nakao and Judith Treas, "Revised Prestige Scores for All Occupations," National Opinion Research Center, Chicago, 1990, quoted in Dennis Gilbert and Joseph A. Kahl, *The American Class Structure: A New Synthesis*, 4th ed. (Belmont, CA: Wadsworth, 1993).

18. For more information on the contrast between these images and the current realities of the industry, please see chapter 1.

19. See, among many others, Hill, "No End of Pledges"; Hill, "Evading the Law"; Hill, *Labor Union Control of Job Training;* Hill, *Black Labor;* Eisenberg, *Pioneering;* Eisenberg, *We'll Call You;* and Jacqueline Jones, *American Work.*

20. This interpretation follows the logic of Kanter, *Men and Women of the Corporation,* though that wasn't recognized by the men.

21. Dirk Johnson, "Facing Shortage, Builders and Labor Court Workers," *New York Times,* March 13, 1999 (emphasis added).

22. Bruce B. Auster, "Women in Hard Hats: The YWCA is Training a New Breed of Construction Worker," *U.S. News and World Report,* February 13, 1995, 39–42.

23. Karen D. Pyke, "Class-Based Masculinities: The Interdependence of Gender, Class, and Interpersonal Power," *Gender and Society* 10, no. 5 (1996): 528.

## Bodies at Work

1. The concept of "feeling rules" is one initially put forth by Arlie Russell Hochschild in "Emotion Work, Feeling Rules, and Social Structure," *American Journal of Sociology* 85 (1979): 551–75, and in her subsequent book, *The Managed Heart.* The idea of linking physiological response with social ideas is derived from the work of Stanley Schacter and Jerome Singer, and other cognitive psychologists (see below).

2. Antony Easthope, *What a Man's Gotta Do: The Masculine Myth in Popular Culture* (1986; repr., Winchester, MA: Unwin Hyman, 1990).

3. This same point is made in Mike Donaldson, *Time of Our Lives: Labour and Love in the Working Class* (Sydney, Australia: Allen and Unwin, 1991); and Robert W. Connell, *Masculinities* (Berkeley: University of California Press, 1995).

4. Linda M. Goldenhar, focus group data (unpublished) from National Institute of Occupational Safety and Health, Cincinnati, n.d.

5. See, e.g., Elaine Blinde and Diane Taub, "Homophobia and Women's Sport," in *Constructions of Deviance: Social Power, Context, and Interaction,* 4th ed., ed. Patricia Adler and Peter Adler (New York: Wadsworth, 2003), 195–206.

6. To state this as an apparent zero-sum relationship, however, is to obscure the true relationship of gender and strength, which I argue is binary only in its social and not its biological articulations. Although it is the case that men in general are stronger than women in general, it is not the case that men are strong and women are not. And though it is certainly the case that some women are not strong enough to do construction work (perhaps not even after targeted strength-building exercises) the same is true for *some* men. And it is simulta-

neously the case that some, even many, women *are* strong enough to do construction work successfully, and more women would likely be able to do the work, if they engaged in systematic—though not necessarily record-shattering—strength building. The reality of gender and strength, then, is that many men and women *are* strong enough to do construction work, and there are also women *and* men who are not.

In our social performances of gender, however, the binary approach to physical strength is often both maintained and treated as if it were natural. That is, men and women tend to live their lives in ways that reproduce the belief that men have strength and women do not. For example, men often lift weights to bulk up and look strong, whereas women often lift to "tone" or burn calories and may intentionally stop short of building visible muscle. Some men offer to carry heavy items for women, thus getting more practice and strength from doing so, and some women let men carry and lift for them, thus failing to develop what strength they do have. In ways similar, then, to the pattern of heterosexual women dating taller men—thereby reproducing the binary belief that men are taller than women—men and women tend to make their bodies relatively strong and weak, thus reproducing the vision that men are strong and women are not.

7. See, e.g., Joe Drape, "Olympians Strike Pinup Pose, and Avoid Setting Off a Fuss," *New York Times*, August 12, 2004, http://www.nytimes.com

8. See Naomi Wolf, *The Beauty Myth* (New York: Anchor/Doubleday, 1991).

9. Susan Bordo, "Reading the Male Body," in *Building Bodies*, ed. Pamela L. Moore, 31–73 (New Brunswick, NJ: Rutgers University Press, 1997); Alison M. Jaggar, "Love and Knowledge: Emotion in Feminist Epistemology," in *Gender/Body/Knowledge*, ed. Alison Jaggar and Susan Bordo, 145–71 (New Brunswick, NJ: Rutgers University Press, 1989).

10. See, among others, Angela Y. Davis, *Women, Race, and Class* (1981; repr., New York: Vintage/Random House, 1983).

11. See, e.g., Reg Theriault, *How to Tell When You're Tired: A Brief Examination of Work* (New York: Norton, 1995).

12. Stanley Schachter and Jerome Singer, "Cognitive, Social, and Physiological Determinants of Emotional State," *Psychological Review* 69 (1962): 379–99; Dolf Zillman, Rolland R. Johnson, and Kenneth D. Day, "Attribution of Apparent Arousal and Proficiency of Recovery from Sympathetic Activation Affecting Excitation Transfer to Aggressive Behavior," *Journal of Experimental Social Psychology* 10 (1974): 503–15; and Theodore Kemper, "How Many Emotions Are There? Wedding the Social and Autonomic Components," *American Journal of Sociology* 93, no. 2 (1987): 263–89.

13. See, e.g., Kemper, "How Many Emotions Are There?"

14. For an example of research on creating arousal through having a subject ride a bicycle in a laboratory, see Zillman, Johnson, and Day, "Attribution of Apparent Arousal." For an example of research creating arousal by having a subject cross a rickety bridge spanning a deep gorge, see D. G. Dutton and A. P. Aron, "Some Evidence for Heightening Sexual Attraction under Conditions of High Anxiety," *Journal of Personality and Social Psychology* 30 (1974): 510–17.

15. One could also, of course, argue that an awareness of bodily feelings of discomfort might be an effective foundation of collective action around issues of working conditions. This second possibility is revealed somewhat more clearly by the issues of safety that lie ahead.

16. See, e.g., Don Sabo, "The Politics Of Homophobia in Sport," in *Sex, Violence, and Power in Sports*, ed. Michael Kimmel and Michael A. Messner, 101–12 (Freedom, CA: Crossing, 1994).

17. Goldenhar, focus group data.

18. Though it might be tempting to read this chapter as evidence that the men (and women) of construction are less intelligent, somehow more gullible, or less aware of their bodies than persons in other situations or occupations, I do not believe this to be the case. Instead, it is simply the case that the experience of doing construction work matches very closely the conditions under which excitation transfer occurs. More important perhaps, this

process was visible to me because I *felt* something to be true yet knew it could not be true. This allowed me to pull these processes apart and explore them. For men in construction, this embodied sense of masculinity would very likely not be a notable feeling or one worthy of attention. I believe that we experience many such embodied confirmations of social rules, yet are generally unable to see them, since they "confirm" what we know to be true. These processes are likely to occur in many situations: they are simply invisible. This matters because it suggests that the body is not simply a vessel though which social reality is interpreted but rather an agent through which social truths are amplified or challenged. This second, larger argument is somewhat beyond the scope of this chapter, though, so I limit my argument here to the body's effects in construction.

19. Similar language and identity issues are described by Joshua B. Freeman in "Hardhats: Construction Workers, Manliness, and the 1970 Pro-War Demonstrations," *Journal of Social History* 26 (1993): 725–44.

20. Similar language and its cultural effects are described in other settings. For example, see Peggy Reeves Sanday, *Fraternity Gang Rape: Sex, Brotherhood, and Privilege on Campus* (New York: New York University Press, 1990) for a discussion of fraternity gang rape; and Helen Michalowski, "The Army Will Make a 'Man' Out of You," in *Gender Images: Readings for Composition,* ed. Melita Schaum and Connie Flanagan, (Boston: Houghton Mifflin, 1992), 627–35, for a description of boot camp resocialization.

21. Robert W. Connell, *Gender and Power* (Stanford University Press, 1987). As I have emphasized elsewhere, such graphics exist in spite of the well-known 1991 Sixth District Federal Court ruling that declared them to be reflecting the employer's opinion of women and creating a hostile environment (*Robinson v. Jacksonville Shipyards* "760 F. Supp. 1486, 1542," 1991, M.D. FL.). The case is discussed in depth in most treatments of workplace sexual harassment, such as Susan L. Webb, *Step Forward: Sexual Harassment in the Workplace, What You Need to Know!* (New York: Mastermedia, 1991); and Ellen Bravo and Ellen Cassedy, *The 9 to 5 Guide to Combating Sexual Harassment: Candid Advice from 9 to 5, the National Association of Working Women* (New York: John Wiley, 1992). In spite of this ruling—and in spite of workplace ideologies alleging that sexual harassment policies mean "you can't say anything anymore" (see chapter 3)—the graffiti still exist in the portable toilets; sexual cartoons are still slid under women's lunch boxes, and "paper pussy" (a term used by Riemer in *Hard Hats* for the posters and calendars pinned up around construction sites) continues to decorate the workplaces.

22. See Easthope, *What a Man's Gotta Do.*

23. These practices have clear ties to and overlap with the practices in organized and professional sports, the military, and even ideologically based movements such as the Third Reich in Nazi Germany; see, e.g., George L. Mosse, *Nationalism and Sexuality: Middle-Class Morality and Sexual Norms in Modern Europe* (Madison: University of Wisconsin Press, 1985).

24. John Stoltenberg, "How Men Have (a) Sex," in *Refusing to Be a Man: Essays on Sex and Justice* (New York: Penguin, 1990), 25–39.

25. H. Andrew Michener, personal communications, 1995.

26. Stoltenberg, "How Men Have (a) Sex."

## "We're Animals . . ."

1. Laud Humphreys, *Tearoom Trade: Impersonal Sex in Public Places* (New York: Aldine De Gruyter, 1975).

2. Lee Lusardi Connor, "Which Husbands Make the Best Lovers? Our 1998 Survey," *Redbook* (September 1998): 116–119.

3. David Nibert, *Animal Rights, Human Rights: Entanglements of Oppression and Liberation* (Lanham, MD: Rowman and Littlefield, 2002).

4. See, e.g., Kelly, *Payback.*

5. Gilb, *Magic of Blood,* excerpted in *Carpenter,* November–December, 1994.

6. See, e.g., LeMasters, *Blue-Collar Aristocrats;* Riemer, *Hard Hats;* Applebaum, *Royal Blue;* and Ben Hamper, *Rivethead: Tales from the Assembly Line* (1986; repr., New York: Warner, 1991).

7. Jacobs, *Revolving Doors, 4,* passim.

8. This means not that these practices and methods are no longer used but rather that they are not formally sanctioned or acceptable. I thank Herbert Hill for emphasizing this distinction (personal communication 1999).

9. Eisenberg, *Pioneering,* 81.

10. Dramaturgical approaches are generally associated with Erving Goffman, *Presentation of Self;* impression management is generally associated with Edward E. Jones, *Interpersonal Perception* (New York: W. H. Freeman, 1990), among others.

11. Michel Foucault, *Power/Knowledge: Selected Interviews and Other Writings 1972–77,* Ed. and trans. Colin Gordon (1977; repr., New York: Pantheon, 1980).

12. LeMasters, *Blue-Collar Aristocrats;* Riemer, *Hard Hats.*

13. See, e.g., Reckman, "Carpentry."

14. For an example in a similar industry, please see Theriault, *How to Tell When You're Tired.*

### Bodily Costs of This Social Wage

1. See, e.g., Simon Carter, "Masculinity, Violence, and Occupational Health and Safety: Observations of Self-Employed Builders" (paper presented at the annual meeting of the American Sociological Association, August 1990, Washington, DC); Nicole Dedobbeleer and Pearl German, "Safety Practices in the Construction Industry," *Journal of Occupational Medicine* 29, no. 11 (1987): 863–68; Carl Graf Hoyos, "Occupational Safety: Progress in Understanding the Basic Aspects of Safe and Unsafe Behavior," *Applied Psychology: An International Review* 44, no. 3 (1995): 233–50; Hongwei Hsiao and Petre Simeonov, "Preventing Falls from Roofs: A Critical Review," *Ergonomics* 44, no. 5 (2001): 537–61; Darcy Lewis, "Behavior-Based Safety Breaks New Ground" *Safety+Health* 159, no. 1 (1999): 54–58; Helen Lingard, "The Effect of First Aid Training on Australian Construction Workers' Occupational Health and Safety Motivation and Risk Control Behavior," *Journal of Safety Research* 33 (2002): 209–30; Martin E. Personick, "Profiles in Safety and Health: Roofing and Sheet Metal Work," *Monthly Labor Review* 113, no. 9 (1990): 27–33; Knut Ringen, Jane Seegal, and Anders Englund, "Safety and Health in the Construction Industry," *Annual Review of Public Health* 16 (1995): 165–88; Frederick P. Rivara and Diane C. Thompson, "Prevention of Falls in the Construction Industry: Evidence for Program Effectiveness," *American Journal of Preventive Medicine* 18, no. 4s (2000): 23–26; R. Blake Smith, "Getting to the Bottom Of High Accident Rates: Labor, Management, and Government Heavily Emphasize Safety Training," *Occupational Health and Safety* 62, no. 2 (1993): 34–39.

2. The idea of consent is most directly associated with the work of Karl Marx in *Capital, Volume I* (1867; repr., New York: Vintage/Random House, 1977); and, more recently, Burawoy in *Manufacturing Consent.*

3. It is clearly an exchange between construction companies and their insurers as well. I will not attempt to address the complexities of that relationship, since it was largely beyond my observation; my knowledge of it reflects largely what I have been told by employers and men in managerial positions.

4. For an example of a publication on training policies, see John C. Bruening, "Tearing Down Obstacles to Safety," *Occupational Hazards* 59, no. 10 (1997): 147–50. For the arguments that the transfer of liability is necessary for employers, see "Employee Accountability Urged for Safety Legislation," *Building Design and Construction* 31, no.9 (1990): 21; and, more recently, RoAnn Destito, quoted in "MoVa Legislators Lend Support for Guild," *Utica Phoenix,* August 16, 2004.

5. Centers for Disease Control and Prevention, "Fatal Occupational Injuries: United

States, 1980–1994" *Journal of the American Medical Association* 279, no. 20 (1998): 1600–1603; United States Department of Labor, *Fatal Workplace Injuries in 1996: A Collection of Data and Analysis* (Washington, DC: U.S. Department of Labor Bureau of Labor Statistics, 1998); United States Department of Labor, *Bureau of Labor Statistics Data: Fatal Occupational Injuries* (Washington, DC: U.S. Department of Labor Bureau of Labor Statistics, 2002) http://data. bls.gov/cgi-bin/surveymost.

6. United States Department of Labor, *Fatal Workplace Injuries in 1996*, 4.

7. See, e.g., Alan M. Klein, *Little Big Men: Bodybuilding Subculture and Gender Construction* (Albany: State University of New York Press, 1993); and Michael A. Messner and Donald F. Sabo, eds., *Sex, Violence, and Power in Sports: Rethinking Masculinity* (Freedom, CA: Crossing, 1994).

8. I use the term "within reason" here somewhat ironically, recognizing that it might be seen as nonsensical to welcome injury of any nature; however, this is, I believe, what the culture requires.

9. Connor, "Which Husbands Make the Best Lovers?"

10. John Anderson, "Construction Safety: Seven Factors Which Hold Us Back," *Safety and Health Practitioner* 17, no. 8 (1999), 16–18.

11. Negotiated down to $2,000 (Kenneth R. Lamke, "Construction Firms Point Fingers at Each Other as Crane Accident Trial Gets Under Way; Mitsubishi, Lampson Say Other Was in Control of Man Lifts," *Milwaukee Journal-Sentinel*, October 19, 2000, B1); insurance picks up the payout ("Citation Dropped, Fine Cut in Worker's Death" [Eau Claire, WI], *Milwaukee Journal-Sentinel*, March 30, 2002; B2).

12. Linda M. Goldenhar and M. H. Sweeney, "Tradeswomen's Perspectives on Occupational Health and Safety: A Qualitative Investigation," *American Journal of Industrial Medicine* 29 (1996): 516–20.

13. It is also important to note that making a belt fit a smaller person might need only the addition of a grommeted hole so that the belt could be cinched more tightly. Thus the cost to provide such equipment could conservatively be estimated as low.

14. OSHA Standard 1926.502(d): "Personal fall arrest systems. Personal fall arrest systems and their use shall comply with the provisions set forth below. Effective January 1, 1998, body belts are not acceptable as part of a personal fall arrest system. Note: The use of a body belt in a positioning device system is acceptable and is regulated under paragraph (e) of this section." Available at http://www.osha.gov/pls/oshaweb/

15. See, e.g., Joan Claybrook and Public Citizen, *Retreat from Safety: Reagan's Attack on America's Health* (New York: Pantheon, 1984); Charles Noble, *Liberalism at Work: The Rise and Fall of OSHA* (Philadephia: Temple University Press, 1986).

16. See for example, John Hood, "OSHA's Trivial Pursuit: In Workplace Safety, Business Outperforms the Regulators," *Policy Review* 73 (1995): 59–64; Thomas J. Kniesner and John D. Leeth, "Abolishing OSHA," *Regulation* 18, no. 4 (1995): 46–56.

17. Occupational Safety and Health Administration, *The Cumulative Impact of Current Congressional Reform on American Working Men and Women*, Special Report Prepared for Secretary of Labor Robert M. Reich (Washington, DC: U.S. Department of Labor, 1995), 4.

18. I draw upon reports provided by the *Milwaukee Journal-Sentinel* and on my own experience within the industry, but my account should not be interpreted by the reader as a legally equivalent or binding assessment of what happened. For more information, please refer to the *Milwaukee Journal-Sentinel* (www.jsonline.com), which has a web archive devoted specifically to this accident and related issues.

19. Steve Schultze, "OSHA Questions 'Man Basket' Use in Miller Park Deaths," *Milwaukee Journal-Sentinel*, August 29, 1999, http://www.jsonline.com/news/metro/aug99/ basket30082999.asp; and Occupational Safety and Health Administration, "Cranes and Derricks.—1926.550," in *Regulations (Standards—29 CFR)* (Washington, DC: U.S. Department of Labor, 2002). The actual OSHA standard is as follows: "*1926.550(g)(2)* General requirements. The use of a crane or derrick to hoist employees on a personnel platform is prohibited, except when the erection, use, and dismantling of conventional means of reaching the work-

site, such as a personnel hoist, ladder, stairway, aerial lift, elevating work platform or scaffold, would be more hazardous or is not possible because of structural design or worksite conditions." Available at http://www.osha.gov/pls/oshaweb/.

20. Kenneth R. Lamke, "Miller Park Roof Lifts Set to Resume Thursday Weather Permitting, Piece Will Be First Installed since Fatal Accident July 14," *Milwaukee Journal Sentinel* (Milwaukee, WI), January 19, 2000.

21. Jo Sandin, "Victim's Wife Says Argument over Wind Preceded Lift," *Milwaukee Journal-Sentinel*, July 15, 1999, http://www.jsonline.com/news/metro/jul99/ jsovictims071599. asp; Kenneth R. Lamke, "3 Ironworkers' Families Sue, Saying Lift Was Unsafe," *Milwaukee Journal-Sentinel*, August 12, 1999. http://www.jsonline.com/news/metro/ aug99/iron13081299.

22. Lamke, "Construction Firms Point Fingers"; Stacy Forster, "Testimony Raises Doubts on Roof Lifts," *Milwaukee Journal-Sentinel* (Milwaukee, WI), November 27, 1999; Kenneth R. Lamke, "OSHA Safety Information Sought Before Roof Lifts Resume," *Milwaukee Journal-Sentinel* (Milwaukee, WI), January 13, 2000.

23. Steve Schultze, Kenneth R. Lamke, and T. Vanden Brook, "Miller Park Investigators Focus on Crane Base; Stadium Official Cites Many Possible Crash Factors, but UWM Expert Points to Wind," *Milwaukee Journal-Sentinel*, July 18, 1999, A1.

24. Kenneth R. Lamke, "Fatal Lift Could Have Been Delayed, Official Says," *Milwaukee Journal-Sentinel*, October 12, 1999, http://www.jsonline.com/news/metro/oct99 stad13101299.asp.

25. Sandin, "Victim's Wife Says."

26. "Wisconsin News Briefs," *Milwaukee Journal-Sentinel* (Milwaukee, WI), September 28, 1999, http://www.jsonline.com/wi/092899/wi—wisbriefs092899.asp.

27. Linda Spice and Kenneth R. Lamke, "Ironworker Says He Warned against Lifting Miller Park Roof Piece," *Milwaukee Journal-Sentinel*, August 20, 1999, http://www.jsonline .com/news/metro/aug99/iron21082099.asp.

28. Sandin, "Victim's Wife Says"; Spice and Lamke, "Ironworker Says."

29. Lamke, "3 Ironworkers' Families Sue."

30. "Responsible Crane Verdict," *Milwaukee Journal-Sentinel*, December 2, 2000, A12.

31. Don Walker, "State Supreme Court Rules on Damages in Crane Collapse," *Milwaukee Journal-Sentinel* (Milwaukee, WI), March 18, 2005; http://www.jsonline.com/news/metro/ mar05/310701.asp.

32. Don Walker, "Huge Roof Payout Put Back in Play," *Milwaukee Journal-Sentinel* (Milwaukee, WI), March 18, 2005, http://www.jsonline.com/news/metro/mar05/310979.asp.

33. Stacy Forster, "Businesses Take Aim at Court Decisions: Ruling to Lift Award Caps Draws Fire," *Milwaukee Journal Sentinel* (Milwaukee, WI), August 2, 2005, http://www. jsonline.com/bym/news/aug05/345686.asp.

### The Wages—and Costs

1. Livingstone and Luxton, "Gender Consciousness at Work."

2. The Village People are one very celebrated example.

3. Akhil Gupta and James Ferguson, "Culture, Power, Place: Ethnography at the End of an Era," in *Culture, Power, Place: Explorations in Critical Ethnography*, ed. Akhil Gupta and James Ferguson (Durham, NC: Duke University Press, 1997), 19.

4. Riemer, *Hard Hats*, 163–166.

5. Michel Foucault, *Discipline and Punish: The Birth of the Prison* (1977; repr., New York: Vintage/Random House, 1995), 201.

6. I should note here that union contracts in construction generally prohibit any sort of maximum output standard to be held by workers. Though I am not advocating such a position (and I would in fact consider a direct quantification of labor problematic in either a prescribing or proscribing fashion, given the large number of factors affecting work output), I am arguing that workers are, at the very least, altering the norms in a manner equivalent to the speeding up of a factory assembly line.

### Appendix

1. Although workers that one sees standing by the roadside would appear to contradict this assertion (something that I found people always wanting to point out to me when I was working construction), highway workers are likely to have persons standing to watch and flag the attention of passing drivers: thus their job is, actually, to be standing there. This is not only likely to be one of the more tedious construction jobs: it is also one of the most dangerous (according to the death statistics): those who seem the least active, the flaggers, are the most at risk of being struck by a vehicle and killed. Additionally, given the strain that roadwork places on traffic patterns, these jobs are generally under pressure to be completed "yesterday" and are likely to be running 12- and 14-hour shifts (Goldenhar, focus group data).

2. Restricting, formally or informally, the amount of time workers can spend in the bathroom or the number of trips any worker can take is clearly an issue for potential ethnographers, but it is also a matter of safety. Such restriction is perhaps most dangerous in hotter environments when workers should be consuming more water in order to stay healthy, but it is a very real issue for workers at any time; the potential long-term ramifications have been detailed by Linder and Nygaard in their volume aptly entitled *Void Where Prohibited*. Among other things, construction workers appear more likely than other workers to die of kidney or urinary diseases, as documented by the Center to Protect Workers' Rights in 1993 (*Patterns of Death Among Construction Workers*). And because of difficulties surrounding menstruation and hygiene, bathroom time is also a gendered issue.

3. Lofland quoted in Punch, *Politics and Ethics of Fieldwork*.

4. Sherryl Kleinman and Martha A. Copp, *Emotions and Fieldwork*, Qualitative Research Methods Series, vol. 28 (Thousand Oaks, CA: Sage, 1993).

5. Frantz Fanon. *Black Skin, White Masks* (New York: Grove Press, 1967). On the effects of discrimination: research suggests, for example, that stress is associated with more rapid aging of the body and also that discrimination is correlated with clogged arteries, not just in occurrence but also by degree. For more information on these topics, see (respectively) Louisa Kasdon, "Women and Worry: DNA Damage from Stress May Be at the Root of Aging," *More*, May 2005, 164; and Miranda Hitti, "Discrimination May Hurt the Heart: Study of Black Women Shows Link between Discrimination and Cardiovascular Disease," my.webmd.com (May 2, 2005), http://my.webmd.com/content/Article/105/107794.htm

6. This point has been explained in different settings by writers such as Nancy A. Hewitt, "The Voice of Virile Labor: Labor Militancy, Community Solidarity, and Gender Identity among Tampa's Latin Workers, 1880–1921," in *Work Engendered: Toward a New History of American Labor* ed. Ava Baron, 142–67 (Ithaca, NY: Cornell University Press, 1991); and Mary Margaret Fonow, "Protest Engendered: The Participation of Women Steelworkers in the Wheeling-Pittsburgh Steel Strike of 1985," *Gender and Society* 12, no. 6 (December 1998): 710–28.

7. Anselm L. Strauss and Juliet Corbin, *Basics of Qualitative Research: Grounded Theory and Techniques* (Newbury Park, CA: Sage, 1990); Anselm L. Strauss, *Qualitative Analysis For Social Scientists* (Cambridge, UK: Cambridge University Press, 1987).

8. Robert M. Emerson, Rachel I. Fretz, and Linda L. Shaw, *Writing Ethnographic Fieldnotes* (Chicago: University of Chicago Press, 1995); Harry F. Wolcott, *Writing Up Qualitative Research* 2nd ed. (Thousand Oaks, CA: Sage, 2001); and Robert S. Weiss, *Learning from Strangers: The Art and Method of Qualitative Interview Studies* (New York: Simon and Schuster, 1995).

9. West and Zimmerman, "Doing Gender."

10. Michael Burawoy, "The Extended Case Method," in *Ethnography Unbound*, ed. Michael Burawoy, 271–87 (Berkeley, CA: University of California Press, 1991).

11. Strauss, *Qualitative Analysis*; Strauss and Corbin, *Basics of Qualitative Research*, esp. chap. 11.

# REFERENCES

Anderson, Evan E., and Rogene A. Buchholz. 1988. "Economic Instability and Occupational Injuries: The Impact of Overtime Hours and Turnover Rates." *Labor Studies Journal* 13 (4): 33–49.

Anderson, John. 1999. "Construction Safety: Seven Factors Which Hold Us Back." *Safety and Health Practitioner* 17 (8): 16–18.

Appelbaum, Eileen, Annette Bernhardt, and Richard J. Murnane, eds. 2003. *Low-Wage America: How Employers Are Reshaping Opportunity in the Workplace.* New York: Russell Sage Foundation.

Applebaum, Herbert A. 1981. *Royal Blue: The Culture of Construction Workers.* Case Studies in Cultural Anthropology. New York: Holt, Rienhart and Winston.

Aronowitz, Stanley. 1992. *False Promises: The Shaping of American Class Consciousness.* Durham, NC: Duke University Press.

Auster, Bruce B. 1995. "Women in Hard Hats: The YWCA Is Training a New Breed of Construction Worker." *U.S. News and World Report,* February 13, 39–42.

Benson, Herman. 2004. *Rebels, Reformers, and Racketeers: How Insurgents Transformed the Labor Movement.* New York: Authorhouse.

Bird, Sharon. 1996. "Welcome to the Men's Club: Homosociality and the Maintenance of Hegemonic Masculinity." *Gender and Society* 10 (2): 120–132.

Blinde, Elaine, and Diane Taub. 2003. "Homophobia and Women's Sport." In *Constructions of Deviance: Social Power, Context, and Interaction,* ed. Patricia Adler and Peter Adler, 195–206. Belmont, CA: Wadsworth.

Bonilla-Silva, Eduardo. 2003. *Racism without Racists: Color-Blind Racism and the Persistence of Racial Inequality in the United States.* Lanham, MD: Rowman & Littlefield.

Bordo, Susan. 1997. "Reading the Male Body." In *Building Bodies,* ed. Pamela L. Moore, 31–73. New Brunswick, NJ: Rutgers University Press.

Bravo, Ellen and Ellen Cassedy. 1992. *The 9 to 5 Guide to Combating Sexual Harassment: Candid Advice from 9 to 5, the National Association of Working Women.* New York: Wiley.

Brinker, Paul A. 1985. "Violence by U.S. Labor Unions." *Journal of Labor Research* 6 (4): 417–427.

Bruening, John C. 1997. "Tearing Down Obstacles to Safety." *Occupational Hazards* 59 (10): 147–50.

Burawoy, Michael. 1979. *Manufacturing Consent: Changes in the Labor Process under Monopoly Capitalism.* Chicago: University of Chicago Press.

———. 1991. "The Extended Case Method." In *Ethnography Unbound,* ed. Michael Burawoy, 271–87. Berkeley: University of California Press.

Carter, Simon. 1990. "Masculinity, Violence, and Occupational Health and Safety: Observations of Self-Employed Builders." Paper presented at the annual meeting of the American Sociological Association, Washington, DC.

Center to Protect Workers' Rights. 1993. *Patterns of Deaths among Construction Workers: California, 1979–81.* Washington, DC: Center to Protect Workers' Rights.

———. 1998. *The Construction Chart Book: The U.S. Construction Industry and Its Workers.* Washington, DC: Center to Protect Workers' Rights.

Centers for Disease Control and Prevention. 1998. "Fatal Occupational Injuries: United States, 1980–1994." *Journal of the American Medical Association,* 279 (20): 1600–1603.

Cherry, Mike. 1974. *On High Steel: The Education of an Ironworker.* New York: Quadrangle/New York Times Book Company.

"Citation Dropped, Fine Cut in Worker's Death" [Eau Claire, WI]. 2002. *Milwaukee Journal-Sentinel,* March 30, B2.

Claybrook, Joan, and Public Citizen. 1984. *Retreat from Safety: Reagan's Attack on America's Health.* New York: Pantheon.

Cockburn, Cynthia. [1983] 1991. *Brothers: Male Dominance and Technological Change.* Concord, MA: Pluto.

Connell, Robert W. 1987. *Gender and Power.* Stanford, CA: Stanford University Press.

———1995. *Masculinities.* Berkeley: University of California Press.

Connor, Lee Lusardi. 1998. "Which Husbands Make the Best Lovers? Our 1998 Survey." *Redbook,* September, 116–19.

Craft, James A. 2001. "Union Violence: A Review and Critical Discussion." *Journal of Labor Research* 22 (3): 679–88.

Davis, Angela Y. [1981] 1983. *Women, Race, and Class.* New York: Vintage/Random House.

Dedobbeleer, Nicole, and Pearl German. 1987. "Safety Practices in the Construction Industry." *Journal of Occupational Medicine* 29 (11): 863–68.

Dedobbeleer, Nicole, Françoise Champagne, and Pearl German. 1990. "Safety Performance among Union and Nonunion Workers in the Construction Industry." *Journal of Occupational Medicine* 32 (11): 1099–1103.

Destito, RoAnn. 2004. Quoted in "MoVa Legislators Lend Support for Guild." *Utica Phoenix,* August 16.

Donaldson, Mike. 1991. *Time of Our Lives: Labour and Love in the Working Class.* Sydney, Australia: Allen and Unwin.

Drape, Joe. 2004. "Olympians Strike Pinup Pose, and Avoid Setting Off a Fuss." *New York Times,* August 12. http://www.nytimes.com.

Du Bois, W. E. B. [1935] 1962. *Black Reconstruction in America 1860–1880.* Studies in American Negro Life. New York: Atheneum/Macmillan.

Dutton, D. G., and A. P. Aron. 1974. "Some Evidence for Heightening Sexual Attraction under Conditions of High Anxiety." *Journal of Personality and Social Psychology* 30: 510–17.

Easthope, Antony. [1986] 1990. *What a Man's Gotta Do: The Masculine Myth in Popular Culture.* Winchester, MA: Unwin Hyman.

Eisenberg, Susan. 1998. *Pioneering: Poems from the Construction Site.* Ithaca, NY: ILR Press.

———. 1998. *We'll Call You If We Need You: Experiences of Women Working Construction.* Ithaca, NY: ILR Press.

Emerson, Robert M., Rachel I. Fretz, and Linda L. Shaw. 1995. *Writing Ethnographic Fieldnotes*. Chicago: University of Chicago Press.

"Employee Accountability Urged for Safety Legislation." 1990. *Building Design and Construction* 31 (9): 21.

Fanon, Frantz. 1967. *Black Skin, White Masks*. New York: Grove Press.

Ferguson, Trudi C., and Madeline Sharples. 1994. *Blue Collar Women: Trailblazing Women Take On Men-Only Jobs*. Liberty Corner, NJ: New Horizon.

Fernandes, Leela. 1997. "Beyond Public Spaces and Private Spheres: Gender, Family, and Working-Class Politics in India." *Feminist Studies* 23 (3): 525–47.

Fonow, Mary Margaret. 1998. "Protest Engendered: The Participation of Women Steelworkers in the Wheeling-Pittsburgh Steel Strike of 1985." *Gender & Society* 12 (6): 710–28.

———. 2003. *Union Women: Forging Feminism in the United Steelworkers of America*. Minneapolis: University of Minnesota Press.

Forster, Stacy. 1999. Testimony Raises Doubts on Roof Lifts. *Milwaukee Journal-Sentinel* (Milwaukee, WI), November 27.

———. 2005. Businesses Take Aim at Court Decisions: Ruling to Lift Award Caps Draws Fire. *Milwaukee Journal Sentinel* (Milwaukee, WI), August 2. http://www.jsonline .come/bym/news/aug05/345686.asp.

Foucault, Michel. [1977] 1980. *Power/Knowledge: Selected Interviews and Other Writings 1972–77*. Ed. Colin Gordon, trans. Colin Gordon et al. New York: Pantheon.

———. [1975] 1995. *Discipline and Punish: The Birth of the Prison*. New York: Vintage/Random House.

Freeman, Joshua B. 1993. "Hardhats: Construction Workers, Manliness, and the 1970 Pro-War Demonstrations." *Journal of Social History* 26: 725–44.

Fuchs Epstein, Cynthia. 1992. "Tinkerbells and Pinups: The Construction and Reconstruction of Gender Boundaries at Work." In *Cultivating Differences: Symbolic Boundaries and the Making of Inequality*, ed. Michèle Lamont and Marcel Fournier, 232–56. Chicago: Chicago University Press.

Fussell, Paul. [1989] 1992. *Class: A Guide through the American Status System*. New York: Simon and Schuster.

Geis, Gilbert, Robert Meier, and Laurence M. Salinger. 1995. *White-Collar Crime: Classic and Contemporary Views*. New York: Free Press.

Gilb, Dagoberto. 1994. *The Magic of Blood*. New York: Grove.

Gilbert, Dennis, and Joseph A. Kahl. 1993. *The American Class Structure: A New Synthesis*. 4th ed. Belmont, CA: Wadsworth.

Goffman, Erving. 1959. *The Presentation of Self in Everyday Life*. New York: Anchor/Doubleday.

Goldenhar, Linda M. n.d. Unpublished focus group data, National Institute of Occupational Safety and Health, Cincinnati, OH.

Goldenhar, Linda M., Steven Hecker, Susan Moir, and John Rosecrance. 2003. "Developing a Model for Overtime in Construction: Not Too Much, Not Too Little, Just Right." *Journal of Safety Research* 34: 215–26.

Goldenhar, Linda M., and M. H. Sweeney. 1996. "Tradeswomen's Perspectives on Occupational Health and Safety: A Qualitative Investigation." *American Journal of Industrial Medicine* 29: 516–20.

Guilbault, Rose Del Castillo. 1993. "Americanization Is Tough on Macho." In *American Voices*, ed. Dolores La Guardia and Hans Guth. Mountain View, CA: Mayfield.

Gupta, Akhil, and James Ferguson. 1997. "Culture, Power, Place: Ethnography at the End of an Era." In *Culture, Power, Place: Explorations in Critical Ethnography*, ed. Akhil Gupta and James Ferguson, 1–29. Durham, NC: Duke University Press.

Hamper, Ben. [1986] 1991. *Rivethead: Tales from the Assembly Line.* New York: Warner.

Hertz, Rosanna. 1996. "Guarding against Women? Responses of Military Men and Their Wives to Gender Integration." *Journal of Contemporary Ethnography* 25 (2): 251–84.

Hewitt, Nancy A. 1991. "The Voice of Virile Labor: Labor Militancy, Community Solidarity, and Gender Identity among Tampa's Latin Workers, 1880–1921." In *Work Engendered: Toward a New History of American Labor,* ed. Ava Baron. Ithaca, NY: Cornell University Press.

Hill, Herbert. 1968. "No End of Pledges: Continuing Discrimination in the Construction Unions." *Commonweal,* March 15, 709–12.

———. 1974. "Evading the Law: Apprenticeship Outreach and Hometown Plans in the Construction Industry." *Civil Rights Digest,* Summer: 1–12.

———. 1974. *Labor Union Control of Job Training: A Critical Analysis of Apprenticeship Outreach Programs and the Hometown Plans.* Occasional Paper. Washington, DC: Institute for Urban Affairs and Research, Howard University.

———. [1977] 1985. *Black Labor and the American Legal System.* Madison: University of Wisconsin Press.

Hitti, Miranda. 2005. "Discrimination May Hurt the Heart: Study of Black Women Shows Link between Discrimination and Cardiovascular Disease," My.webmd.com (May 2). http://my.webmd.com/content/Article/105/107794.htm.

Hochschild, Arlie Russell. 1979. "Emotion Work, Feeling Rules, and Social Structure." *American Journal of Sociology* 85: 551–75.

———. 1983. *The Managed Heart: Commercialization of Human Feeling.* Berkeley: University of California Press.

Hoffmann, Elizabeth A. 2004. "Selective Sexual Harassment: Differential Treatment of Similar Groups of Women." *Journal of Law and Human Behavior* 28 (1): 29–45.

Hood, John. 1995. "OSHA's Trivial Pursuit: In Workplace Safety, Business Outperforms the Regulators." *Policy Review* 73: 59–64.

Hoyos, Carl Graf. 1995. "Occupational Safety: Progress in Understanding the Basic Aspects of Safe and Unsafe Behavior." *Applied Psychology: An International Review* 44 (3): 233–50.

Hsiao, Hongwei, and Petre Simeonov. 2001. "Preventing Falls from Roofs: A Critical Review." *Ergonomics* 44 (5): 537–61.

Humphreys, Laud. 1975. *Tearoom Trade: Impersonal Sex in Public Places.* New York: Aldine De Gruyter.

Jacobs, Jerry A. 1989. *Revolving Doors: Sex Segregation and Women's Careers.* Stanford, CA: Stanford University Press.

Jaggar, Alison M. 1989. "Love and Knowledge: Emotion in Feminist Epistemology." In *Gender/Body/Knowledge,* ed. Alison Jaggar and Susan Bordo, 145–71. New Brunswick, NJ: Rutgers University Press.

Janeway, Elizabeth. 1974. *Between Myth and Morning: Women Awakening.* New York: William Morrow.

Johnson, Dirk. 1999. "Facing Shortage, Builders and Labor Court Workers." *New York Times,* March 13, A1, A8.

Jones, Edward E. 1990. *Interpersonal Perception.* New York: W. H. Freeman.

Jones, Jacqueline. 1998. *American Work: Four Centuries of Black and White Labor.* New York: Norton.

Kanter, Rosabeth Moss. [1977] 1993. *Men and Women of the Corporation.* New York: Basic Books.

Kasdon, Louisa. 2005. "Women and Worry: DNA Damage from Stress May Be at the Root of Aging," *More,* May 2005, 164.

Kelly, Thomas. 1997. *Payback.* New York: Knopf.

Kemper, Theodore. 1987. "How Many Emotions Are There? Wedding the Social and Autonomic Components." *American Journal of Sociology* 93 (2): 263–89.

Kinn, Steven, Sadik A. Khuder, Michael S. Bisesi, and Sandra Woolley. 2000. "Evaluation of Safety Orientation and Training Programs for Reducing Injuries in the Plumbing and Pipefitting Industry." *Journal of Occupational and Environmental Medicine* 42 (12): 1142–47.

Klein, Alan M. 1993. *Little Big Men: Bodybuilding Subculture and Gender Construction.* Albany: State University of New York Press.

Kleinman, Sherryl, and Martha A. Copp. 1993. *Emotions and Fieldwork.* Qualitative Research Methods Series, vol. 28. Thousand Oaks, CA: Sage.

Kluegel, James R., and Eliot R. Smith. 1986. *Beliefs about Inequality: Americans' Views of What Is and What Ought to Be.* New York: Aldine De Gruyter.

Kniesner, Thomas J., and John D. Leeth. 1995. "Abolishing OSHA." *Regulation* 18 (4): 46–56.

Korman, Richard, et al. 1998. "The Jokes Aren't Very Funny Anymore." *Engineering News Report,* September 7, 26–30.

Lamke, Kenneth R. 1999. "3 Ironworkers' Families Sue, Saying Lift Was Unsafe." *Milwaukee Journal-Sentinel,* August 12. http://www.jsonline.com/news/metro/aug99/iron13081299.asp.

———. 1999. "Fatal Lift Could Have Been Delayed, Official Says." *Milwaukee Journal-Sentinel,* October 12. http://www.jsonline.com/news/metro/oct99/stad13101299.asp.

———. 2000. "Construction Firms Point Fingers at Each Other as Crane Accident Trial Gets Under Way; Mitsubishi, Lampson say Other Was in Control of Man Lifts." *Milwaukee Journal-Sentinel,* October 19, B1.

———. 2000. "Miller Park Roof Lifts Set to Resume Thursday Weather Permitting, Piece Will Be First Installed since Fatal Accident July 14." *Milwaukee Journal-Sentinel* (Milwaukee, WI), January 19.

———. 2000. "OSHA Safety Information Sought before Roof Lifts Resume." *Milwaukee Journal-Sentinel* (Milwaukee, WI), January 13.

Lamke, Kenneth R. and Steve Schultze. 1999. "Charges in Crane Collapse Called Unlikely." *Milwaukee Journal-Sentinel,* July 26. http://www.jsonline.com/news/metro/jul99/miller27072699.asp.

Leidner, Robin. 1993. *Fast Food, Fast Talk: Service Work and the Routinization of Everyday Life.* Berkeley: University of California Press.

LeMasters, E. E. 1975. *Blue-Collar Aristocrats: Life Styles at a Working-Class Tavern.* Madison: University of Wisconsin Press.

Lewis, Darcy. 1999. "Behavior-Based Safety Breaks New Ground." *Safety+Health* 159 (1): 54–58.

Linder, Marc, and Ingrid Nygaard. 1998. *Void Where Prohibited: Rest Breaks and the Right to Urinate on Company Time.* Ithaca, NY: ILR Press.

Lingard, Helen. 2002. "The Effect of First Aid Training on Australian Construction Workers' Occupational Health and Safety Motivation and Risk Control Behavior." *Journal of Safety Research* 33: 209–30.

Lipset, Seymour M., and Ivan Katchanovski. 2001. "The Future of Private Sector Labor Unions in the U.S." *Journal of Labor Research* 22 (2): 229–44.

Livingstone, D. W. and Meg Luxton. 1989. "Gender Consciousness at Work: Modification of the Male Breadwinner Norm among Steelworkers and Their Spouses." *Canadian Review of Sociology and Anthropology* 26 (2): 240–75.

Martin, Molly, ed. 1988. *Hard Hatted Women: Stories of Struggle and Success in the Trades.* Seattle, WA: Seal.

Marx, Karl. [1867] 1977. *Capital, Volume I.* New York: Vintage/Random House.

Messner, Michael A., and Donald F. Sabo, eds. 1994 *Sex, Violence, and Power in Sports: Rethinking Masculinity.* Freedom, CA: Crossing.

Michalowski, Helen. 1992. "The Army Will Make a 'Man' Out of You." In *Gender Images: Readings for Composition,* ed. Melita Schaum and Connie Flanagan, 627–35. Boston: Houghton Mifflin.

Milwaukee Journal-Sentinel. 1999. Wisconsin News Briefs. *Milwaukee Journal Sentinel,* September 28, 1999, http://www.jsonline.com/wi/092899/wi—wisbriefs092899.asp.

Mosse, George L. 1985. *Nationalism and Sexuality: Middle-Class Morality and Sexual Norms in Modern Europe.* Madison: University of Wisconsin Press, 1985.

Nakao, Keiko and Judith Treas. 1990. "Revised Prestige Scores for All Occupations." National Opinion Research Center, Chicago.

Nibert, David. 2002. *Animal Rights, Human Rights: Entanglements of Oppression and Liberation.* Lanham, MD: Rowman & Littlefield, 2002.

Noble, Charles. 1986. *Liberalism at Work: The Rise and Fall of OSHA.* Philadephia: Temple University Press.

Norwood, Stephen H. 2002. *Strikebreaking and Intimidation: Mercenaries & Masculinity in 20th Century America.* Chapel Hill: University of North Carolina Press.

Occupational Safety and Health Administration (OSHA), United States Department of Labor. 1995. *Occupational Safety and Health Standards for the Construction Industry.* Chicago: CCH.

———. 1994. Personal Fall Arrest Systems. In *Regulations* (Standard 1926.502[d]), Washington, DC: U.S. Department of Labor, http://www.osha.gov/pls/oshaweb.

———. 1995. *The Cumulative Impact of Current Congressional Reform on American Working Men and Women.* Special Report prepared for Secretary of Labor Robert M. Reich. Washington, DC: U.S. Department of Labor.

———. 2002. Cranes and Derricks—1926.550. In *Regulations* (Standards—29 CFR) Washington, DC: U.S. Department of Labor, http://www.osha.gov/pls/oshaweb.

Oppedahl, David B. 2000. "Understanding the (Relative) Fall and Rise of Construction Wages." *Chicago Fed Letter,* 155. http://www.frbchi.org.

Paap, Kirsten (Kris). 1995. "Working-Class Women, Occupational Realism, and Occupational Choice: Beliefs and Knowledge of Working-Class Women at First Workforce Entrance." Paper presented at annual meeting of the American Sociological Association, Washington, DC.

Personick, Martin E. 1990. "Profiles in Safety and Health: Roofing and Sheet Metal Work." *Monthly Labor Review* 113 (9): 27–33.

Pierce, Jennifer L. 1995. *Gender Trials: Emotional Lives in Contemporary Law Firms.* Berkeley: University of California Press.

Price, Vivian. 2002. "Race, Affirmative Action, and Women's Employment in US Highway Construction." *Feminist Economics* 8 (2): 87–113.

Punch, Maurice. 1986. *The Politics and Ethics of Fieldwork.* Qualitative Research Methods Series, vol. 3. Thousand Oaks, CA: Sage.

Pyke, Karen D. 1996. "Class-Based Masculinities: The Interdependence of Gender, Class, and Interpersonal Power." *Gender and Society* 10 (5): 527–49.

Reckman, Bob. 1979. "Carpentry: The Craft and Trade." In *Case Studies on the Labor Process,* ed. Andrew Zimbalist. New York: Monthly Review Press.

Reiman, Jeffrey. 1998. *The Rich Get Richer and the Poor Get Prison: Ideology, Class, and Criminal Justice.* Boston: Allyn and Bacon.

"Responsible Crane Verdict." 2000. *Milwaukee Journal-Sentinel,* December 2, A12.

Riemer, Jeffrey W. 1977. "Becoming a Journeyman Electrician." *Sociology of Work and Occupations* 4 (1): 87–98.

———. 1979. *Hard Hats: The Work World of Construction Workers.* Beverly Hills, CA: Sage.

———. 1982. "Work Autonomy in the Skilled Building Trades." In *The Varieties of Work*, ed. Phyliss Stewart and Muriel Cantor, 225–34. Beverly Hills, CA: Sage.

Ringen, Knut, Jane Seegal, and Anders Englund. 1995. "Safety and Health in the Construction Industry." *Annual Review of Public Health* 16: 165–88.

Rivara, Frederick P., and Diane C. Thompson. 2000. "Prevention of Falls in the Construction Industry: Evidence for Program Effectiveness." *American Journal of Preventive Medicine* 18 (4S): 23–26.

*Robinson v. Jacksonville Shipyards*, 760 F.Supp. 1486, 1542. 1991. M.D. Fla.

Roediger, David R. [1991] 1999. *The Wages of Whiteness: Race and the Making of the American Working Class*. New York: Verso.

Royster, Deirdre A. 2003. *Race and the Invisible Hand: How White Networks Exclude Black Men from Blue-Collar Jobs*. Berkeley: University of California Press.

Rubin, Lillian B. 1994. *Families on the Fault Line: America's Working Class Speaks about the Family, the Economy, Race, and Ethnicity*. New York: Harper/Perennial.

Sabo, Don. 1994. "The Politics Of Homophobia in Sport." In *Sex, Violence, and Power in Sports*, ed. Michael Kimmel and Michael A. Messner, 101–12. Freedom, CA: Crossing.

Sanday, Peggy Reeves. 1990. *Fraternity Gang Rape: Sex, Brotherhood, and Privilege on Campus*. New York: New York University Press.

Sandin, Jo. 1999. "Victim's Wife Says Argument over Wind Preceded Lift." *Milwaukee Journal-Sentinel*, July 15. http://www.jsonline.com/news/metro/jul99/jsovictims071599. asp.

Schachter, Stanley, and Jerome Singer. 1962. "Cognitive, Social, and Physiological Determinants of Emotional State." *Psychological Review* 69: 379–99.

Schroedel, Jean Reith. 1985. *Alone in a Crowd: Women in the Trades Tell Their Stories*. Philadelphia: Temple University Press.

Schultze, Steve. 1999. "OSHA Questions 'Man Basket' Use in Miller Park Deaths." *Milwaukee Journal-Sentinel*, August 29. http://www.jsonline.com/news/metro/aug99/ basket30082999.asp.

Schultze, Steve, Kenneth R. Lamke, and T. Vanden Brook. 1999. "Miller Park Investigators Focus on Crane Base; Stadium Official Cites Many Possible Crash Factors, but UWM Expert Points to Wind." *Milwaukee Journal-Sentinel*, July 18, A1.

Schuster, Michael, and Susan Rhodes. 1985. "The Impact of Overtime Work on Industrial Accident Rates." *Industrial Relations* 24 (2): 234–46.

Silver, Marc L. 1982. "The Structure of Craft Work: The Construction Industry." In *The Varieties of Work*, ed. Phyliss Stewart and Muriel Cantor, 235–52. Beverly Hills, CA: Sage.

———. 1986. *Under Construction: Work and Alienation in the Building Trades*. SUNY Series in the Sociology of Work. Albany: State University of New York Press.

Smith, R. Blake. 1993. "Getting to the Bottom of High Accident Rates: Labor, Management, and Government Heavily Emphasize Safety Training." *Occupational Health and Safety* 62 (2): 34–39.

Spice, Linda, and Kenneth R. Lamke. 1999. "Ironworker Says He Warned against Lifting Miller Park Roof Piece." *Milwaukee Journal-Sentinel*, August 20. http://www. jsonline.com/news/metro/aug99/iron21082099.asp.

Stiehm, Judith Hicks. 1989. *Arms and the Enlisted Woman*. Philadephia: Temple University Press.

Stoltenberg, John. 1990. *Refusing to Be a Man: Essays on Sex and Justice*. New York: Penguin.

Strauss, Anselm L. 1987. *Qualitative Analysis for Social Scientists*. Cambridge, UK: Cambridge University Press.

Strauss, Anselm L., and Juliet Corbin. 1990. *Basics of Qualitative Research: Grounded Theory and Techniques.* Newbury Park, CA: Sage.

Swidler, Ann. 1986. "Culture in Action: Symbols and Strategies." *American Sociological Review* 51: 273–86.

Tanenbaum, Leora. 1999. *Slut! Growing Up Female with a Bad Reputation.* New York: Seven Stories.

Terkel, Studs. 1974. *Working.* New York: New Press.

Theriault, Reg. 1995. *How to Tell When You're Tired: A Brief Examination of Work.* New York: Norton.

Thieblot, Armand J., Jr., and Thomas R. Haggard. 1983. *Union Violence: The Record and the Response by Courts, Legislatures, and the NLRB.* Labor Relations and Public Policy Series No. 25. Philadelphia: Industrial Research Institute, Wharton School.

United States Department of Labor. 1998. *Fatal Workplace Injuries in 1996: A Collection of Data and Analysis.* Washington, DC: U.S. Department of Labor Bureau of Labor Statistics.

——. 2002. *Bureau of Labor Statistics Data: Fatal Occupational Injuries.* Washington, DC: U.S. Department of Labor Bureau of Labor Statistics, http://data.bls.gov/cgi-bin/surveymost.

——. 2002. *Bureau of Labor Statistics Data: National Employment, Hours, and Earnings.* Washington, DC: U.S. Department of Labor Bureau of Labor Statistics, http://data.bls.gov/servlit/.

——. 2002. *Bureau of Labor Statistics News: Median Weekly Earnings of Full-Time Wage and Salary Workers by Union Affiliation, Occupation, and Industry.* http://www.bls.gov/news.release/union2.to4.htm.

Walker, Don. 2005. "Huge Roof Payout Put Back in Play." *Milwaukee Journal-Sentinel* (Milwaukee, WI), March 18. http://www.jsonline.com/news/metro/mar05/310979.asp.

——. 2005. "State Supreme Court Rules on Damages in Crane Collapse." *Milwaukee Journal-Sentinel* (Milwaukee, WI), March 18, http://www.jsonline.com/news/metro/mar05/310979.asp.

Webb, Susan L. 1991. *Step Forward: Sexual Harassment in the Workplace, What You Need to Know!* New York: Mastermedia.

Weiss, Robert S. 1995. *Learning from Strangers: The Art and Method of Qualitative Interview Studies.* New York: Simon and Schuster.

West, Candace, and Sarah Fenstermaker. 1995. "Doing Difference." *Gender and Society* 9 (1): 8–37.

West, Candace, and Don Zimmerman. 1987. "Doing Gender." *Gender and Society* 1: 125–51.

Wolf, Naomi. 1991. *The Beauty Myth.* New York: Anchor/Doubleday.

Wolcott, Harry F. 2001. *Writing Up Qualitative Research,* 2nd ed. Thousand Oaks, CA: Sage.

Zillman, Dolf, Rolland R. Johnson, and Kenneth D. Day. 1974. "Attribution of Apparent Arousal and Proficiency of Recovery from Sympathetic Activation Affecting Excitation Transfer to Aggressive Behavior." *Journal of Experimental Social Psychology* 10: 503–15.

# INDEX